Z

Ascendant

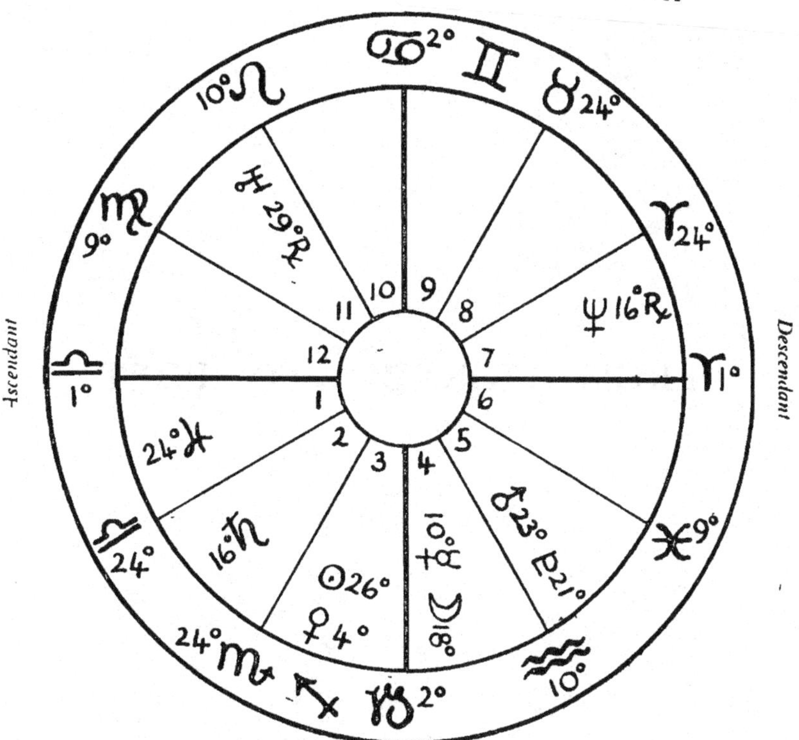

Descendant

Nadir

HOROSCOPE OF MARY, QUEEN OF SCOTS

Born 8th December 1542, about Midnight Lat. 56

Ruler Venus, the Archangel Anael

Planets in the Elements	Planets in the Qualities
4 in fire	4 cardinal
3 in air	4 fixed
1 in water	2 mutable
2 in earth	0 exalted

SUN in Sagittarius
MOON in Capricorn
Ascendant LIBRA

FROM PIONEER TO POET

FROM PIONEER TO POET

OR

THE TWELVE GREAT GATES

AN EXPANSION OF THE SIGNS OF THE ZODIAC ANALYZED

BY

ISABELLE M. PAGAN

Author of "An Astrological Key to Character"

THE THEOSOPHICAL PUBLISHING HOUSE LONDON LTD

68 Great Russell Street, London, W.C.

INDIA

THE THEOSOPHICAL PUBLISHING HOUSE

Adyar, Madras, 20

U. S. A.

THE THEOSOPHICAL PRESS

Wheaton, Ill.

Published in 1911
2nd Edition 1926
3rd Edition 1930
4th Edition 1954

PRINTED BY THE REPLIKA PROCESS
IN GREAT BRITAIN BY
LUND HUMPHRIES
LONDON · BRADFORD

And there came unto me one of the Seven Angels, and . . . carried me away in the spirit to a great and high mountain, and showed me that great city, the holy Jerusalem, descending out of heaven from God having the glory of God: and her light was like unto a stone most precious, even like a jasper stone, clear as crystal; and had a wall great and high, and had TWELVE GATES *and at the gates* TWELVE ANGELS, *and names written thereon which are the names of the* TWELVE TRIBES *of the children of Israel.*

REVELATION, *xxi.* 9.

The Heavens declare the glory of God;
And the firmament showeth his handywork
Day unto day uttereth speech,
And night unto night showeth knowledge.

PSALM XIX. 1.

Look, how the floor of heaven
Is thick inlaid with patines of bright gold;
There's not the smallest orb which thou behold'st,
But in his motion like an angel sings
Still quiring to the young-eyed cherubins.

The Merchant of Venice.

Ever consider this Universe as one living Being, with one material substance and one spirit.

Contemplate the fundamental causes, stripped of all disguises. . . . Consider well the nature of things, distinguishing between matter, cause, purpose.

MARCUS AURELIUS.

CONTENTS

FOREWORD TO THE THIRD EDITION

This book goes forth with warm gratitude to fellow-students, far and near, for their counsel and encouragement A learned Hindu sent his thanks to me for strengthening his own conviction—by my *Synthesis of Powers* (p 310)—that a careful study of Greek Philosophy and Religion would best provide the ground on which the East and West could meet with understanding From Finland to the Cape, from Australasia to California, letters have come containing helpful comments, some of which have now been embodied in the text, with thanks to kind critics Some errors were due to fatigue, the book having been completed while on a lecture tour, and partly written in the train. The Arietian type should have been credited with a special gift for arousing the enthusiasm and loyal devotion of children and of child-like races, and Faust's Gretchen might be added to the list of Librans in fiction Further, I have been told that my *Suggestion*, tucked into the Appendix (p 306), ought to have been placed at the beginning, "to disarm stern critics!" More detail about houses and planets will be found in my *Palace of the King*, a rhymed encouragement for beginners, but for technical achievement readers must supply themselves with the works of other writers, the handiest for travellers being Waite's pocket *Compendium of Natal Astrology*, containing all that is necessary for drawing out horoscopes accurate enough for such analysis as is taught here on p 228, and even for generalised forecasting by students who stop short of dating probable events I avoid prediction as a rule *Sufficient unto the day is the evil thereof*, and few have enough fortitude to face forecasts of calamity without loss of energy, while many, assured of coming luck—especially financial—are inclined to take things easy But, on December 1st, 1914, I ventured comments on the horoscopes of the Nations then engaged in war, and so far none of my forecasting has been falsified From the minute book of the somewhat sceptical private Club to which I spoke, I quote some secretarial jottings at the time "The Kaiser will be called on to renounce all his ambitions," and "the Czar will lose his autocracy—if not his throne" During King George's reign "increase of British territory" is indicated by his horoscope, but "the most remarkable change will be in the religious life of the nation, which will have a great development towards higher spirituality" Some of us rejoice to see that change at hand, and one symptom of it will be the renewal of a wholehearted belief in the existence of the Heavenly Hierarchy, and a reverent and open acknowledgment thereof If this book helps to forward that dawning realisation, its end will have been achieved

ISABELLE M PAGAN,

Edinburgh, April 4th, 1930

FOREWORD TO THE FOURTH EDITION

I have been asked to decide on any corrections desirable in this edition of my book, and I find changes are required on pages 223 and 275, and also note many desirable alterations of a more trifling nature. Some of the latter have been dealt with in footnotes, but the frequent references to Pluto will have to stand. They were written before the position of that planet was ascertained, but later analysis suggests that I was somehow guided aright as to his function, as well as when bestowing on him the name chosen later by astronomers. I may add, however, that the title VILJE—the Will—given to this representative of the third Person of the Trinity in Scandinavian lore, has since helped me to understand his influence; for his position in sign and house does give an indication of how the Will is set, and the sphere in which it will operate most easily. If Pluto is in good aspect, the will is well attuned to circumstances, which the native can face and use aright; but bad aspects show failure to do so, through some degree of "wilfulness", which is, in its essence, Will-Power misdirected, either through lack of wisdom, or want of common sense. When adding Pluto to the twelve charts illustrating the zodiacal types, I have appended brief notes on his influence—longer in the case of the royalties analysed on pages 275 and 303 a necessary step, for both royalties lost their thrones after my book was written, and only the addition of Pluto to their charts suggests the likelihood of such a misfortune. The same adverse influence is seen even more clearly in the chart of another dethroned royalty, that of Mary, Queen of Scots, which is now inserted as a frontispiece, for Pluto's conjuction with Mars in the fifth house—the house of popularity and notoriety—is seen there in *opposition* to Uranus in the tenth—a house concerned with friends and possible helpers—indicating the disastrous and ultimately fatal results of her own wilfulness. Note that her ruler, Venus, as well as the Sun, is in Sagittarius, a genial sign that likes to go its own way, ignoring convention and demanding freedom from restriction in matters of the heart, even to the point of rebellion She was born so near midnight between the 7th and 8th of December that her exact birthday was in doubt, but she always held it on the 8th, so this chart shows the Sun already in the third house, a position suited to a writer of songs. She herself said, "My end is my beginning", and that tragic ending carried her story far and wide, inspiring great poets and dramatists in many lands.

Her horoscope must have puzzled astrologers until Neptune was discovered. He is placed in the seventh house (marriage and partnership) with three bad aspects, reminding us of her three unfortunate marriages. The first brought early widowhood, which ended her time of girlhood's happiness as Queen of France. Her second choice, Darnley, gave her a faithless, inconsiderate, drunken husband; and her third too-hasty union, with Bothwell, brought about the loss of her crown and kingdom, followed by weary years of exile and imprisonment, ended by her execution in 1587.

The midnight hour of her birth confirms the old tradition that she was born under Venus—and certainly a Libran ascendant is well suited to her natural grace and charm, and many gifts. But while accepting this and other old documentary records of famous births as likely to be right, I have learnt caution when drawing horoscopes of the present day, especially when the medical man concerned in the birth has a special degree of learning and skill. Rightly he uses that to lessen suffering, and when a birth is delayed—or hastened—by drugs or surgery—or prematurely brought about by accident—the result may disconcert the astrologer, whose reading, based on the signs rising and at the zenith, may be a misfit as regards his description of outer personality, self-expression, and natural endowment leading to choice of career. The horoscope of our own Queen Elizabeth II needs rectification, and the circling zodiac on her chart should be wheeled round to bring the royal sign of Leo to an angle—preferably setting, which would show the Sunshine that brightens the house of partnership and marriage, helping the success of the career. That would make the very fair sign of Aquarius ascend—much better suited to her Majesty than Capricorn; and the ruler would be Uranus—most appropriate for one who prefers to travel by air when possible! I judge that the birth was hastened.

In the case of the Duke of Windsor there was considerable delay, resulting in a striking astrological misfit. He was about 23 hours late, and the Moon had passed into Pisces from Aquarius during the delay. The actual hour of birth announced gives him the stately sign of Aquarius rising and the Moon in Pisces; but these signs should be reversed. A chart for the previous day, with Pisces rising and the Moon in Aquarius, is much better suited to the personality, its special talents, tastes, and tendencies, and literary style; and it also accords well with events in his life; for the ruler of Pisces is Neptune, whose insistent call to his children is, "Give it up! Renounce!" That call has been obeyed in a very striking fashion.

Socrates said that every man belonged to the choir of one or other of the gods, and that he himself belonged to the choir of Zeus—and well and truly he answered to the call of that Power. Even his choice of sculpture as a profession in his early days fits the type to which he belonged; for sculptors, like geologists, are nearly all "Jovial", astrologically. Chisel and hammer are their tools, metaphorically as well as actually. It is useful to know to what "choir" we ourselves belong, and a great help in understanding others, such classification making it easier to recognise their virtues and make allowance for their shortcomings, often due to the influence of their "Guardian Angel", or Ruler, not yet rightly understood. Parents and teachers find specal interest—and often amusement—when their task is lightened by even such limited knowledge of astrology as is given in this book, and married couples may harmonise all the better when each has learnt to understand and appreciate something of the special "music" required by the Master who is conducting the "choir" to which the chosen partner belongs.

ISABELLE M PAGAN,
Edinburgh, April 1954

INTRODUCTION

FROM the time of the "Three wise men of the East" and long before their day, Astrology has been held in honour by its students in every quarter of the globe. The false pretensions and superficial acquirements of the quack and the charlatan have done much to discredit it, but in spite of that it has always found its devotees, even in the materialistic West, and the open-minded attitude of the present generation has brought it once more into the field of inquiry as a curious and interesting branch of the more occult sciences—a study so ancient and of such persistent vitality as to merit earnest attention. Among the famous men who have considered it worth examination in the past we find the names of Francis Bacon, Sir Isaac Newton, Kepler and other scientists. Napier invented logarithms while seeking new methods of astrological research. Goethe, Dryden, and Scott felt the fascination of the subject, Sir Philip Sidney speaks of "The dusty Souls" of those who "scorn Astrology." Dante refers to his own horoscope and classifies the planetary types. Shakespeare makes constant use of astrological terms and references. This being the case, it is idle to brush the matter aside as beneath the notice of the scientist and the scholar. Predictions may be verified or falsified —that will largely depend on the insight and intuition of the astrologer; but the time-honoured beliefs on which such prophecy is based are, to say the least of it, very interesting, and those who can find enough patience to give them their honest and unprejudiced attention will certainly find their reward. Astrology is to Astronomy what Psychology is to Physiology; and like Psychology, it is a study that is still in its infancy. Scientists as a rule reject it entirely, because astrologers continue to use mediæval terms, and to work out the planetary positions in a horoscope with the earth as the centre of the solar system. Critics of such a mode of procedure forget that man is always the centre of his own universe, and that consequently the centre of his horoscope—which is the symbol of his life here below— is naturally the place for the particular planet on which he lives. In natal astrology—which is the only department of a very vast subject to which reference is made in this book—we are only concerned with the relations of the *natives* (the technical term for the subjects of astrological prediction or analysis) to the great Powers, or forms of energy, which stimulate human consciousness, arousing in it some kind of spiritual, mental, or emotional response, which works out, ultimately, in the field of action, and so forwards the evolution of the race and of the individual. Tradition tells us that these Powers have their special centres of activity in definite regions of the starry heavens, and that a special form of energy is associated with each sign of the Zodiac. It also recognises in the solar system forms of energy similar to, and harmonising with, the activities of the Zodiacal Powers, each of which finds a sympathetic echo in one or other of the planets. And here the scientist receives another shock, for the astrologer's "*Signs* of the Zodiac" no longer correspond with the *constellations* of the Zodiac, and among the so-called planets, he persists in reckoning the Sun and the Moon! Further, in the various powers in the mind and soul of man, the astrologer recognises something akin to those varying attractions and repulsions and thought-vibrations which he believes to be behind the various movements of the heavenly bodies; for man is the microcosm, the whole Universe the macrocosm, Rightly considered, such dogmatic assertion is only another form of the familiar teaching given to every Christian child, that the heavens are full of God's shining angels, who are constantly raining down influence upon the children of men. Man responds to such influences, or stimulus, well or ill according to his stage of evolution, and that stage is marked by the kind of character and the amount of faculty, intuition and imagination with which he is endowed.

This is not a scientific treatise or defence of Astrology, but merely the record of the impressions of a student whose efforts to understand the subject have been limited almost entirely to the department of natal astrology, and to that only in so far as it is connected with the evolution of character; but a few words as to the astrological point of view may be of value by putting the reader into touch with the line of thought followed up in this volume. Like all really great religious and philosophical systems Astrology proclaims that *The Lord our God is One*, and that His Universe also is One. But the One manifests as the many, and in the attempt to understand the

Divine Energy and its methods of work, many systems of Cosmology and Theology have been built up, all of which agree in beginning with some symbolic presentation or abstract definition of the threefold nature of primary manifestation; or, in other words, by the assertion, in one form or another, of the doctrine of the Trinity.

The astrological Trinity consists of what are technically expressed as the Three Qualities—the Cardinal, the Fixed, and the Mutable. The Cardinal quality may be defined as the driving force of the Universe, that type of energy which sets in motion, creates and vivifies and desires to manifest; the active quality of Love. The Fixed quality represents Power; and is associated with that which is steadfast, enduring, unchanging, persistent and strong, the force that manifests in stability and repose. The Mutable quality represents Wisdom, the form of energy which adapts, harmonises and evolves, the source of order and method in the Cosmos. These three correspond, to some extent, with the three Gunas of the Hindoo; and it should be realised that they can only be separated theoretically, and that they are indissolubly bound together as one in manifestation. Perfect Love cannot manifest without Wisdom to guide it; Wisdom cannot manifest without Power; and in the manifestation of Perfect Power, both Love and Wisdom are seen.

These three qualities therefore are combined in all manifestation, and according to tradition, each of the three has four modes of manifesting, thus making twelve Powers or Orders, each of which finds its symbol or representative in one of the signs of the Zodiac. The four Fixed signs are Taurus, Leo, Scorpio and Aquarius; the four Cardinal signs are Aries, Cancer, Libra and Capricorn, the four Mutable signs—also called *Common*—are Gemini, Virgo, Sagittarius, and Pisces. Each of these signs represents to us a form of the Divine Energy, a Principality or Hierarchy, consciously assisting the great Creator of the Universe, working out His purposes and fulfilling His designs, possessing distinct and individual characteristics, but blending harmoniously into the great Whole. The four Fixed signs seem to be selected by Sacred Writers as in some way summing up and representing all the rest; as may be seen in the Visions of Ezekiel and St. John, where the four Living Creatures are the symbols of Taurus the Bull or Calf, Leo the Lion, Aquarius the Man, and Scorpio the Scorpion, which is described by its older name of the Eagle.

The four modes in which the three qualities find expression are defined in terms of what the ancients called *the four elements,* and the signs are consequently described as being fiery, airy, watery or earthy. Aries, Leo and Sagittarius are fiery. They work harmoniously together, and sympathetically with the airy triplicity—consisting of Gemini, Libra and Aquarius. For fire and air uniting produce flame, which is the emblem of the Holy Spirit. The three watery signs, Cancer, Scorpio and Pisces, work sympathetically with the three that are described as earthy—Taurus, Virgo and Capricorn. For earth and water together make a fruitful soil. A well-balanced horoscope has the four elements equally accentuated, and it is a handicap for a man to be too fiery or too airy, too watery or too earthy; for each of these elements symbolises a plane, or realm of activity, spiritual, mental, emotional or physical, and if our evolution is to advance through the equal development and co-ordination of all our faculties we must not specialise in any one direction to such an extent as to let the others atrophy from disuse.

Human nature is complex, and full of mystery, and if we are to understand it aright, we must first contrive to unravel the various strands of which it is woven, and to separate them out for individual study, so that we may master the characteristics of each, and recognise them surely and certainly when we meet them in their working out. That being done we must learn to combine them again, and to realise how they ought to blend and harmonise, and so by sympathetic comprehension to school ourselves to deal wisely with all those with whom we are called upon to work. "*Tout comprendre c'est tout pardonner*"; and a careful study of the twelve types here set forth will prove suggestive and helpful to many. If such study is assisted by the collection of specimen horoscopes among those personally known to the student, there is no fear that the subject will be found a dull one. It must of course always be remembered that no character is spun from one thread alone, and that every man is more or less under the influence of all the twelve signs, so that he is, potentially at least, the Warrior, Builder, Poet, Prophet, King and so forth. But at the same time there is always one of these functions more congenial than the rest; one path on which progress will be more encouraging and rapid, because it is the path of least resistance; and it is distinctly consoling to find that in spite of false starts and blunders, that path is generally taken in the end, and that the round man in the square hole is much more rare than we imagine. Analysis of the horoscopes of a score or so of men and women of the age of forty years or more will prove that destiny has generally given them their true position. The king is called to administer and organise, even although he may have, like the Prince in the fairy tale, "but a very small kingdom." The warrior will fight—on the right side or on the wrong according to his powers of discrimination and stage of evolution—but he will most assuredly fight, and preferably against heavy odds. The poet will find some corner of the world in which to see his visions and dream his dreams in peace. The mediator becomes a middle-man of some kind, and the prophet gathers his little school of disciples around him—even if they can only meet by his own fireside. All along the line it is not what is outwardly achieved, but the progress made towards unity and perfection of character that really counts, and if even a few of those who take up this volume are impelled by the perusal of its pages to face the possibilities of their own lives fairly and squarely, determined to make the best of their own type whatever that type may be, and so far as in them lies to make allowances for types that differ from their own, the purpose of the author has been achieved.

For the benefit of readers who are unfamiliar with Eastern religions and philosophies, it should perhaps be pointed out that in the following pages the truth of the doctrine of re-incarnation is taken for granted, and that the Astrology which ignores that great teaching is apt to be too fatalistic and depressing. The horoscope is viewed here in the Eastern way as the symbol and to some extent the guiding chart of a man's life; but that life is looked upon as only one link in a great chain of lives, each following logically and naturally upon its predecessor. Consequently, the fact that one man is born under a strenuous and much enduring sign, and has to fight his way through difficulties, or bear the burdens of others all his days, and that another is born in comfortable circumstances, and is blessed with the type of personality that will smooth his path and make the acceptance of help and favour come easy to him, has to the astrologer nothing in it of hardship or injustice. The wheel of life continues to revolve, and the influence of each great Power makes itself felt in turn; and only after many attempts to play Warrior, King, Counsellor or any other *rôle*, can mastery of the part be attained. The order in which the different tasks are attempted and the way in which they are worked out in detail, will vary with every individual; and it is probably this endless variety in the sequence of experience that differentiates one character from another so strongly. Roughly speaking, every man has to go through the mill over and over again, until each separate power and quality is evolved to perfection; and the "Great Bible of the Zodiac," as it is sometimes called, gives us a hint of the normal order of development in humanity at large. Hope and courage and enterprise naturally head the list, for without them no achievement is possible. So the first place is given to Aries, the sign of the Warrior or Pioneer; and among primitive savages the Arietian is the type of man that stands for the ideal. After war comes peace, and with the dawn of civilisation we associate Taurus, the sign of the Builder, patient, persistent and steadfast, learning to follow the plough and to profit by the recurrent seasons of seed-time and harvest; gathering and putting to practical use the kindly fruits of the earth. Then comes the development of intellectual activity, the sign of Gemini suggesting to us the twin birth of science and of art. Cancer, the fourth sign, speaks to us of the growing love of home, the dawn of true patriotism and the gradual evolution of a noble pride of race, culminating in the activities of the kingly sign of Leo, which lifts the national life to a higher plane, organising and establishing and glorifying its administration. The true crown of Kingship is service, and after thinking out the principles of right government, the mind of man turns once more to the governed, so that the next step is active and willing service, without thought of glory or reward, and the cleansing and healing and nourishing of the national life goes forward under the influence of Virgo, the sign of purity and of health. The first part of the pilgrimage is now over, and with Libra, the sign of the Balance, we pause and sum up, adjusting and equalising and perfecting, with due regard to fair proportions and to harmony and beauty of the whole scheme. Then with fresh impulse we start on the return journey, and Scorpio, the most forceful sign, takes imperious hold of us, demanding more energy in the rulers, greater fortitude and endurance in the people, the complete mastery of nature's secrets, and the exercise of power everywhere; till Sagittarius in its greater wisdom calls a halt, speaking to us of reason and of conscience, and of the great teachings of philosophy, and also of that law of liberty which gives freedom not only to the body, but to the mind and to the soul. Only three more signs remain. Capricorn, which gives the splendid spur, awakening ambition and aspiration, and carrying a man upwards to the highest attainment of which he is capable; Aquarius, which sweeps away all false ideals, hypocrisies and shams, and seeks underneath accepted formulæ and conventions for principles and fundamental laws; and lastly Pisces, the sign of the dreamer, the interpreter and the poet. This gentle influence inspires the mystic to look inward towards the heart of all things, making him see the One in the many so clearly, that he may become a channel of illumination, revealing and interpreting God to humanity. Aries, the first sign, chants the great song of the coming forth from God. Pisces, the last sign, proclaims that coming forth an illusion, for in Him, at all stages of our pilgrimage, we live and move and have our being. The circle is complete—yet not a circle, but a spiral; and after the Poet has sung his song and given his message and taken his rest, he once more resumes his work as Pioneer, issuing forth more fully armed and better prepared than before to renew the combat, rising on every round to higher and ever higher levels, morally, mentally and spiritually.

But although the above sequence of lives may be looked upon as natural and normal, it does not follow that it is inevitable. It is quite conceivable that many of the woes we have to face arise from our own blind determination to take up the work that looks attractive without waiting to consider whether we are really fitted for it or not; and it is scarcely necessary to add, that in classifying the different kinds of human activity as the work of the Warrior, Statesman, Governor and so forth, the writer takes for granted that the very widest and most general application possible will be given to these descriptive words. The born fighter is not necessarily an army man; and he who has the insight of the poet does not always possess the power of expressing his vision in the form of verse.

What it is that actually determines the choice of the outer personality to be worn by the individual in any one incarnation is another question, and can hardly be discussed at length here. As has already been indicated, the author leans to the opinion of many thinkers that it is probably man's own free will. It seems only reasonable and just that the secret ambitions we nurse, the aspirations and ideals we cherish in one earthly life, should forge the chains which will draw us steadily along some particular line of development in the next. If, besides desiring a special sphere of action, we have actively prepared for it, we shall probably carry out our appointed tasks successfully. If we misuse present opportunities, neglect the development of our faculties, and merely spend our time in idly yearning and craving for something different from what we have, the succeeding life will assuredly be a failure, for at the end of each stage in the journey, we are told that "To him that hath shall be given, and from him that hath not, shall be taken away even that which he hath." Still, through that very failure we may learn something of the humility which is the beginning of wisdom, so that, with or without our voluntary co-operation, the great work of character-building goes on.

Readers who desire to study this fascinating subject in its modern dress are referred to the manuals on the *Evolution of Consciousness*, on *Reincarnation*, on *Karma*, and on kindred subjects, issued by the Theosophical Publishing Society. Those who prefer to dig for such information in ancient literature will find it variously expressed by many philosophers in the Classical as well as in the Oriental schools. One of the quaintest and most vivid presentations of this belief is to be found in the closing paragraphs of Plato's *Republic*, in the Vision of Er, a Grecian warrior slain in battle, who was allowed to return to earth and to describe the marvellous things he had seen on the other side of death. The teaching given in this Vision is practically the same as that familiar to students of Hinduism. "Your genius will not choose you, but you will choose your genius" is the solemn announcement made to the army of souls awaiting judgment; and owing to their lack of experience, or "because their minds have been darkened by folly or sensuality" in a previous life, many of them chose lamentably amiss; so that "the spectacle of the election was most curious—sad, and laughable, and strange." The lives were arranged in lots by those who had the guidance of all things, and every life had, of necessity, its own limitations and its own handicaps; but those who chose in a hurry forgot to consider that and were often appalled by their own choice after it was ratified. The greatest fool among them chose the

On the East, three Gates; on the North, three Gates; on the South, three Gates; and on the West, three Gates. And the wall of the city had twelve foundations, and in them the names of the twelve apostles of the Lamb.

REVELATIONS xxi. 13.

Part I.

DESCRIPTIVE

Come and see the mystery of the word ELOHIM. There are three degrees, and each degree by itself alone; yet notwithstanding they are all ONE and joined together in ONE and cannot be divided from each other.

RABBI BEN JOCHAI.

matter fairly, and from every point of view, they will speedily realise that the mere lengthening of the earthly pilgrimage does not in any way weaken or disturb the fundamental and essential teachings of the Great Founder of Christianity in the very least, but quite the contrary. It actually reconciles apparent contradictions, and makes much that was perplexing and difficult, show itself in its true light as reasonable and just; and the sooner the Church as a body awakens to the fact, the better for itself and for humanity at large.

greatest possible position as a tyrant; and found himself face to face with such blood-curdling tragedy in his own family life, that he would fain have resigned this coveted honour to another; but the wise Odysseus went about "seeking the life of a private man who had no cares," and "had some difficulty in finding this, which was lying about, and had been neglected by everybody else."

Plato's assertion that some poor suffering souls, sickened by the sorrows and disappointments of human experience, chose to return as birds or beasts, is naturally repugnant to the modern mind, accustomed as it is to a more orderly conception of evolution on the physical plane. It is suggestive that the great philosopher invariably attributes this retrograde choice to anger, resentment, bitterness or hate;—emotions which always lead to blunders. Perhaps if Plato had had our modern theories of evolution to work upon, this particular suggestion as to modes of rebirth might have been omitted. "As above so below"; and if lines of evolution neither cross nor intermingle on the physical plane, it seems probable that the evolution of consciousness will follow the same laws. The large and increasing body of Christians of the present generation who are inclined to accept the doctrine of reincarnation as a reasonable explanation of many social and psychological problems, will probably agree with those early Church Fathers who condemned *Plato's version* of the transmigration of souls; but a more acceptable form of the theory seems likely to be hammered out by certain investigators of psychic phenomena, who have taken up the comparative study of what are usually described as cases of recovered memory. An increasing number of persons in this present generation have apparently developed enough of the psychic or intuitive side of their natures to give them occasional glimpses of their own personalities and experiences in past lives. Such knowledge has been claimed by exceptionally great and gifted people—such as Pythagoras—in the past; but it is only in recent years that it has shown symptoms of becoming so common as to excite comparatively little comment. When such assertions become so precise as to be capable of proof by documentary evidence still existing, the theory of reincarnation will no longer be regarded as a hypothesis, but as a fact; and already the recording of such cases has begun. Such a statement may be a shock to those who cling to the orthodox teaching of their childhood; but if they consider the

♈ ARIES ♈

THE RAM.

The Sign of the

WARRIOR OR PIONEER

A cardinal fiery sign.

Keynote—Hope.

Watchword—Action.

Ruler—Mars.

♂

Mystical Gems—Amethyst, Diamond.

Colour— Red. *Metal*—Iron.

Physical Manifestation—Impetus.

Mental Manifestation—Enterprise.

Fight the Good Fight!

For we wrestle not against flesh and blood, but against principalities, against powers, against the rulers of the darkness of this world, against spiritual wickedness in high places. Wherefore take unto you the whole armour of God, that ye may be able to withstand in the evil day, and having done all, to stand. Stand therefore, having your loins girt about with truth, and having on he breast plate of righteousness; and your feet shod with the preparation of the gospel of peace. Above all, taking the shield of faith, wherewith ye shall be able to quench all the fiery darts of the wicked. And take the helmet of salvation, and the sword of the Spirit, which is the word of God.—Ephesians vi. 12.

CHAPTER I.

THE ARIETIAN TYPE

"Heavenly Glory . . . stuck upon him, as the Sun
In the grey vault of heaven; and, by his light,
Did all the chivalry of England move
To do brave acts." *K. Henry IV.*

Ruler

THE ruler of Aries is Mars, the planet which is declared to be the chief centre of Divine Energy in our planetary system. In the ancient world the intelligence associated with this planet was looked upon as the God of War, an essentially masculine power, ardent, active, energetic and fearless. Mars is defined as "The Source of division and of motion, separating the contrarieties of the Universe," and it is said that he "requires the assistance of Venus so that he may insert order and harmony into things contrary and discordant"; a saying well worthy of note. The form of energy which manifests in Action, can achieve nothing by itself alone; and it must be guided by Love or Wisdom or rather by both, before it can bring anything to perfection. The particular limitations of this aspect of deity are more easily grasped than those of any of the other gods. The old classic myths which describe his characteristics, represent him as peculiarly liable to err, especially when acting on his own initiative. He rushes into the fray recklessly, without examining into the justice or even into the origin of the quarrel; and he very frequently fights on the wrong side. Whenever he is firmly opposed by one of the other deities, and notably by Pallas Athene, he is defeated; for the haphazard employment of energy, which is the primitive form of warfare, is always ineffectual, and if Wisdom undertakes to control it, she can do with it what she will. The wife of Mars is Neris, Enterprise, and his sister is Bellona, War. In his train follow Honour and Courage, Horror and Fear, and finally, after the conflict, Peace and Security. Mars had many temples and shrines—some attended by women as well as men; but his worship was most characteristically and fittingly carried on in the great institution of the *Ludi Martiales*, and in the other games and gymnastic competitions held in his honour. He has his counterpart in all systems of religion. The Greeks called him Ares, the Scandinavians Tyr; and in Christian lands he is honoured under the names of various warrior saints, especially St. George.

Evolved Type

The type of fight congenial to the true Arietian is the "Forward charge!" He is the Captain, the Leader, the Pioneer among men; going out in sympathy to new thought, rapidly assimilating fresh ideas, always in the van of progress in whatever kind of work—intellectual, artistic or practical—he may take up. He gets to close quarters in his battles, and when highly developed fights best with his head; that is to say, in the field of thought. Enterprise and ardour are the characteristics of the type, and the channels into which these are directed will vary according to the condition and limitations of the individual and the particular stage of his evolution. Most Arietians show a definite preference for work which gives some opportunity for personal leadership and sufficient scope for their martial ardour. They really enjoy facing and overcoming difficulties, and will go out of their way to challenge opposition rather than forego the exercise of their faculties. Hope and enthusiasm are with them wherever they go and their happy knack of forgetting failure helps them through times of stress and strain and anxiety that would break down the courage of any other type. Rarely hampered by diffidence and shyness, and never by pessimism, they carry through their undertakings with a confidence and dash and brilliancy that disarm criticism.

The type is generally softened when manifesting in womankind, but it still displays its characteristic warmth and vitality; and even when hampered by ill-health, the daughter of Mars is apt to have a good deal of the warrior about her. She cannot abide half-hearted work or want of enthusiasm in those around her, and finds the cautious ultra-scrupulous person who weighs every word and deliberates over every decision, a terrible trial; a fact which she can generally make abundantly evident to the individual in question. She very often craves for more scope for her energies, and larger opportunities of swaying and leading her fellow-creatures than can be found in the ordinary routine of domestic duties; and is frequently to be found on committees and on deputations connected with social and political reforms.

Tranquillity and serenity are seldom appreciated at their true value by this type, and still more seldom achieved; but Arietians are nevertheless delightfully refreshing to meet, for they are bright and lively in society, and a boon and a blessing to all those who desire help in arousing public interest in their social and charitable undertakings. Other and very different types of humanity may excel in planning details and in organisation, but without efficient aid from the children of Mars, the most desirable projects will make little headway, and the best-laid schemes fall to the ground.

Primitive Type

At the early stages of evolution the Martial type naturally suffers from excess of the qualities associated with it. Courage, hope and enthusiasm in enterprise, become recklessness and heedlessness and fanaticism. These people must always be doing something; and, if their energies are not carefully guided for them, they rush headlong into activities which they are incapable of carrying to a successful issue. They fail utterly in work requiring tact and patience and self-control, and their eager desire to see immediate results is often both a misery and a temptation to them. They overwork their splendid bodies till they break down, and when they have got into hopeless difficulties, they exhaust their intellect by devising expedients till they can no longer distinguish the path of rectitude, which is always and ever the only reliable short cut. In order to bring about conditions or events on which they have set their hearts, they will sweep aside every obstacle that confronts them, without scrutinising very closely the means they employ to get rid of it; and the result is naturally disastrous. For "the mills of God grind slowly," and the attempt to hasten them in ways which are not God's, simply dislocates the machinery and results in useless friction, fierce opposition and endless delay. After such a state of affairs has been brought about, our unfortunate warrior waxes more militant than ever—fighting failure instead of accepting it, and blaming others for the miscarriage of his plans, instead of realising that his own deficiencies and shortcomings have led to the catastrophe. Consequently he is the last person to think of the true remedy for the muddle he is in; which is generally a patient retracing of the steps taken, and a careful undoing of the heedlessly tangled threads. The cutting of the Gordian knot by abandoning the enterprise is a much more congenial method of extricating himself from an awkward position; and this having been done the restless energy pours itself forth into fresh channels, until brought up by further obstacles.

At this early stage, the typical hopefulness concerning the future, takes the form of rebellion against the limitations of the present, and a constant source of trouble is the intense desire to "play lead" or to dominate others personally, before the qualities of the born leader are more than half developed, and naturally the simplest way of attaining that ambition is to shun the society of one's equals and superiors—who are usually qualified to criticise—and to associate only with intellectual inferiors, who are unlikely to foresee difficulties because they lack imagination. At the same time this craving for personal leadership in action is not associated with the desire for positions of responsibility in which the work is centralised and organised. Our Arietian is the Captain—not the General; and although he demands—and indeed insists upon—a free hand in carrying out orders, he generally takes service under a banner of some kind; but in early youth he is apt to make a very bad subordinate and is happier when working at a distance from headquarters, where close supervision is impossible. One source of trouble is that he has as a rule very little power of reading character correctly. This tells especially in his blundering choice of a hero to worship or a king to serve, and he is extremely self-willed about the matter, refusing to listen to reason, or to hear any criticism whatever of the idol of the moment. This power of shutting the ears and eyes is one which gives us a clue to what seems a most perplexing contradiction in the children of Mars. No type gives the impression of such perfectly straightforward sincerity; and yet none can begin to compete with it in sheer audacity and effrontery in uttering and maintaining what it knows—or ought to know—to be untrue. These people can make themselves blind and deaf to whatever they please; and having deceived themselves have very little difficulty in deceiving others. Their position may be utterly untenable, their facts without any shadow of foundation, but they stick to their guns nevertheless, determined to drive their schemes forward at all hazards, and bringing out their wildest assertion with such earnestness and conviction that only those of their hearers who have already caught them tripping can find any room for doubt. This trait is partly responsible for the loss of old and trusted friends, a misfortune which befalls our warrior somewhat frequently; for it requires great magnanimity to forgive falsehood, and the shock of repeatedly detecting discrepancies and inconsistencies in the statements of someone previously held in honour and esteem, proves too much of a strain on the patience and forbearance of the majority of mankind. Attempted explanation or justification merely increases the difficulty, for the plea of expediency is accepted only by the few; and the martial craving for immediate results is only foolishness to those who understand the value of clearness and accuracy, or who rate stability of construction higher than rapidity of achievement. Another source of woe is the tendency of the Arietian to make very rapid progress in development, and so to grow away from his old friends, disconcerting and distressing them by sudden and unexpected changes in his convictions and opinions; and further complications arise from the fact that it is practically impossible for him to regain, even temporarily, his former point of view. His custom is always to throw the past behind him and go forward; and those who attempt to cry halt, are very frequently swept out of the way with a contempt which arouses all their resentment.

Love and Friendship

Enthusiastic friendship fills a large place in the emotional life of the sons and daughters of Aries, and the same impetuosity and ardour that is shown in this direction, also characterises their love affairs. No type is warmer-hearted, or more frank and generous in showing affection; but, even among the highly developed, these tendencies are apt to lead to trouble, and the sorrows that follow upon rash engagements and imprudent marriages are among the forms of discipline that they are called upon to face. They not infrequently mate with a husband or wife who can hold his or her own, and may succeed in making of matrimony a more or less merry duel; for as a rule the children of Mars are blest and assisted by a sense of fun and a real gift of enjoying a situation; but there is apt to be a good deal of sparring, and of wasted energy in consequence. Occasionally, however, our warrior contrives to settle down, as peacefully as in him lies, with some gentle and adaptable mate who admires his energy while finding it impossible to emulate it, and who makes up for the Martian's slap-dash way of going at his work, by patiently following after him, adjusting the difficulties his impetuosity has occasioned, and filling in the details his haste has overlooked.

If falling in love is, even for the highly developed specimens, a dangerously headlong performance, falling out of love is, at the primitive stage, more dangerously headlong still, for loyalty and tenacity are not among the virtues of this sign, and the desire for change of surroundings and companionship is difficult to master. Repentance, once begun, has all the characteristic energy of the type, and it frequently finds an outlet in definite action. Broken troth and cancelled wedding are the natural results of this tendency, and decrees of separation or divorce are resorted to in circumstances which would not be found unendurable by those born under the more adaptable and forbearing signs.

In Drama and Fiction

The Arietian type is a favourite one in fiction, and supplies the hero of many a dashing exploit and hair-breadth escape; for the fact that the sons of Mars lead their followers *personally*, taking the lion's share of any danger involved, and never shrinking or shirking or sparing themselves, makes them peculiarly fitted to arouse popular sympathy. Shakespeare has drawn for us a splendid example in Harry Hotspur, the fiery son of old Northumberland; and the elder Dumas has filled volumes with the adventures of that hero's astrological brethren. Hotspur's tendency to hyperbolic eloquence, criticised by some as rhodomontade inappropriate to a soldier and a man of action, is quite characteristic of the type, and the glowing declaration:

> "By Heaven, methinks it were an easy leap,
> To pluck bright honour from the pale-faced moon;
> Or dive into the bottom of the deep,
> Where fathom-line could never touch the ground,
> And pluck up drowned honour by the locks;"

could only have been uttered by a son of Mars at white heat. Striking portraits of more primitive specimens are also to be found in light literature — headstrong rebels, bumptious bullies and dangerous demagogues, many of whom play important parts in old-world plays and romances and in modern penny dreadfuls. The foibles and follies of Arietians at the early stage of their evolution are nowhere better hit off than in the personage of Jack Cade as drawn by Shakespeare in his historical drama of "Henry VI." It is characteristic of the type that Cade was a mere tool in the hands of an abler and still more unscrupulous man; for leaders of popular rebellions are generally the sport—and the victims—of the wire-pullers behind. His intolerance of superior culture in others is also typical. Having no education himself, he cannot endure those who have; and so refuses to countenance any man with learning enough to sign his own name. The applause of the majority, even if that majority be but a miserable rabble, is the breath of his life, and however high-handed a bully he may show himself in his treatment of individuals, he is careful to do nothing that will seriously endanger his popularity with the mass of his followers. His victory depends on their adherence, and no misstatement is too wild and exaggerated if it will increase their loyalty, and give his enterprise a better chance of success.

In Real Life

One of the finest and most interesting of the various Arietian personalities connected with recent history is that of Charles Gordon, who was in his youth the dauntless leader of "the ever-victorious army" during the Taeping rebellion in China in the year 1862; and later in life, the General entrusted by the Khedive with the task of suppressing the slave-trade, subduing the forces of the Mahdi, and establishing order in the Soudan. His birth-hour, recorded in his father's family Bible, shows 13° of Aries rising; and a careful perusal of his biography* will prove most helpful to any student desiring to understand this type. Even in minor details of personal appearance, manner and gait, he falls exactly into his correct class as a son of Mars. He had the orthodox, keen-sighted blue eyes, with a fearless and somewhat dominating look in them. His hair was crisp and brown and inclined to curl. His manner was extremely unaffected and sincere, and "he had plenty of imperious authority at command when required." "The pale blue eye could flash with the fire of a born leader of men. . . . The square jaw denoted unshakable resolution" and "in congenial company Gordon was never tranquil, pacing up and down the room, with only brief stops to impress a point on his listener by holding his arm for a few seconds, and looking at him intently to see if he followed with understanding and interest the drift of his remarks; lighting cigarette after cigarette to enable him to curb his own impetuosity, and demonstrating in every act and phrase the truth of his own words that inaction was intolerable to him." . . . "In spite of the beautiful goodness of his heart, and the great breadth of his charity, Gordon was far from possessing a placid temperament, or from being patient over small things. Indeed

* *Life of Gordon*, by D. C. Boulger, published by T. Fisher Unwin Information as to the hour kindly given through "Kymry," from Sepharial's Almanac.

his very energy tended to make him impatient and irritable whenever any person or thing interfered with his intentions and desires. . . . There was no trace of timidity in his composition. He had a most powerful Will. When his mind was made up on a matter, it never seemed to occur to him that there could be anything more to say about it. Such was his superb confidence in himself."

The student will note with some satisfaction the faithfulness to type indicated by the escapades of his early youth—the practical jokes and thoughtless mischief of his schoolboy and cadet days—the unnecessary ringing of doorbells and light-hearted smashing of other people's windows—and other examples of crazy foolishness all faithfully chronicled and thoroughly characteristic, being simply the outcome of a superabundant vitality not yet under proper control.

It is interesting also to read that his biographer records a distinct modification in Gordon's character, or rather a complete change in the *direction* of his energies after his thirty-second year. The Gordon of the Soudan, he remarks, was not the Gordon of China. There was no loss of power or activity, but during what is described as a transition period, spent in engineering work at Gravesend, philanthropy began to occupy the foremost place in a mind where formerly professional zeal and a keen appreciation of the glory of warfare had reigned supreme. The astrologer will note that this transition period includes the thirty-fifth year of his life; the year in which, in most cases, the influence of the sign in which the Sun is found, begins to show itself strongly and definitely, carrying a man into the sphere in which he will most readily find success. In Gordon's horoscope, the Sun is in Aquarius, the most humanitarian and fraternal of all the signs, and it is certainly on his philanthropy as much as on his soldiership that his fame rests. Had he thought more of his own personal glory and less of the poor folks, white or black, around him, he might possibly have been more successful—as the world counts success; and though he was a warrior to the end, the fitting monument raised to his memory by his sorrowing fellow-countrymen is the Gordon Boys' Home—a charitable institution for waifs and strays.

Literary Style

Gordon's journals partake too much of the nature of hurried notes and jottings to be characteristic examples of Arietian style; but they show something of its vigour and go, and are true to the type in that they are concerned almost entirely with action, with what people were doing or leaving undone all around him. Possibly had some shorthand reporter preserved for us his rousing extempore addresses to his classes of working lads at Gravesend, we should have had something more strikingly Martial to remember him by; for it is in oratory rather than in literature that Arietians find scope for the exuberant energy of their natural expression. Their style is free and flowing, abounding in apt illustration and telling phrase, and tending to well-rounded periods and measured cadences rather than to precision and accuracy of statement. It is consequently exceedingly well adapted to public speaking, either in the pulpit or on the platform, and has a special value for those engaged in preaching a crusade of any kind. The somewhat belligerent enthusiast of the street-corner often betrays in the measured swing of his flights of eloquence the characteristics of this class, even when his grammar is defective and his logic nowhere; and at all great crises of national history, when civil or religious liberty is in danger, or when great forward movements are just beginning, the tongues and pens of the sons of Mars will find full employment. Students who desire to analyse such outpourings will find material for their study in the *verbatim* reports*—published in pamphlet form—of the discourses of Mrs. Annie Besant. In her autobiography she gives us her horoscope map, which shows 10° of Aries rising, and Mars not very far below the horizon, and perusal of the pages which deal with her early life, and its record of opposition challenged and difficulties overcome, will show how energetically she answered to the imperious call of her ruler. Her work in the slums of London was of the typical Arietian quality, and it is interesting to note her preference for nursing cases of dangerous illness—cases which could give her the thrilling sensation of "carrying on a hand-to-hand conflict with death." Her rapid growth away from the training and teaching of her childhood is also typical; for many Arietians change their religion, or at any rate its outer form; probably because action seems to them so very important, that to take part in a ritual which no longer represents their beliefs is much more difficult for them than for other people. Hence possibly the amount of non-conformity in England, which is, according to astrological tradition, ruled by Aries.

* Theosophical Publishing Society

It is sometimes profitable for the analyst of any particular type to pass in review the various notabilities who have done the characteristic work of the particular sign in the past, and to note how far their personalities and style correspond with what we have observed in specimens studied close at hand to-day. We may look for possible sons of Aries among popular leaders and great orators of all ages, and by comparing the biographical and descriptive details available about them, draw our conclusions, learning incidentally much that will help us in the study of character, as well as something of literary criticism, for "the style is the man."

Religion

As it is only in the domain of religion that enthusiasm can reach its greatest heights, so it is among the pioneers of the great religious movements that we naturally seek for the most strongly accentuated specimens of the Arietian brotherhood. Among them, two rise before us, and stand out with special clearness—Mahomet, the enthusiastic and well-beloved prophet of the dusky sons of the desert; and Moses, the leader and law-giver of Israel. The scriptural assertion—surely a mistranslation!—that the latter was a "meek" man, may give the reader pause; but analysis of his life* and character leaves little room for doubt, and the four magnificent orations ascribed to him in the book of Deuteronomy, show the martial characteristics so strongly that the astrologer should find little difficulty in accepting the idea that the scribe was actually "inspired" to give them accurately. A typical passage is to be found in the thirtieth chapter:

"For this commandment which I command thee this day, it is not too hard for thee, neither is it far off. It is not in heaven, that thou shouldst say, 'Who shall go up to heaven and bring it unto us and make us to hear it that we may do it?' Neither is it beyond the sea that thou shouldst say, 'who shall go over the sea for us, and bring it unto us and make us to hear it that we may do it?' But the word is very nigh unto thee, in thy mouth and in thy heart, that thou mayst do it."

The sterner passages are simpler in construction, but equally characteristic in their oratorical ring.

"I call heaven and earth to witness against you this day, that I have set before you life and death, the blessing and the curse."

We find equally good examples of this style in the Koran,

* Consider the sudden slaughter of the Egyptian, the breaking of the tables of stone, the striking of the rock and the grinding to powder of the golden calf.

especially in the more rhetorical passages such as the opening paragraphs of Chapters 79, 81 and 82; and the Prophet's reply to his relatives when they tried to dissuade him from uttering his message would, taken by itself, be enough to proclaim the son of Mars. "Though you set the sun against me on my right hand, and the moon upon my left, I will *never* give it up!" The arduous pilgrimage to Mecca is a fitting expression of devotion to the teaching of this warrior prophet; for it is a strenuous and even a dangerous undertaking, and makes a considerable call on the physical strength and endurance of the faithful.

Reference has already been made to the *Ludi Martiales* of ancient Rome. Perhaps Western Nations have been too prone to let the religious element disappear from the field of athletics. The development and domination of the physical body can be undertaken with as much religious fervour as the training of the emotions or the mind; and the ambition to make that body a fit temple for the indwelling spirit should be held up as an ideal by every teacher of physical culture. Our modern athletes have probably lost more than they realise through the fact that their competitions are no longer dedicated to the Gods; but the old conviction that such a dedication was called for, dies hard, and, in England at any rate, there are certain forms of exercise that rank as ritual still. Games such as football and cricket are looked upon as symbolic presentations of the greater game of life, and insisted upon by our highest educational authorities as part of the school curriculum. Training in these exercises is considered the best possible method of teaching a boy to strive for the welfare of the whole corporate body, and not merely for personal glorification. Shakespeare, in reference to the astrological tradition mentioned above, called England "this seat of Mars," and the choice of St. George as the patron saint of the country is peculiarly appropriate. The nation has answered nobly in the past to its Ruler's call for energy and enterprise; but a word of caution on this matter may not be out of place. It is a serious form of error—although a very common one—to exalt and worship one aspect of deity alone, and to neglect the reverence due to all the rest; and there is no doubt that England gives Mars a dangerously prominent place among deities. When a popular poet recently dared to voice a protest on this subject, his utterance was treated as rank filial impiety and his somewhat scathing reference to "flannelled fools and muddied oafs" was condemned by people and by press as little short of blasphemous. Mr. Kipling's pessimistic views may or may not have been exaggerated in their expression, but the conviction that athletics can be overdone, and so defeat their own end, is gradually forcing itself upon the parents and teachers of England. Fair play is the jewel John Bull wears next his heart, and Right Action is his ideal; but his belief that it doesn't matter what a man thinks or feels so long as he *does* the right thing, is a most dangerous form of heresy; and a ritual calculated to purify the emotions and awaken the mind is just as important as a ritual designed primarily for the development of the body. However valuable the discipline of going into rigorous training may prove for the athletes themselves, it can do little or nothing for the unthinking multitudes who attend matches and races in order to enjoy vicariously the unearned sensations of effort and achievement. It should also be remembered that their unrestrained emotional excitement, especially when it is stimulated by betting on the possible results of the competition, spells nothing but danger.

Physical Characteristics

The Arietian type expressed in physical form is active, energetic and muscular. The bones are large and the hair either crisp, wiry and curly, or softer and of very thick growth. It is said to be generally of a strong colour, brown, red or warm blond, but Aries is a sign of very short ascension in the North, and specimens are much rarer than is the case with most of the other types; so it is difficult to test the truth of these traditional assertions. The writer has seen both black hair and golden in the daughters of this type, and it is really more easily recognised by its keen glance, bright vivacious manner, and impetuous habit of rushing at a subject or a bit of work, than by its actual colouring. The masculine type has a fine forehead, a somewhat short nose, an orator's mouth, and a powerful jaw. Other specimens have longer faces, and in their case there is a more prominent or even aquiline nose, and a longish upper lip. The movements are quicker and more impulsive and the whole personality is intensely alive. The athletic young Englishman at his best shows the type to advantage, as also does the Prussian soldier. *Both* countries are said to be under the sway of Mars; which is probably why there is a tendency for them to come to loggerheads at times: for competition and emulation play a large part in Arietian progress, and have their unlovely aspects as well as their beneficent and stimulating effects upon national life and character.

Arietians are often attracted into the army, and many of those who are not, take an active part in territorial work and do volunteering of various kinds—fire-brigade by preference! They are also drawn in more peaceful ways to the use and manipulation of fire and steel. Many are distinguished as surgeons. Humbler brethren are gun-makers, cutlers, engine-drivers, stokers and chauffeurs. The caricature of the type is naturally to be sought at the lowest levels, and may be seen in the pugilist or "chucker-out" of the comic papers; or, in grimmer guise, in the Bill Sykes type of criminal, big boned and brawny and prone to sudden gusts of fury and ferocity.

As regards physical health and energy this is a magnificent type, **Health** but its very excess of vitality is a danger, and maladies are not infrequently induced by over-work, which brings its own nemesis of enforced idleness—a cruel discipline for the child of Mars. The headstrong tendency to carry an enterprise through in wholly adverse circumstances or at an unsuitable time is naturally responsible for frequent disappointment; which results in irritation, anger and impatience, sometimes inducing severe headaches, followed by brain-fag or neuralgia, which may be precursors of gastric and kidney derangements. In some specimens, religious and other enthusiasm degenerates into fanaticism or monomania of some kind; a form of malady very hard to combat, and not infrequently dangerous.

The remedy of remedies for this type is constant self-control—the cultivation of patience, tranquillity, gentleness, forethought and humility. Faith in others, whether superiors or equals, may also be recommended; for during illness the Arietian's fond delusion that no one can really do anything properly but himself, altogether runs away with him, and no amount of mistakes and blunders on his own part will cure him of it. The old-fashioned remedy of blood-letting is, in certain cases, to be recommended; but it is better to regulate the circulation by right thinking, and by the cultivation of moral strength and all the truly virile qualities. If impatience and childish ill-temper and irritability are held in check, the headaches which presage a break-down and which are generally accompanied by an unpleasant rush of blood to the brain, will soon disappear. Vigorous daily exercise in the open air is very desirable for this type, and those belonging to it should never touch alcohol or any exciting drug ; for control of the passional nature is quite hard enough already without making matters worse by stimulating it. At the same time doctors and nurses would do wisely to remember that Arietian patients are driven almost to frenzy by a too insistent use of the negative, and that what their souls invariably crave for most is the "Everlasting Yea." The ten times repeated *shalt not* of the Hebrew commandments is enough to make our invalid warrior—in certain moods—half crazy with longing to break them all; whereas the glorious affirmatives of the Founder of Christianity will go straight to his heart. "Thou shalt love the Lord thy God with all thy heart and with all thy soul and with all thy mind. This is the first and the greatest commandment, and the second is like unto it, *thou shalt love thy neighbour as thyself.*" On these two commandments do most truly hang "all the law and the prophets," and the sons and daughters of Mars who dedicate their splendid energies to the attempt to carry them out, will have nothing to fear from the energy and enthusiasm which are their greatest gifts.

♉ TAURUS ♉

THE BULL.

The Sign of the

BUILDER OR PRODUCER

A fixed earthy sign.

Keynote—Peace.

Watchword—Stability.

Ruler—The Earth.
The Negative side of Venus ?)

⊕

Mystical Gems—Moss-agate, Emerald.

Colour—Indigo blue ? *Metal*—Copper ?

Physical Manifestation—Inertia.

Mental Manifestation—Steadfastness.

Not every one that saith unto me Lord, Lord, shall enter into the kingdom of heaven; but he that doeth the will of my Father which is in heaven. . . . Therefore whosoever heareth these sayings of mine, and doeth them, I will liken him unto a wise man, which built his house upon a rock: and the rain descended, and the floods came, and the winds blew and beat upon that house, and it fell not; for it was founded upon a rock.—MATTHEW vii. 21.

In the elder days of art
Builders wrought with greatest care
The unseen and hidden part,
For the Gods see everywhere.

* * * *

Build to-day then, firm and sure
On a broad and ample base,
And ascending and secure
Shall to-morrow find its place.

LONGFELLOW.

CHAPTER II.

The Taurean Type

Were we not born under Taurus?—*Twelfth Night.*

In ancient days only five planets were known—Mercury, Venus, Mars, Jupiter, and Saturn—and between the influences of these five planets and the influences associated with the Great Powers symbolised by the Signs of the Zodiac astrologers discerned a sympathetic relationship. Certain planets seemed merely to echo or repeat the influence of certain signs. To each planet were then assigned two signs as sympathetic, and with one of these two signs the bond was so strong that the planet was said to rule it *positively*. With the other, the bond was weaker and more indefinite, and the planet was only said to rule it *negatively*. This arrangement provided ten of the twelve signs with rulers, and the two remaining signs were given to the Sun and the Moon respectively. Since these days, two more planets, Neptune and Uranus, have been added to the list, and astronomers suggest that there are more. One called Vulcan is* believed to have its orbit nearer still to the Sun than Mercury; but the radiance of the great luminary makes it invisible. The existence of two others beyond Neptune is suspected. The asteroids are believed to represent one that has been shattered, and last but not least the Earth itself has been classified as one of these beautiful orbs, holding its stately course in the shining heavens, and subject to the same laws as its brethren. Astrologers have consequently had to revise their theories; and among other changes the negative rulers of the signs have had to be dethroned. When a planet is described as the positive ruler of a sign, we know where we are. As we have already seen, Mars is the positive ruler of Aries; and when it rises in a horoscope we know that the native—the individual to whom that horoscope belongs—will show the martial qualities of courage, enterprise and self-confidence; but a planet rising never brings up the qualities of a sign over which it is said to hold a negative sway. When therefore we find it asserted that Taurus is ruled by the negative side of Venus, we are justified in Ruler

* Because of certain irregularities in the movements of Mercury.

doubting the assertion and in asking whether no more suitable ruler can be suggested; for certain it is that Venus rising does not bring up the essential Taurean quality of steadfastness,* but quite the reverse; and it is that quality we must look for in the power or deity associated with this sign.

The true ruler of Taurus is probably the angel or planetary spirit of our own kindly Mother Earth, a deity worshipped under many names. As Vesta† she is defined as the goddess presiding over the hearth and home, the protectress of the state and of the empire. She is described as "giving to the orbs of the planets the sameness of their revolutions"; and her sacred fire is said to burn ever steadily at the heart of things. Another classical personification of this steadfast and immutable aspect of deity is Juno, the representative and upholder of divine law. She is the ox-eyed goddess of the strong arms, the protector of family life and the guardian of all social contracts, including the marriage contract, and also the Mother of Health and Energy in the persons of Hebe and of Mars. In Northern lands she is Frigga, the wife of Odin. In Christendom she has been replaced by the Madonna in her aspect of earth mother, the aspect in which she is pictorially represented as sheltering her children under a long flowing cloak. The month of Mary is the month of May, when the Sun is in Taurus, and special honours are then paid to the Blessed Virgin in all Roman Catholic countries. It is to her that her children turn when seeking for peace and rest, and to her that petitions for material prosperity are most frequently addressed. The Latin litany still chanted in her praise is said to include lines from an ancient hymn to Juno; and the later Christian artists have identified her with the heavenly being, "The woman" of the Book of Revelation, who is said to be supported and helped by the earth, which gives her an abiding place in the day of her need, and which devours or absorbs those waters—or astral energies—which would otherwise have swept her away. She is described as being clothed with the Sun and crowned with the twelve stars, and having the Moon—the satellite

---

* Or, in its imperfect form, obstinacy.

† For the definition of this deity I am indebted to quotations in G R S. Mead's *Orpheus, the Theosophy of the Greeks* The student of physics may see in this power something akin to inertia, which gives physical stability and is connected with the law of gravitation.

of the earth—*under her feet;* and she is destined to bring forth at the appointed time the Redeemer of all mankind. The whole of this description is full of meaning to the student of astrology, and indeed, many passages in that marvellous book, with its constant references to angels and archangels and signs and wonders "seen in the heavens," must necessarily remain unintelligible to those who persist in ignoring this particular key to their interpretation.

Evolved Type

The chief characteristic of the highly developed Taurean is his stability of character and of purpose. His is the steadfast mind, unshaken in adversity, and his the power of quiet persistence in the face of difficulties. He has found his true position with regard to the Universe, and that position is the centre. Identified with the Self of all selves, one with the very heart of things, he refuses to be hustled or hurried or frightened or pushed into any false position, either mental or physical; and generally excels in work requiring a sense of true proportion and a just appreciation of relative values. He thoroughly understands the importance of system, method and order, enjoys routine and regularity, and often shows constructive ability, especially in matters concerning the foundations and beginnings of enterprise. He works best when spurred by necessity or inspired by the love of others, and especially by love of his wife and family, and in hard circumstances his patience and perseverance are marvellous. He generally has a horror of debt, and shows much care and prudence in the administration of affairs, succeeding particularly well in businesses such as banking, life assurance and trust work of all kinds. The office of acting as mainstay or prop in material ways is peculiarly congenial to the type, and it consequently provides many ideal trustees and guardians—people who will make large sacrifices of time and energy, rather than fail those who have confided in them. The widow and the fatherless find in them towers of strength, and the commercial integrity which qualifies them for such posts also fits them for many kinds of public office. People of this type suit subordinate positions, junior partnerships, and so forth, preferring to have boundaries and limits set them by someone in supreme authority, for obedience comes easy to them when they have once given in their allegiance or accepted an office; and they understand its advantages too well to waste time in fruitless rebellion even when their taskmaster is a fairly severe one. When nagged beyond endurance, however, they can make a stand, and their occasional out-bursts of righteous wrath are sufficiently vehement to cause considerable consternation to those who have aroused them. Besides excelling in the building up of commercial and other undertakings, Taureans are very successful in agricultural and other rural pursuits, and in the cultivation and garnering of the kindly fruits of the earth. Farming and gardening give employment to many children of this sign, the humbler of whom dig and delve, follow the plough and the harrow, or carry the milking pail. Others take part in practical constructive work, laying bricks, or piling stone upon stone, generally in a leisurely fashion, and always under the direction of others. Not a few find snug and easy births as janitors, hall-keepers and trusted custodians of places of public interest; and others hold government appointments as custom-house officers, collectors of revenue or members of the police force.

The quick recognition of relative and essential values which shows in all the sons and daughters of this sign, gives them almost invariably the delightful gift of humour. Their feet never lose touch with the solid ground, and they generally know not only where they stand themselves, but where other people stand also; so that the preposterous claims of the braggart and the charlatan and the hysterical exaggerations of more excitable individuals merely move them to mirth. Their laughter has, however, no touch of malice in it, and the true Taurean enjoys a joke against himself as whole-heartedly as any. It is consequently difficult to ruffle him, and his kindly tolerance and warmth of heart are calculated to make him a favourite among his fellow men and women; many of whom find his leisurely ways and tranquil presence very soothing when they are fretted or fatigued. This gift of restfulness makes people of this type particularly welcome in the sick-room, and some of them, while engaged in nursing, develop a healing touch; especially if an unselfish impulse to pass on the superabundant vitality is encouraged, and the principles of magnetic healing are assimilated.

Primitive Type

The primitive specimen naturally prefers to keep his good things to himself and often by seeking to save his life loses it; for excess of vitality stored up, instead of overflowing for the benefit of others, is a danger, and not an advantage, to its owner. At the early stages our Taurean, instead of finding his own centre in the Divine Centre of the Universe, is self-centred in the ordinary sense of the words, and quite incapable of seeing anyone's point of view but his own. His steadfast nature and splendid persistence only show as a mulish obstinacy and a pig-headed determination to hold his own. Tranquillity and restfulness are represented by laziness and sloth, and the inherent loyalty characteristic of the developed type, as well as its strength and solidity of character, are only recognisable in an ignorant and foolish dislike of change, and a dogged disinclination to strenuous exertion of any kind. The primitive Taurean is absurdly over-cautious and exasperatingly deliberate; and his filial devotion to his Mother Earth and gratitude for her gifts are often perverted to a gross materialism accompanied by much self-indulgence, which saps the energy and leads to mental stagnation. He is never aggressive in battle, and avoids it if possible; but when pushed to the wall, or persistently goaded, will sometimes astonish his opponent by an outburst of fury, dangerous while it lasts, but quickly succeeded by a resumption of stolidity. Even at this early stage, the sense of humour is conspicuous, and although his little joke may take some time in the making, it is usually a genuine achievement of its kind, even if it hardly rises above the level of the grotesque and is distinguished rather for its breadth than for its depth.

Love and Friendship

The Taurean shows himself exceptionally capable of faithful and enduring friendship and affection. His loyalty lives on in spite of neglect or rebuff, thus partaking of the persistent and somewhat dogged nature of the essential qualities of the sign. In both sexes there is a tendency to fall in love early and keep it up late, and the devotion of people of this type is almost invariably offered to living, breathing realities, and not to ideal or abstract heroes and heroines. At the primitive stage the nature is somewhat over-amorous and sensual, and even when well developed there is enough of the *earthy* or physical element about the affection to make the Taurean friend or lover crave very strongly for the actual physical presence of the beloved. Telepathic communication or spiritual companionship have not enough body in them to satisfy; and when the emotions come strongly into play they are almost always betrayed, sooner or later, by the tendency to give them a tangible form. Every excuse for a personal interview is snatched at. Any pretext that will give an opportunity for communication of a definite kind is seized and held on to with dogged persistence. Trouble and inconvenience and even absurdity are of no account, if a chance arises to deliver a note or lend a book or bestow a photograph, flower or gift of some kind. The onlooker may deride, the adored one may grow restive and even cross, but the steady pursuit goes on till it ends either in victory or in unmistakable defeat and the triumph of a rival. In the latter case a certain amount of philosophy comes to the rescue, and the very lovable humility of the type asserts itself. The bright particular star has proved to be really out of reach, but the disappointment is accepted without bitterness or resentment, for Taureans are rarely handicapped by pride and self-conceit though frequently by shyness and self-consciousness. If victorious, the marriage preparations go forward with zest, and the union is generally satisfactory ; for a sense of proportion prevents a Taurean husband or wife from exacting too much, and the natural kindliness and warmth of heart blossom beautifully in the parental instinct. Marriage with a primitive specimen is, however, naturally somewhat of a trial, and trouble may arise on account of his or her laziness and self-indulgence. The women make splendid mothers physically and welcome their offspring with great delight, preferring to nurse and tend them personally if possible, and never wearing out their childish nerves by the fussy attentions, constant supervision and correction that sometimes pass for parental care in the case of more worried and worrying individuals. It is hardly necessary to point out the dangers to which the primitive maiden of this type is exposed. Physical well-being and comfort are apt to be given a very high place, and when a life of comparative idleness and luxury is possible, conditions are not too closely scanned. A mercenary marriage suggests itself as a comfortable solution of many difficulties, and the weaker sisters, especially when hard-pressed by poverty, fall lower yet. The favourite slave of a Turkish Harem, if she is to be really happy and contented, should be born under this sign, but naturally these remarks are only applicable to those whose spiritual energies are not yet awakened. After the great work of regeneration has begun, the soft and sensuous parts of the nature, purified and transmuted to gentleness and compassion, take their place as jewels in the glorious crown of Taurean womanhood and no type can excel this one in tenderness and charm.

Religion The religious tendency of the Taurean is occasionally conspicuous by its absence; but even in the most materialistic of the sons and daughters of the sign, there is always an inclination to hold settled convictions, one way or another, rather than to be swayed and harassed by difficulties and doubts. They generally know what they believe and what they disbelieve, and have no objection to stating it if challenged. The lowly souls among them find sufficient outlet for their religious feelings in intense gratitude to the Giver of all good, the aspect of deity which appeals to them most being that covered by the country parson's invocation in his grace before a *real* banquet—"O Bountiful Providence!" Their gratitude is, not infrequently, of the type which is strengthened by a lively hope of further favours to come. The more highly evolved find their reverence deeply stirred by the conception of God as Builder of the Cosmos, and the beautiful ritual of freemasonry is valuable and helpful to many sons of this sign, who learn through its symbology and teaching to build up their own characters in accordance with the plan of the Great Architect of the Universe. If environment has made them more or less orthodox and inclined them to church observance, they like services to be well and even sumptuously rendered. In sects where images are forbidden, the comfortable church with a well-paid choir and a first-class organ is preferred. The Taurean *paterfamilias* gives handsomely to the collection and is probably one of the treasurers or business managers of church committee or building fund, and may frequently be descried in the corner of his own well-cushioned pew, enjoying a quiet siesta during the sermon. He inclines to accept the teaching that has come his way in early youth, and is averse to change, though tolerant of that kind of development which accompanies the gradual building up of a more substantial position for the church with which he happens to be connected. In forms of faith in which the use of material symbols—incense, rosaries, images and other physical aids to concentration and devotion—are permitted, he finds great satisfaction; and probably no religious development which the world has ever seen has been more typical of this sign than the ancient religion of Egypt, the land of Taurus or the Golden Calf. The Great Pyramid, the most lasting and stable of all sacred buildings, firmly based on solid foundations and tapering to a mere point at the highest levels, is its fitting monument; the impressive and highly symbolical ritual of the *Book of the Dead* is its ideal prayer-book. No race has more fully realised the value of symbolism, or used it more freely. These people believed in a future life and another world no doubt, but the claims of the physical plane, its uses and significance, were ever present to their minds. With tranquil serenity they looked forward to the heaven-world and accepted in theory the immortality of the soul; but they lived upon earth, and strove to immortalise the body by making a mummy of it. A natural result of this procedure is the erection of costly shrines and tombs, and the development of rites and ceremonies which show honour to those who are gone, and this also produces a kind of religious observance congenial to our Taurean, who, in spite of his steady-going stay-at-home temperament, inclines to take a pilgrimage at times and prefers to visit places hallowed by association with revered teachers or saints. He likes to tread the soil they have trod, to see and if possible handle the objects connected with them. He prefers that his impressions concerning the activities of the higher planes should be helped by stimuli to the physical senses. There is consequently some danger of idolatry—of exaltation of the relic or symbol over what is actually intended to be remembered or symbolised. In Northern lands this custom has been somewhat sternly suppressed, but it is interesting to note how the inherent tendencies of human nature will find an outlet somewhere, and it is open to question whether the substitution of the worship of the almighty dollar for that of the Golden Calf has really anything to recommend it.

Literary Style

The Taurean habit of mind is contemplative, and his literary expression indicates the fact. He is apt to take his time about telling a story, and to dwell at considerable length on points which interest him or strike him as important, especially if they have anything to do with the foundations of the plot or the essential qualities to be shown by the characters. His sense of proportion, however, keeps this ruminating tendency in check; and when critically examined these meditative passages are generally found to be integral parts of the whole. His attention to solidity of structure naturally makes for permanence and durability, and Taurean work stands the wear and tear of time better than most, because it gets down to bed-rock, and is very little affected by the passing fashions of a day. He has the builder's instinct for what is really essential, and never troubles his head about decoration till he has his proportions fixed and his walls fair and square before him. Consequently the ornament introduced is always well chosen, emphasising all that is good and permanent in the structure, and thereby adding greatly to the effect of the whole. He gives us no misshapen curve, no confused outlines. If there is any carelessness it is in the matter of finish, but even then his roughness and lack of polish are due rather to the coarse grain of the material handled than to want of judgment in the builder; and often what is condemned as gross by people of culture and refinement is nevertheless artistic, because it is thoroughly appropriate to the subject in hand, which may actually demand breadth and freedom in its treatment. For to the true-born son of Taurus nothing is common or unclean. Anything that concerns the ordinary daily life of toiling, suffering, slowly-evolving humanity seems to him legitimate and suitable as a subject for literary treatment. The physical plane is his chosen field of operations, and he takes it as he finds it. Even when dealing with the loftiest topics he gives us their relationships to the here and now, and prefers to show forth the higher qualities dramatically, as they work out visibly in human experience. Consequently the parable or allegory at its best and pithiest may be looked for from writers with a strong Taurean strain in them, and their illustrations, metaphors and similes are never strained or far-fetched, but fall into their place so naturally and harmoniously that it is impossible to cut them out without serious injury to the passage in which they occur. One of the finest examples of Taurean achievement in this line is the short meditation in which the melancholy Jaques tells the forest exiles in "As You like It," that

> "All the world's a stage,
> And all the men and women merely players."

Shakespeare's actual birthday is unknown, but we do know that the Sun was in Taurus when he was born, and can see for ourselves how strongly he answered to this influence. Among other famous literary men associated with this accentuation are Robert Browning and Henry Fielding, both born with the Sun in Taurus; while we find Milton, Dumas (*père*), Thomas Campbell, Matthew Arnold and Ibsen with the Moon in Taurus. Unfortunately no literary genius of the first rank is recorded by astrologers in the past as having been born *under* this sign; and the actual personal traits and literary tendencies have had to be selected by careful comparison of the personalities and the letters of friends born with Taurus as ascendant.

The study of those and the attempt to realise strongly what qualities were shared by the literary giants aforesaid brought up so insistently the thought of two poets who show Taurean traits that they must be mentioned here, although, as a matter of fact, their hour of birth is not known. Geoffrey Chaucer and Robert Burns have all the kindliness, the humour, the breadth and soundness and fidelity to nature, of the sons of this sign. Nothing was too lowly or insignificant for them to mention. Burns could find inspiration in the sight of a field mouse; and the "modest crimson-tippit flower" that moved him so deeply also inspired Chaucer to sing

"Yet love I most these floures white and rede
Such that men callen daisies in our toun.
To them have I so great affectioun!"

The characters in Burns' "Cottar's Saturday Night," "The Holy Fair," and "Tam O'Shanter" have the same warm-blooded humanity about them as the pilgrims of the famous Prologue to the "Canterbury Tales." Both poets allowed their humour to degenerate into coarser pleasantry, and consequently offend the fastidious critics of the present day, but the coarseness was inherent in their subjects. Biographical details also suggest Taurus as ascendant. Burns followed the plough in his youth, and was later made an exciseman. Chaucer's government post was in the custom-house and both poets knew what poverty meant and were kept plodding all their days. The Sun in Taurus brings material success and prosperity (see Shakespeare, Browning, Fielding, Marconi, Huxley and many others) but an incarnation spent with Taurus as ascendant merely indicates that the kind of work demanded of them will probably be connected with laying foundations of some sort; or that it will be of a type that is either durable itself or such as makes permanent constructive work easier for others, who will possibly gather in most of the fruits of the labour.

Physical Characteristics

Manifesting physically this sign is said to give a certain comeliness of proportion, usually on a generous scale, average height or over, broad shoulders, full throat, fine dark eyes, rather heavily lidded, with long dark curling eyelashes and rich masses of glossy hair, either straight, silky, and very thick, or thinner, with a becoming ripple in it. In colour it is brown or black, and does not fall off or turn grey readily. The voice is round and musical, very pleasing to the ear, both in speech and song. There is also a more feminine type, of slighter build—throat long rather than full, shoulders sloping rather than broad, colouring fairer, and voice higher in pitch though always sweet and musical. This type is associated with Taurus rising with a fair planet—Jupiter or Neptune—in it. The gentle dark eyes and pencilled eyebrows are perhaps the least variable of the physical characteristics, and although it is one of the most clearly marked and easily recognisable of the twelve types, students should be cautioned against assuming that Taurus is *rising* in a horoscope because personal appearance suggests this sign. If the typical traits show forth strongly the sign will certainly be accentuated in the horoscope, but a Taurean Zenith seems to give the Taurean build and movements and predilections almost as often as the Ascendant does; and it was the marked physical effect of this sign in that elevated position that first convinced the writer that the average astrologer did not lay sufficient stress on the importance of the Zenith as regards both physical and emotional traits, especially the latter.

In Real Life and in Fiction

The burly policeman, beloved and trusted by the nervous spinster and the forlorn child, is a good specimen of the work-a-day Taurean; who is also seen to advantage in John Bull at his best. and in the ample serenity of the Junoesque young matron. In fiction, lovable specimens of the Taurean abound. Kent in "King Lear" is one of them; and among Shakespeare's women may be mentioned Helena, the amorous heroine of "All's Well that Ends Well," who along with many attractive qualities shows some of that deliberate disregard of the conventions which makes one of the dangers of this sign wherever the passions are concerned. Another lovable heroine who suggests the type is George Meredith's beautiful young opera singer, Sandra Belloni—the wonderful "Vittoria" of a later novel.

The burlesque Taurean is fat, thick-necked, gross and overfed looking, and often has a great love of low comedy, heartily relishing a joke of considerable breadth, and delighting the easily tickled among his fellow men by his grotesque clowning and facial play. Among the yokels who compete for prizes by grinning and grimacing at each other through horse-collars at country fairs, it is probable that the winner will have a strong Taurean strain. Sir Toby Belch in "Twelfth Night" and the drunken porter in "Macbeth" were of this fraternity; and surely Sir John Falstaff had some flavour of the same influence about him, although naturally no one sign could possibly account for the whole of him!

Health The dangers to health that threaten this type are ignorance, inertia and self-indulgence; to which may be added, in the case of primitive specimens, sensuality, gluttony and drunkenness. The natural vitality, always abundant, should be guided into proper channels, and given out freely and generously for the pleasure or benefit of others. Otherwise it consumes itself and morbid conditions develope rapidly. Death in these circumstances is usually sudden, and frequently from apoplexy. The remedies are to be found in the cultivation of the religious sense, and in the practice of the three graces, Faith, Hope and Charity; also in constant warfare against laziness and self-indulgence. Of games in early years the favourite will probably be football, and when that is outgrown it is well to see that something else takes its place, even if it is only a quiet hour occasionally spent on the bowling green, or a peaceful and leisurely stroll through rural scenery in the gloaming; but the finest and healthiest and most congenial exercise of all will probably be singing, and it is the duty of most people born under this sign either to cultivate their tuneful voices for solo singing, or to train them for co-operative work and give their practical support and help to some choral union or church choir.

♊ # GEMINI ♊

THE TWINS.

The Sign of the

ARTIST OR INVENTOR

A mutable airy sign.

Keynote—Joy.

Watchword—Variety.

Ruler—Mercury.

☿

Mystical Gems—Beryl, Aquamarine.

Colour—Yellow. *Metal*—Quicksilver.

Physical Manifestation— { Expansion. Contraction.

Mental Manifestation— { Joy. Sorrow.

Even as an arrow which smiteth the targe ere ever the cord be still, so sped we to the second realm [Mercury]. When my Lady had placed herself in the light of that heaven, she forthwith became so joyous that the very planet shone the brighter for it. And if the star itself was changed and laughed, what then did I, who of my own nature am ever variable in every kind of way!

* * * *

So did I see more than a thousand splendours draw nigh unto us; . . . and as each one approached [even] the shadow [in it] was seen to be filled with joy, by the clear radiance that streamed from it.

* * * *

In so short a space . . . I saw the sign that followeth the Bull, and was within it.

O glorious stars! Light full of mighty power, from which I gratefully acknowledge [that] all my genius, such as it is [doth flow]! He who is the Father of every mortal life, [the Sun], was appearing and disappearing together with you, what time I first drew breath in Tuscany; and, further, when grace was granted me to take my place in the Great Wheel [of the Zodiac] which turns you round, it was your region that was assigned to me.—DANTE. IL PARADISO, *Cantos* v. 88, xxii. 109.

CHAPTER III.

THE GEMINIAN TYPE

THE ruler of Gemini is Mercury, the servant of Jupiter and messenger of the Gods, whose function it is to reveal the mind of Deity to man. His mission is expression, and his chief characteristics are versatility and adaptability. His influence shows in intellectual agility and bodily dexterity. The mythological stories connected with him are full of instances of his skill in adapting means to an end; and not infrequently of his ingenuity in adapting other people's means to his own ends. Deity manifesting on the physical plane must express the Self in terms of that plane, limited and bounded by physical conditions; must build up a personality—an efficient body—by means of which expression is possible. The building of such a personality is, in its essence, egoism; *i.e.*, the separating of a part of the greater self, the process of allowing it to become an "own self," something different from all other selves; a process which, like many other forms of birth or of growth, involves pain, and in a certain limited sense, loss to the parent self. But when the work is complete and full expression is achieved, the travail of the night is forgotten because of the joy which cometh in the morning, and Mercury, in spite of his lawlessness and thievish propensities, is the well-beloved of Jupiter, his chosen delegate and interpreter. **Ruler**

The chief characteristic of this type is a certain exuberance or overplus of intellectual energy, which must find expression, and prefers to express itself, if possible, in a variety of ways. This craving for diversity and impatience of repetition or sameness, leads, in the case of fully developed Geminians, to brilliant results, alike in experimental science, in literature and in art. Mercurians only really strike the true keynote of their being, JOY, when in the act of expressing some essential part of themselves; and having attained such expression they are rarely content to rest upon their oars, but "forgetting those things which are behind, and reaching forth unto those which are before, press forward towards the mark for the prize of their high calling." Theirs is a charming type, whose true function it is to make life more interesting and more beautiful for themselves and others; to stimulate, refresh and revive their fellowmen by force both **Evolved Type** of exhortation and of example, inducing those whose spirits are flagging and who are in danger of sinking into dejection or apathy to rouse themselves to fresh effort. A keen desire for intellectual satisfaction is the driving force of this sign, and when the religious sense is awakened, much suffering is sometimes undergone by advanced souls of this type; for they *must* understand and reason upon the faith that is in them, and if their surroundings are unsuitable, and the teaching offered to them uncongenial, many doubts and difficulties arise which must be overcome by hard wrestling before peace is attained. Their craving for perfect expression and desire to influence those around them makes it impossible for them, in such conditions, to suffer in silence and alone. Friends and relatives are perforce obliged to face the same problems so far as in them lies, often to their great bewilderment and perplexity; and if it is impossible for them to understand and sympathise, the intellectual suffering of the Geminian increases to such an extent that it becomes a martyrdom of misery, the very intensity of which brings relief through compelling increased endeavour after progressive thought, and consequently the definite attainment of some logical result. The reaction from this period of anguish often takes the form of a joyous excitement which eagerly seeks an outlet, and generally finds one in striving to arouse answering vibrations in others. Any kind of sympathetic appreciation is welcome at such times, but intellectual approbation is particularly prized. If literature is the chosen vehicle of expression something in the nature of a rhapsody or song of triumph may be looked for. There is always a strong effort after achievement of some kind and the exaltation accompanying such achievement is not infrequently followed by a keen and critical examination of the work achieved. If the verdict is unsatisfactory the artist will probably abandon that particular line of endeavour for the time being and start off on another tack, but will very likely resume the abandoned task as suddenly as he dropped it, and carry it through brilliantly to a successful issue. These quick changes, which are especially noticeable in childhood and early youth, are often a source of perplexity and dismay to the parents and guardians responsible for the upbringing of this type, but the developed Geminian knows his own business best, and should be left free to follow his apparently erratic course and, above all, never tied too closely to drudgery or routine of any kind. A profession which allows of variety of occupation should invariably be selected, and if that is impossible, same absorbing hobby should be encouraged which will give the necessary relief and become to some extent a secondary profession. These people generally enjoy their work and often hold strong convictions as to the duty of taking a bright view of life, and throwing oneself heart and soul into one's business or occupation: a trait which is a source of great refreshment and inspiration to those who work with them. In marriage they look for intellectual sympathy and companionship, ignoring differences of age and condition if they can find the response, appreciation and support for which they crave.

Religion

The type of religion most congenial to the Geminian is best understood by a careful study of the writings of St. Paul, who, it will be remembered, was mistaken by the inhabitants of Lystra for an incarnation of the God Mercury, and consequently must have belonged physically as well as mentally to this type. His epistles are excellent examples of the Geminian style, and in them we find much that is characteristic of it, *e.g.*, many sudden digressions, interpolations and changes of subject often making the train of thought hard to follow; a curiously impulsive insistence in following out any separate thread of reasoning, and a frequent abandonment of the argument before it is sufficiently clear to carry conviction to the reader—though to the writer the logical sequence is apparently complete; a strong tendency to self-analysis and introspection and a constant recurrence of the first personal pronoun; an intense interest in his own intellectual development, and an eager desire that others should understand his particular difficulties, trials and temptations, and rejoice with him in his victories. The particular point of view held at the moment is always considered the right and only one, not merely for himself but for others. While it is narrow and rigid he persecutes the Church. When it changes he becomes a missionary of the gospel of universal salvation. Outward forms and ceremonies are to him of little importance compared with the holding of sound dogma concerning life and religion. An intellectual understanding of man's relation to the Deity, to the Christ, and to his fellowmen is of paramount importance; and he realises with keen delight that certain of the Greek poets had also proclaimed the Fatherhood of God,* and with keen sorrow, that, in

* Acts xvii., 28.

spite of that glorious message, the Athenians of his day continued to make their religious life chiefly consist in the offering of propitiatory sacrifices to minor deities. The constant repetition of the words "Joy" and "Rejoice" in these epistles is particularly typical, as also the writer's alternations between the bright hope of universal salvation, and an exaggerated despair over his own slavery and that of others in "the bondage of sin." Another significant detail for the astrologer is the fact that he followed two professions—continuing voluntarily to work at his trade as a tent-maker long after he had become a noted preacher and teacher, and might have claimed the support of the Church as such.

Primitive Type

At the early stages of evolution the thievish propensities of the Mercurian are much in evidence on all the planes. The primitive Geminian will take from anyone; not merely accepting but exacting as his due, sympathy, attention, consideration, admiration, time, energy and pecuniary assistance; in fact, anything and everything that will feed his egotism or further his physical and intellectual development. He writes "I" with a particularly large capital, and is apt to feel that nothing which does not intimately concern his own happiness, well-being, and comfort, is of any importance whatever. Sickness, suffering, sorrow and loss are tragedies indeed when they touch him, and as such to be proclaimed aloud, reiterated, and lamented until everyone in the neighbourhood is convinced of their existence and magnitude. When they only affect others they are merely a nuisance and a discomfort, representing the negative and unimportant part of life; dull and depressing subjects, not to be dwelt upon any longer than is absolutely necessary; sordid details, to be ignored, shoved aside and put out of sight as quickly as possible. The craving for joy and variety which, later on, will act as a splendid spur, at this period takes the form of a effervescent restlessness and perpetual dissatisfaction. A constant demand for entertainment, novelty and excitement results in a tendency to shirk uncongenial duties, and leave "the trivial round, the common task" as much as possible to others. Routine work of any kind is particularly resented as an affliction, and until the advantage of regular and punctual attention to minor details in housekeeping, office work, etc., is intellectually understood and appreciated, the Geminian doomed to such labour feels like a bird in a cage, and expends far more energy in beating against the bars with his wings than would suffice to fulfil his obligations three times over. The root of all such unhappiness and rebellion is generally the secret conviction that he or she, however heedless and incompetent, is meant for better things, and is consequently thrown away on drudgery of any kind. There is always a strong desire to be "in the running"—in the very centre of things; and if these people find themselves in any way inferior to those around them, and are consequently compelled to take a back seat, they feel very sore and ill-used—and show it. They are bad listeners, and often resent the suggestions of others, however practical and sensible they may be; shying away from any plan proposed, and frequently substituting some quite crazy scheme of their own. Geminians are also very prone to rapid and complete changes in their point of view, and are generally utterly incapable of realising either that they have changed, or that it is possible and even right for other people to hold different convictions and opinions from themselves. They are deplorably lacking in persistence and tenacity, and often strikingly deficient in memory and imagination; which defects make it peculiarly difficult for them to realise the value of old associations, to put themselves in the place of others, and to acknowledge and discharge debts of gratitude. Nevertheless they are generally wonderfully business-like and exact when there is any question of what is owing to them, for even when quite comfortably off, they always feel hampered by poverty. The desire to spend and to acquire is always in excess of the means, and though there may be occasional fits of lavish generosity, such outbreaks are often made an excuse for subsequent meannesses or demands. Many of them manage to combine a hysterically sensitive disposition with an astonishing amount of cold-blooded selfishness, verging, not exactly on *deliberate* cruelty, but on a type of cruelty which is born of an innate desire to abolish sorrow in whatever form it may be met with, and get away from it into the sunshine again. Thus the sick and suffering are either neglected altogether, or tormented by ill-judged ministrations, and inopportune admonitions. Sometimes futile attempts are made to goad them into cheerfulness and serenity, either by ineffectual argument or by such insistent exhortation as leaves them utterly exhausted physically and mentally, and more desperately in need of help and consolation than ever. In love affairs they keep a cool head and a keen look-out for their own advantage, are rarely carried away by passion, and can generally steer clear of awkward complications, carefully avoiding or slipping out of anything that will hamper their career or tie them down to an uncongenial life. The question that they ask themselves clearly and definitely about marriage is, almost invariably, "What will this give me?" Rarely or never "How much can I give?"

Physical Characteristics

Manifesting physically, the Gemini type is generally associated with a slender figure, agility of movement, small features, pointed chin, and hair "between colours"—*i.e.*, indefinite brown or blond. The eyes are gray or hazel, bright but not very large; complexion pale as a rule, even when quite healthy, but inclined to flush or darken, and very easily tanned. The feminine edition is particularly fascinating, and the more artistic and sensitive among the men partake of the same charm. There is something of "the dainty rogue in porcelain" about them, especially in childhood and early youth. Sir Joshua Reynolds loved to paint this type, and some of the lightly built and finely poised statues of Mercury express it to perfection. The more masculine edition, which is less versatile, sensitive and fastidious, and generally turns to practical science rather than to art, has a more muscular and wiry build and stronger and more definite features—prominent nose, high cheek-bones and decided chin; hair dark brown or black. The type is most easily recognised by its alert, eager bearing, sympathetic manner (verging on the gushing) and quick unexpected movements. The sandals of Mercury are winged, and though probably the symbol was chosen chiefly as representing speech—the winged words which are set free through the working of the intellect—it is peculiarly appropriate in other ways too; for there is something of the song-bird about Geminians. The movements, both physical and mental, are unexpected. There is a tendency to advance in short, quick flights; to alight again as suddenly, and apparently on impulse, to survey the surroundings with eager curiosity and interest, and, when the point of view has nothing fresh to offer, to dart off again—generally in some unforeseen direction—to exhaust the possibilities of the new vantage ground, and so on indefinitely throughout the whole pilgrimage. Sometimes they seem to take a half-mischievous delight in their own power of disconcerting and astonishing other people by their methods of procedure; and the song-bird's preening of his feathers and triumphant little gush of song after alighting on a particularly congenial bough, are very well paralleled by the Geminian's artless and open satisfaction over his own achievements. Peter Pan, with his irrepressible "cock-a-doodle," was of this family, and is also definitely stamped "mercurial" by his refusal to grow any older: for these people retain much of the spontaneity and charm of childhood even in extreme old age. The above is specially true of the feminine or artistic type; the masculine edition suggests the hawk rather than the song-bird. The flights are longer and more sustained, and generally mean business. There is less loquacity and more watchfulness; less of the characteristic "temperament" and a keener intellect.

North America is said to be very largely under the influence of this sign, and among the brilliant financiers of its great cities, and also among their highly sensitive, adaptable and charming women —women whose native element is "Society"—excellent examples of the two classes described above are to be found. More primitive specimens may also be recognised in the same country; unscrupulous but clever men, to whom sudden and shifty financial moves are as the breath of life; and high-strung, restless women who exhaust their energies in a mad chase after excitement and variety, defying every rule of hygiene, rebelling against all the dictates of common sense as regard diet, clothing, sleep, etc., and then making the resultant nervous prostration an excuse for every kind of petting and self-indulgence. Neurasthenia and its half-sister hysteria are the curse of that tribe, and the best cure for both is the cultivation of a sense of duty, self-control, and self-sacrifice.

In Fiction

Burlesque editions of the Geminian are to be seen in the caricatures of Brother Jonathan at his 'cutest, in the "Artful Dodger" of Charles Dickens, and, generally speaking, among the whole confraternity of those of the nimble-fingered gentry whose ability in their profession shows intellect, though of a perverted type, and whose motto may be written: "All that's thine is mine; but what is mine is my own"

Health

The physical constitution of Geminians has already been touched upon. Their type of energy is what is described as *nervous*, and it will carry them through almost anything they want to do, but fails them as soon as the work becomes irksome, uncongenial or dull, unless a very high degree of mental and moral development makes it possible for them to replenish it from spiritual sources. The chief dangers that threaten the finer types of Geminian, are physical exhaustion due to the strain of artistic production—or, in the case of women, due to the labour of child-bearing and rearing; and to these may be added in some cases intellectual agony arising from religious doubts and difficulties. In the less evolved specimens, vanity and egoism are the origin of the trouble, and their victims become excessively exacting to those around them, imagining that no one really understands or appreciates them, and giving way to tearfulness, wayward temper, childish rebellion, hysteria and all the other manifestations of overstrung nerves. The cultivation of an earnest desire to cease giving trouble to others is the true remedy for this condition. Geminians are more or less children as regards health all their days, and those forms of treatment generally applied to children, suit them best. Fresh air and sunshine, regular hours, a light diet consisting largely of milk, and above all *plenty of sleep* will soon pull them round, even if, as sometimes happens, the lungs are threatened. Traditionally, Gemini is said to rule the arms and the lungs, and the breathing capacity should be carefully watched. Ten full inspirations and expirations thrice daily, taken in the fresh air if possible, will prove very beneficial, especially if the inbreathing is accompanied by the mental affirmation "I am drinking in fresh supplies of health and energy and vitality," and the outbreathing by the thought "I am getting rid of what is useless and deleterious and injurious to health." Light gymnastic exercises that expand the lungs and develop a perfect carriage are also to be recommended. Probably the very best of these—for male Geminians at any rate—is fencing.

* * *

The foregoing description of the sons and daughters of Gemini, which appeared in the June number of *Modern Astrology* for 1908, is the only one of my contributions to that magazine which provoked its readers to expostulate with me on my over-severity and exaggeration; which is rather curious, for exaggeration is the fault of the sign, and the impulse to meet criticism and to fight it is generally very strong indeed. Having sinned in the first way, I shall venture to adopt the second practice also, and so find courage to make reply forthwith.

One of my critics asserts that all Geminians are gentle and easily led and quite incapable of self-defence, and that when friction arises stronger types invariably get the better of them, the Geminian simply allowing himself to be pushed into the background. So he does—in matters to which he is indifferent; for he is not belligerent, and never fights for fighting's sake. But as to being easily led, and incapable of self-defence, that is quite another matter; and no type is more strongly convinced of the duty of self-defence. War, it must be remembered, is not always carried on in a series of pitched battles, and the hardest type of fighting to put down is persistent or recurrent guerilla warfare; for when that is going on, the opposing army knows neither peace nor rest. I have heard a student compare a Geminian's method of attack to that of a mosquito; and in an ancient list of creatures said to be ruled by this sign, I have discovered, to my amusement, *the house sparrow and—the common flea.* Geminians are masters of light skirmishing and are consequently hardly ever really beaten. They understand instinctively the advantages of a sudden change of front, of unexpectedness of attack, and of rapidity of retreat. Let the reader watch our lively little friends the sparrows—and he will see the Geminian method of warfare exactly. All is peace and harmony, and the spectator is admiring the beautifully ordered lives of the little creatures and their admirable social instincts; when suddenly one of them fluffs out his feathers and goes for some astonished rival or opponent with all his might, gives him a disconcerting and decidedly painful peck, and promptly retires into safety. The Geminian child in any nursery or schoolroom, may be seen following the same tactics. He is generally the centre of joyous activity and merry play. He likes everything to go on happily and brightly, but he prefers to strike the keynote in the harmony himself. If his will is crossed, and the others take a negative attitude when he makes a suggestion, he may stand it the first time, and even oftener—particularly if highly developed—but sooner or later he rebels and flies out suddenly, to the consternation and discomfort of the whole group; especially as he usually ends by a burst of passionate weeping which brings out a body-guard of some sort in the shape of nurse or governess, and ensures him an easy victory next time. For it must be remembered that a reputation for "tantrums" can be used as a very efficient piece of armour. These little outbursts are naturally most frequent during periods of rapid growth and consequent nerve fatigue; and Geminians are a terror while teething—not merely at the baby stage, but while the twelve-year molars are arriving, and even during the advent of the wisdom teeth. Which things are an allegory; for during productive periods we are all prone to take from our fellow men far more than we give.

While thus faithfully chronicling further details of the failings of this sign, it behoves me to add that there is a type of Geminian who is practically an unknown quantity to the astrologers of the North, although he is presumably quite common at the Equator. All the sons and daughters of Mercury born in Great Britain and in corresponding latitudes are bound to have either Capricorn or Aquarius at the Zenith; but nearer the Equator it is possible to find people whose horoscopes show Gemini rising with Pisces at the Zenith; which will naturally give a very different type of temperament and personality from either of the other two possible combinations. Pisces is a gentle and poetic sign, much more plastic than Capricorn, much more romantic than Aquarius; and it generally arouses in those under its influence certain wistful cravings connected with the spiritual element in human nature. Any modification of faculty or of character due to this mystic influence is certain to be interesting, and in the case of highly evolved Geminians might conceivably give very brilliant results, possibly connected with high achievement in the domain of music, literature or art. In the less advanced specimens, however, the gentleness might only show as weakness, and at the primitive stage of evolution the plasticity and receptivity of Pisces, added to the fickleness and waywardness of Gemini might prove a fatal bar to a successful career in any walk of life. The peculiar helplessness and childish irresponsibility of the native would however, be due rather to the sign at the Zenith, than to the sign ascending, as will be fully demonstrated in the tables of analysis which will be found in the third part of this volume; tables which give a much greater importance to the Zenith than is usually assigned to it by astrologers, but which if carefully tested by students, will nevertheless be found to be fairly accurate. The point is worth insisting on here, because this variation in the Zenith is often largely accountable for the fact that there are two or three widely differing types found among those born under the same sign; and if we bear in mind that a large number of Geminians are drawn by an Aquarian Zenith towards scientific investigation, and that others are dominated by the aspirations and ideals of the poet, we shall be better able to understand the enormous difference between the two most famous sons of the sign.

Dante Alighieri attributes to the glorious stars* of the constellation which follows the Bull—that is to say, to *Gemini*—all his greatest gifts, or at any rate his intellectual superiority, and Francis Bacon also informs us—indirectly—that he was born under this sign of the Twins. Surely no student of the biographies of these two men will venture to assert that they were easily led and incapable of self-defence! Yet it is true that their enemies did get the better of them, for the poet died in exile, and the great philosopher and scientist was publicly disgraced for taking bribes which his predecessors in office had pocketed for generations with impunity. The writings of the two men should be very carefully contrasted and compared. Bacon shows little or no tendency to intensity or exaggeration either in feeling or in expression; but the failings with which his biographers reproach him—ingratitude and lack of loyalty—are certainly associated with this sign; and his tendency to complicate his style by parenthesis is also characteristic. Clearness and simplicity of diction is always a difficulty for the eager Geminian, and it is generally extremely hard work to commit his prose paragraphs to memory. The music of Dante's lovely verse is partly due to the exquisite beauty of the Tuscan dialect in which he wrote, but he must also have had a wonderfully delicate ear for language; for although he does sometimes involve his readers in difficulties by the agility of his thought and the parenthetical interpolations with which his verse abounds, there are passages of such extraordinary beauty that they linger long even in the memory of a foreign student. It should be noted that although the poet tells us in his Paradiso (quoted on page 34) that the Sun rose and set in Gemini at the season when he first drew breath, he avoids claiming it as actually ascending at the moment of his birth, and attributes his gifts entirely to the power of his rising sign. This distinctly suggests that the great luminary was already well above the horizon before he was born, for astrologers both ancient and modern are generally agreed that the Sun rising is more apt than the Moon or any planet to bring up its own characteristics and make them predominate in a personality. In fact, it very

* *Paradiso*, Canto 22, l 109

often modifies the rising sign to such an extent as to make it barely recognisable, and especially is this the case with the Mutable signs; for the influence of the Sun is fixed and dignified and regal. Dante is believed by his biographers to have been born in the second week of May (old style), when the Sun was just entering the sign of Gemini, and if the Sun was already *well* up before he was born, then a very late degree of the sign was rising; which in the latitude of Florence would allow this Piscarian Zenith—so eminently suitable from the Astrologer's point of view—to grace his horoscope, calling him to the career of the Visionary, Interpreter and Poet.

Another son of this sign, George Bernard Shaw, was born in Dublin between 12.30 and 1 a.m. on July 26th, 1856—so I was told by his mother and older sister. This gives Gemini rising, with his ruler, Mercury, in the imaginative sign of Cancer. The Sun in Leo in the third house proclaims *the man with a message;* and its conjuction with Venus betokens power to deliver it in artistic form. The Moon, Uranus and Pluto are in Taurus—giving business ability, a sense of humour, and of proportion. Pluto has three severe aspects and two mildly favourable. A brilliant horoscope, well worth study, and full of contradictions. Jupiter in the warrior sign of Aries enjoys a fight; but, in the eleventh house, makes many friends; and he helps success in the delivery of the message, for he smiles at the Sun and Venus.

Note.—Some astrologers consider that Bacon's assertion that he was born neither under Sol nor under Jupiter, but that *the contemplative planet* carried him away entirely, means that Saturn was his *ruler:* but others agree that it must have been rising; which makes Gemini the ascendant. In the writer's mind there is no room for doubt. The style is unmistakably Geminian. See the letter, quoted in his biography (Vol. I.) which gives this information, and which holds a record for repetition of the first personal pronoun.

♋ CANCER ♋

THE CRAB.

The Sign of the

PROPHET OR TEACHER

A cardinal watery sign.

Keynote—Patience.

Watchword—Sympathy.

Ruler—The Moon.

☽

Mystical Gems—Moss-agate, Emerald.

Colour—Violet. *Metal*—Silver.

Physical Manifestation—Flexibility.

Mental Manifestation—Imagination.

Lives there the man with soul so dead
Who never to himself hath said
"This is my own, my native land"?
Whose heart hath ne'er within him burned
As home his footstep he hath turned
From wandering on a foreign strand?

* * * *

O Caledonia, stern and wild,
Meet nurse for a poetic child!
Land of brown heath and shaggy wood,
Land of the mountain and the flood,
Land of my Sires! What mortal hand
Can e'er untie the filial band
That knits me to thy rugged strand.

SIR WALTER SCOTT.

CHAPTER IV.

The Cancerian Type

The ruler of Cancer is the Moon—Artemis, Diana, Selene—the feminine deity especially adored in sultry climes and under Southern skies, where the scorching heat of the summer noontide makes mortals crave for the coolness which accompanies the midnight radiance of the lesser luminary. She sees the labours of man with a favourable eye and rewards his toil by giving him a plenteous harvest. All over the world this power has been held in reverence as possessing a peculiar influence in such matters as concern the dawning and early development of life, both vegetable and animal. The bursting of the swelling seed, the first feeble shooting of the tender plant, the times and seasons and ceremonies connected with the generation, birth and nurture of all young creatures, these are matters that enter into the dominion of Diana and come naturally under her sway. She is the power behind the parents, regulating the Karma of heredity in all that concerns the physical vehicle; linking the present to the past in accordance with nature's law. Adaptability with Tenacity—in one word Patience—that is the essential force of this sign and of its ruler. The Moon waxes and wanes, shines in full radiance or suffers eclipse, but in all its varying stages is ever constant in its inconstancy. Cancer, the crab, when once he has seized an object, and means to have it, will rather lose his claw than let go, and having lost it will grow another to take hold again. "Mother Nature" is the modern name for this Power—a goddess much reverenced by our leading biologists. The ancient Jewish Priests and Astrologers called the Archangel of the Moon, Gabriel, "the hero of the Lord," and it is interesting to notice that St. Luke names him as Messenger of the Annunciation, both in connection with the coming of the Christ and the birth of St. John the Baptist. In the Christian Calendar the patron saint of child-birth is St. Margaret; who, according to the legend, was swallowed by a Dragon, but had power to burst his body asunder and so to emerge unhurt; an appropriate parable, suggesting the Chinese myths connected with seasons of lunar eclipse, and also picturesquely representing many forms of growth and development—the bursting of the bud, the emergence of the nestling from

Ruler

the shell, and the liberation which attends all birth, on every plane.

Evolved Type

The highly evolved Cancerian is the master of many moods, both in himself and in others; for when he has fully developed the faculty of expression he is the musician to whose piping all the world must dance. His true function is to vitalise and inspire the men and women of his own generation and especially the youth of his native land, by raising their ideals; and when he takes up the harp of life he smites "on all the chords with might," making each in turn vibrate and quiver to its fullest extent. The whole gamut of emotion lies open to him. He can feel, and make others feel, joy, sorrow, compassion, horror and despair as no other type can, seizing the imagination and holding it by the power of his imagery and the intensity of his own feelings; and behind this exercise of imagination and play of emotion there is always a purpose—a purpose closely connected with the evolution of his race. The past and future are as real to him as the present. Memory is very retentive, the history of his own nation, family or class immensely important in his eyes; and he holds aloft the torch lit by past experience to illuminate the future and guide the steps of his fellow men. He is the teacher *par excellence;* and cares little for smoothness of outline or grace of form so long as he can drive his lesson home. His style is picturesque, vivid—often very dramatic; and he continues to deliver and redeliver his message, changing and adapting its form while preserving its essence, until he succeeds in arousing the attention of his audience and kindling its enthusiasm. Successful preachers and public speakers of all kinds are found under the influence of this sign, as also editors and literary men who have a strong personal hold over their readers, and actors and dramatists in whom imagination is a predominant feature. These people love to come into touch with the public, to claim its interest, to stimulate its imagination and to sway its moods; and if large audiences are unattainable and a public career impossible, as in the case of most women, the natural bent will find scope and outlet in the nursery, in the school-room or among the friends and relatives of the home circle. A great degree of happiness often accompanies the exercise of faculty even in this limited field, for the affections are very strong and the maternal element particularly marked. No lapse of time or separation by distance ever seems materially to lessen love or friendship or weaken family ties in the case of these people. The grey-haired son in Canada or Australia is as near to the heart and as present to the mind of the Cancerian parents in the mother country as he was in the days of his infancy; so that the sense of separation hardly exists, and long voyages and arduous journeys to far distant lands are permitted or undertaken by this type with a composure and even with a pleasure which many less deeply devoted to home and fatherland cannot begin to understand. Early memories of childhood and old ties of friendship are a peculiar and sacred treasure for Cancerians, who will correspond for years with people to whom they have been attracted in their early teens, have never met since and are not in the least likely to meet again. The striking success of this type in the field of teaching is partly due to this tenacity of recollection, and to the vivid pictures of childhood and youth which remain with its representatives, helping them to understand and come into touch with the undeveloped of all ages. Their memory not infrequently carries them back to babyhood, faithfully recording striking experiences of the third and fourth years and sometimes even the emotions experienced at eighteen or twenty months in connection with certain clearly recorded scenes. This fact, together with the strongly sensational tendency of the sign, makes early training and education extremely important, and the injudicious or unsympathetic disciplinarian of the budding prophet may unwittingly cause him suffering quite out of proportion to his childish faults and shortcomings. Injustice rankles long, and even when the victim is sufficiently evolved and large-minded to understand and forgive it, his retentive memory makes it impossible for him to forget. Further, it is not always easy to hit on the right discipline for this type. Severity is useless, coercion almost impossible; brute force and castigation may ensure outward obedience for a time, but they always engender fierce resentment and dislike, and sooner or later the inborn tenacity re-asserts itself, and the small sinner goes on his own way at the first opportunity. Nevertheless, the nature is loving, loyal and very sympathetic, and if those in authority can manage to put a high ideal before the child, appealing strongly to his imagination, victory is easy and assured. Hero-worship is a strong factor in the upward growth, and rightly guided and directed will prove the best of aids. Old ballads and tales of chivalry and heroism—especially those associated with home, heredity and fatherland—are excellent food for the active and ever-growing imagination, which craves constant nourishment, and which, if starved, is apt to become morbid and diseased, leading to untruthfulnes, both wilful and unconscious.

Love and Friendship This type is very romantic and imaginative where the affections are concerned, though often too shy or proud to betray the fact; for ridicule is torture to the Cancerian. In consequence, the story of his love-affairs is frequently a tragic sequence of misunderstandings and heartaches; which condition of things may continue for many years, for the patience and tenacity of the sign show in this as in all other matters, and a misplaced affection, even if apparently conquered for a time, will recur and reassert itself in spite of everything that reason and common-sense and worldly wisdom may say against it. When such a love as this—so strong and lasting—is based on real sympathy and understanding, and is triumphant in the end, the happiness attained is as intense as the previous suffering was severe; for where feeling is concerned this type knows no half-measures, and its love, which, as has been said, has much of the maternal element in it, is characterised by a great yearning to give, while asking for little or nothing in return.

Religion The religious tendency inspired by this sign is best understood by studying the writings of the prophets of all times and nations, and one of the most striking examples is to be found in Jeremiah, whose lamentations and other writings, full of wonderful imagery and of deep feeling, show strongly and unmistakably the influence of Cancer. In fact the very quintessence of Cancerian style may be seen in some of his more vivid and dramatic passages; as, for example, in the closing verses of the fifth chapter of his prophecies:

> "A wonderful and horrible thing is committed in the land,
> The prophets prophesy falsely,
> And the priests bear rule by their means;
> And my people love to have it so:
> *And what will ye do in the end thereof?*"

The tragic intensity of the passage has rarely been paralleled; and the nature of the situation, set forth in so few words and with such marvellous power and pathos, is such as must appeal with peculiar force to all who are born under this sign. That the teaching of the nation should be corrupt, that its prophets should hold up false ideals, that its priesthood should find it convenient to accept them, and—most poignant cry of all—that the people should *love to have it so!* there lies the true tragedy of national life; the very root and source of corruption laid bare. Very characteristic also are Jeremiah's pessimistic moods when over-humility, doubt and discouragement overwhelm him and threaten to paralyse his energy. Very human is the cry, "Ah, Lord God! Behold, I cannot speak; for I am a child"; and again, "Woe is me, my mother, that thou hast borne me a man of strife and contention to the whole earth! . . . Everyone of them doth curse me." But these times of misery and depression pass away, and with Cancerian tenacity he continues to teach, in spite of the bitter humiliation of the stocks and the dreary desolation of his sojourn in the dungeon.

In Real Life

All along the line of prophets, the same characteristics repeat and re-assert themselves. Carlyle is a modern example who will probably occur to the minds of most students. It is recorded that he was born "late in the evening" of December 4th. At that time of year it is dark at four o'clock in the district around Ecclefechan, and the Scottish peasant is often a-bed before nine, so that the word "late" must be given a relative value. The choice of ascendant consequently lies between Cancer and Leo, and no astrologer will hesitate in pronouncing in favour of the former. The style is quite unmistakable, and is specially and characteristically Cancerian in his wonderful *History of the French Revolution*, which is so far dramatic in form that it has been neatly described as a "compendium of stage directions." Apart from Carlyle's manner of expressing himself, his success as a public lecturer, his love of home life, the tenacity and warmth of his affections and friendships,* his moodiness and fits of deep depression, and last, but not least, his chronic indigestion, would be enough to announce the influence of this sign, even if no word of his writings remained to us and we had to depend on biographical details only. Another modern prophet born with Cancer rising was Madame Blavatsky, one of the founders of the Theosophical Society, who also, in her day and generation, lifted up her lament against the prophets who prophesy falsely and the priests who bear rule by their means; urging her pupils and followers, in the true Cancerian vein, to turn their thoughts back to the days of the Fathers and Founders

* Note especially his friendships with Emerson and Goethe; warm friendships which lived and throve on correspondence alone.

of religion, and forward to the glory that shall be when Truth reigns over all. Those who had the opportunity of coming under her personal tuition declare that never was there a teacher more marvellously inspired with the power of making a pupil understand, assimilate and remember any lesson, however difficult, which she undertook to expound; and the style in which she expounded was of the most ultra-Cancerian type; for like many foreigners she never learned to draw the subtle line between metaphor and slang, and accepted any phrase, however ludicrously informal and unscholastic, which helped to make her meaning clear and drive her thesis home. The tenacity of her memory, stretching back to very early childhood, was phenomenal, her wide range of emotion and sympathy particularly striking, and her range of mood of such endless variety that those who knew her best described her as apparently many people rolled into one.

Primitive Type

Primitive Cancerians are the slaves, instead of the masters, of their moods; inefficient minstrels, vainly trying to string and to tune the harp of life, ever striving to find the key to its harmonies, and ever doomed to disappointment; altering its pitch fitfully and spasmodically, sweeping its chords ignorantly and impatiently, and making of its music a miserable jangle. Helplessly they wander from string to string, forcing each to vibrate in turn; now calling arrogantly to their little world to listen to their attempts, and anon relapsing into the silence of despair. They are a constant prey to sentimentalism, sensationalism, and exaggerated emotion of every kind—mere aggravating bundles of contradictions and inconsistencies in the eyes of the majority of their fellow men; for it is hard to understand that the instrument must be perfected before the music can find a voice, and that he who has the power to perceive the discords of life and to suffer from them is already half way to the point at which he will begin to listen to its harmonies and help to produce them. At the early stages this is often a very unhappy sign. A sense of latent power, as yet unexpressed and inexpressible, gives the undeveloped specimens an absurd idea of their own importance, and of the deference and consideration due to them by others. Moods of exalted self-sufficiency are followed by others of exaggerated shyness and humility. Fierce pride and independence alternate with the helplessness and loneliness of the child who has lost his way. There is as wide a difference between the two conditions as there is between the crab in his normal state, *i.e.*, encased in his natural armour of plated bone, all knobs and joints and elbows and claws—ever ready for defence, if not for aggression—and the same creature at its period of growth, when it slips off its old shell and becomes scarcely recognisable—a thin-skinned, helpless, semi-transparent object, lying hidden in the crevices of the rock and trembling at the approach of every foe. In like manner, Cancerians will sometimes shun their fellow creatures for weeks, giving way to unreasoning terrors or to morbid feelings of self-consciousness, shyness and depression; after which they will emerge into the light of publicity again and make some desperate effort to challenge the attention of their fellow-men and regain their own self-respect. Even in the advanced specimens we find a tendency to dramatic methods. The ideal lecturer illustrates his theme freely, using blackboard, lantern slide, or striking scientific experiment to supplement his discourse; the Prophet Ezekiel goes through elaborate dumb-show action with tiles and iron pots and what not, to attract the attention of his audience before he opens his mouth to speak; and there is no end to the attitudinising and eccentricity of the primitive specimen, when he desires to come into touch with his public. The false prophet, the cheap-jack, the impostor and the charlatan are treading the early stages of this path of evolution; and much that is otherwise inexplicable in their conduct becomes easy of interpretation to those who can recognise their type and understand the intense craving for emotional experience which leads them at times to such heights of folly. Children under this influence pass through analogous phases of development, even when the ego is already well advanced; *e.g.*, a school-girl of this type has been known to find a morbid pleasure in giving her class-mates the impression that she had gone mad; and a bright and intelligent boy of sixteen, born with the Moon rising in Cancer, has actually presented himself at school with his head elaborately bandaged, and posed for a whole blissful day as the hero of a dangerous accident, revelling in the sympathy and interest of masters and boys, recounting and elaborating with ever-increasing gusto the exact circumstances connected with his wholly imaginary injury. He was even heartless enough to present himself at home in the same guise, frightening a sensitive and excitable mother almost into fits, and accepting subsequent rebuke and punishment quite coolly, as just so much more food for sensation, both in himself and in others. Of the same breed was "Tom Sawyer," and it is not surprising to find that the horoscope of Tom Sawyer's biographer, Mark Twain, shows us Jupiter, the planet representing the mental activity, in this imaginative sign of Cancer.

Physical Characteristics

Manifesting physically, this sign confers a form more interesting than beautiful; for even on this lower plane the type shows a tendency to model itself on its symbol. The bony structure is generally the most striking feature of the Cancerian. The limbs, and especially the arms, are long in proportion to the body; the shoulders are broad, the hands and feet exceptionally large, the skull of a generous size with an over-hanging brow, high cheek-bones, and a decided lower jaw, sometimes garnished with irregular and rather prominent teeth. The nose in the plainer specimens is often insignificant or peculiar; even in the handsomer varieties it tends to width of nostril and has an inclination to turn up. The mouth is wide and expressive, with a generous smile and great possibilities both of sweetness and of grimness. The eyes are blue or grey, generally short-sighted, deep-set, and wide apart. The eyelashes are long and curling, the eyebrows very distinctly marked, sometimes almost meeting, with a decided downward curve, just over the bridge of the nose. They are inclined to be bushy and over-prominent in old age. The hair is soft and plentiful, silky and wavy, flaxen, blond or light brown; and it frequently fades early to the silvery whiteness which suggests moonshine. In the case of women the structural characteristics are naturally softened to a less bony build, and many of them have considerable grace of movement, though it is rather the free grace of Diana and the wood nymphs than the conventional feminine grace of the drawing-room. The best-looking among them more than make up in expression for any want of regularity in feature, and many successful actresses suggest the type, notably those who excel in intensity and in imaginative power.

Astrological tradition declares that Scotland—especially at the University city of St. Andrews,—is particularly sensitive to the Cancerian vibrations; and certainly the Caledonian prophet or teacher has made his influence felt for many generations and in many distant lands, his energy finding scope even beyond the borders of the British empire, among alien races and under foreign skies. Prof. Richard

Lodge, after some years' residence in Edinburgh, has pronounced the Scottish people one of the most adaptable races on the face of the earth. It is certainly one of the most tenacious, and if it has, as he declares, largely borrowed its education, its theology, its architecture, and its art from other lands, it has made them its very own, and developed them along its own lines. The race is not a beautiful one, and its defects are pre-eminently Cancerian, but there are dignified and impressive specimens to be met with among the stately Highlanders and village prophets of the North. The burlesque edition of the type is to be seen in the raw-boned "Sandy" of the comic papers, whose character is what he himself would call "a wee thing cranky," and whose national, racial, and local prejudices are much in the foreground. He clings to his convictions like a limpet to the rock, and assumes the defensive at a moment's notice if the faintest breath of criticism is breathed upon his customs, his country or his clan. His outlook is apt to be pessimistic and he is too often tempted to force a change of mood by taking refuge in alcohol. But all this moodiness, crustiness, and angularity is only on the outside, and beneath the hard shell beats a heart full of warmth and of genuine romance, tender almost to sentimentalism whenever it has to deal with sickness or suffering, with the impotence of infancy or the helplessness of old age. His religion is simplicity itself as far as rites and ceremonies are concerned, but he lays tremendous emphasis on "the preaching of the Word," on soundness of doctrine, and on efficient religious instruction in the schools. The sermons in Scottish churches are considered of greater importance than all the rest of the service put together, and the prayers—generally extempore—embody and summarise national and local ideals, abounding in references to the fathers of the Church, and almost always including an earnest petition for the right guidance of "schools, universities, and all places of learning," as also for a special blessing upon all teachers, "that they may be given power and ability wisely to train the youth of the land." It is interesting to compare this characteristic custom with the usages of the sister Church across the border, whose Book of Common Prayer practically ignores the existence of secular education; for the patron saints or ruling Powers of England favour a different ideal from that which holds sway in the North; and the Saxon goes about his business, leaving prophecy alone.

Health

This type is reputed a delicate one, but the delicacy is of a kind that can be mastered and held in check by Cancerians who are advanced in evolution. The emotional nature is generally too strong for the physical, and when they have been upset by bad news, or are anxious about some loved one, there is a very strong tendency to exaggerate the symptoms and to become a prey to serious apprehensions of a complete break-down. These terrors are increased if such a collapse would mean finâncial difficulties for the wife and family; and as worry is one of the most fruitful causes of illness, grave symptoms may actually develope, brought about entirely by ill-controlled feelings and morbid imagination. Naturally at the primitive stage matters are still more apt to go wrong. Touchiness, bitterness, resentment and hurt pride are three very serious factors to be dealt with in trying to keep the body healthy; for the more they engender indigestion, the more indigestion serves to engender them. Gloomy forebodings begin to hold complete sway, and the efforts of the much-tried relatives to cheer the sufferer are too often treated as heartlessness and want of sympathy. In fact, what the primitive Cancerian enjoys is a good old revel in awful possibilities; and in certain moods, if he hasn't got a serious complaint to discuss, he wil actually create one—symptoms and all—by the sheer force of concentrated thought. The pangs due to insufficient mastication are translated into heart symptoms, bronchial catarrh into consumption, and so forth. Hypochondria is one of the very hardest maladies to tackle, and also one of the most difficult to nurse sympathetically, for it is always apt to make a patient exasperatingly depressing. Doctors and attendants when dealing with such cases should never forget that though the malady is real enough to require treatment, it is rooted in an exceptionally active imagination, which needs to be kept clean and healthy and well-fed exactly as the body does. The invalid should nourish the understanding, enlarge the horizon, turn the flow of sympathy outwards instead of inwards and attend to the dictates of common-sense in the matter of fresh air and exercise. Diet is very important; for Cancer, according to tradition, "rules the stomach." If eczema or other gouty symptoms appear, meat should be strictly avoided. Worry, anxiety, and fears for the future sometimes end in morbid growths, and although these may in many cases disperse and vanish when the period of stress and strain is over, surgical treatment is occasionally necessary. The best remedies are courage and hope, virtues which should be sedulously cultivated; and the duty of forgiveness and the killing out of all bitterness and resentment cannot be too strongly urged. Regular gymnastic exercise will help matters from the physical side by stimulating the circulation and working off unwholesome secretions; but as the type is seldom muscular the exercise taken should not be too severe. Celtic dancing and especially *highland* dancing of the more elaborate type (as seen in the Sword Dance, *Shian Trews*, etc.) is ideal for the purpose, demanding, as it does, perfect balance, freedom of movement and agility, without any probability of wrench or strain. These dances should, by preference, be practised from quite early childhood and so become familiar while the constitutional habits are being built up. Parents of young Cancerians will find their infancy an anxious and sometimes perilous time; and should give particular heed both then and later to diet, guarding against the unlawful consumption of sweets and the bad habit of eating "snacks" between meals. Children of this type are generally of the sweet-toothed order, and can scarcely be restrained from over-indulgence in chocolates and other sugary confections if they are obtainable either by fair means or foul. Naturally after feasting to satiety in kitchen cupboard or store-room, the small sinner disdains the dinner provided by his mother, and the foundations are laid of some functional irregularity that will possibly be an affliction throughout life. Among health-giving recreations and pursuits for Cancerians, gardening should be given a large place. The characteristic tenderness of the sign comes out strongly in the care lavished on seedlings and saplings and in the delight taken in their growth; and those born with the Sun in this sign, as well as those born with it rising, are sometimes extremely successful in their horticultural efforts. This is not reputed a long-lived type, chiefly perhaps because extreme delicacy during the first few weeks carries off an undue proportion, and brings down the average age attained. Of those who do survive to old age, too many are hampered by recurrent attacks of various commonplace and unromantic afflictions —generally preventible—which interfere with their usefulness and their serenity, especially if they are men. But there are specimens who stand the discipline magnificently and without complaining, steadily growing in sympathy and consideration for other sufferers all their days.

Contemplate the courses of the stars as one should do that revolves along with them.

Consider frequently the connection of all things in the Universe, and their relation to each other. All things are in a manner intermingled with each other, and are therefore mutually friendly. For one thing comes in due order after another, by virtue of local movements, and of the harmony aud unity of the whole.

The Universe, compact of all things, is One. Through all things runs one divinity.—Marcus Aurelius.

♌ LEO ♌

THE LION.

The Sign of the

KING OR PRESIDENT

A fixed fiery sign.

Keynote—Glory.

Watchword—Faith.

Ruler—The Sun.

☉

Mystical Gems—Ruby, Diamond.

Colour—Orange. *Metal*—Gold.

Physical Manifestation—Radiation.

Mental Manifestation—Comprehension.

The glorious planet Sol . . . whose med'cinable eye corrects the ill aspects of planets evil.—Troilus and Cressida.

O thou that rollest above, round as the shield of my fathers! Whence are thy beams, O Sun, thou everlasting light? Thou comest forth in thy awful beauty; the stars hide themselves in the sky; the Moon, cold and pale, sinks in the western wave; but thou thyself movest alone. The oaks of the mountains fall, the mountains themselves decay with years, . . . but thou art for ever the same, rejoicing in the brightness of thy course. When the world is dark with tempests, when thunder rolls and lightning flies, thou lookest in thy beauty from the clouds, and laughest at the storm. . . Exult then, O Sun! in the strength of thy youth!

JAMES MACPHERSON. (*Ossian*)

CHAPTER V.

The Leonian Type

The ruler assigned to Leo is Phœbus Apollo, or the Sun; the Defender, the Bright One, the Lord and Giver of Light; the heart and centre of the Solar System, the type and symbol of the Logos Himself. This power sums up and harmonises the characteristics of all the others. He is the companion and leader of the muses, the oracle of poets and musicians, the protector of all the arts and of many of the sciences. He perfected the lyre invented by Mercury, adding to it many strings and drawing from them harmonies unheard before He built the stately walls of Troy and the fortress of Megara. He slew the Cyclops and strangled the Python; and when banished from High Olympus by the will of his father Jupiter, he descended upon earth and became the Good Shepherd who tended the flocks of Admetus, bringing to men many gifts while he sojourned among them. In connection with this influence all the Solar Deities and heroes may be profitably studied, from Baldur in the North to Horus in ancient Egypt. Indeed the worshippers of the Sun God are to be found everywhere, and the brightness of his majesty is accepted as a symbol of Divine Glory in every religion all over the world. The Christian poet hails the Christ as the "Sun" of his soul, and Jewish astrologers associated the Archangel Michael with the chief luminary. He is depicted as young and handsome, with flowing golden curls, and holds in one hand a sword, and in the other the scales of justice, and the dragon of evil (the Python of Apollo) writhes at his feet, the angel's victorious pose suggesting the triumph of good over evil. Modern scientific research has added yet another interpretation to the ancient allegory by proving that microbes and bacteria faint and perish when bathed in the light of the Sun; another suggestion that great truths are true on all the planes. **Ruler**

It is said that no one can stand before the statue known as the Apollo Belvedere without instinctively straightening his shoulders and drawing himself up to his full stature. The fully developed Leonian has something of the same effect upon his fellow-men, morally and mentally as well as physically. His faith and trust in humanity, his **Evolved Type** serene conviction that those who are working for him will always do their best, and that even those who fail him will redeem themselves and do better in the future, all combine to awaken a generous response in the hearts of others, and by thus touching the mainspring of action, he gives to those around him fresh courage, and sets them striving with might and main to fulfil his expectations. He is the ideal head of any large enterprise, institution, or undertaking. Many-sided himself, he understands and appreciates the qualities of all the other types, and never wastes his energy by asking from anyone what it is not in his or her power to give. Therefore he is particularly successful in organising activities and distributing duties, giving to the specialists facilities and opportunities for exercising their various faculties. Like a wise monarch he sends the warrior to the field of battle, the sage to the council-chamber; the governor to discipline the unruly province, the ambassador to offer terms of peace. Royal commands, to be effective, must be easily understood, and therefore his style is simple and straightforward. Royal approval is definite and unmistakable, and is emphasised in the sight of all men by the order, the ribbon and the star. Royal displeasure is intimated without hesitation or circumlocution, and with sufficient decision to prevent the recurrence of its occasion. The kingly study is contemporary history, the kingly tense the present indicative. The ideal monarch holds the past in reverence, as the parent of the present, and looks forward to the future as its child; so he has himself crowned by the priest, thus endowing him with position and authority to uphold tradition; and welcomes the advent of the prophet, giving to him the rostrum provided by an unfettered press. He encourages both science and art by his personal interest and patronage, and takes special measures for the well-being of the sick and the suffering, the poverty-stricken and oppressed. He practises constant self-denial and shows constant consideration for others by his punctuality, method and forethought; and though his own life is simple and his days full of labour, he can show regal hospitality, shining as host, and delighting to give of his best to the guest and stranger. In this department of kingship almost every man is called upon at times to play his part, and the "Queen Consort," whose dignity is gentle and gracious rather than commanding, finds special opportunities of distinction. It is characteristic of the Leonian type of hospitality that it is always the welcome that really crowns it with success, and never either the richness of the feast, nor the splendour of the entertainment. In fact both may leave something to be desired, especially in humble homes; for the mastery of detail is difficult for this type; but the harmony of the gathering will be undisturbed; each guest will be given a chance to excel in his own special line, or made to feel that he has in some way contributed to the general enjoyment, and so will depart with reluctance and with a lively goodwill to return.

Love and Friendship

The loves and friendships of the Sun-God are seldom fortunate, and Apollo's devotion to Hyacinth, to Daphne and to other youths and nymphs left him unsatisfied and sorrowful. The emotions of this type tend to be over-generous and too wide-spread, and the characteristic faith in human nature frequently results in misplaced affections and unwise friendships. Heart-aches, broken engagements, and unhappy marriages are frequent; but on the other hand the inborn magnanimity and power of forgiveness are such that in many cases the sufferer can adjust himself or herself to apparently impossible conditions, avert a tragedy and bring success out of failure by a sheer act of faith.

Religion

The type of religious expression natural to the Leonian is the psalm or hymn of praise; the joyous procession of youths and maidens "lifting up their voices with their harps, with their psalteries, with their instruments of ten strings." The temples of Apollo were specially designed to suit such ceremonial—"all beautiful, without and within"; and the worshippers who met to do him honour in the days of ancient Greece and Rome, passed in triumph through his courts, and out along the highways, crowned with garlands and chanting his praises. Games were organised in his honour and some of the grandest dramas the world has ever seen were declaimed at his special* festivals; and though many of these are deeply sad, they are always beautiful—symmetrical in proportion, clear and dignified in narration, concerned with the fortunes of princely personages and carefully preserving the unities. The mystery play, recently revived, is their successor. The simpler functions referred to above find their modern representatives in such celebrations as the Christian feast of Corpus Domini—always

* Or at the festivals of Bacchus and Dionysios, who were also representatives of the Sun God, wine symbolising the vitality or life-blood, which flows from the heart and centre of being

held about mid-summer, when the Sun reaches his highest point in the heavens. Then happy bands of rose-wreathed children and white-veiled maidens pass along the village streets of Catholic countries, singing praises and scattering flowers before the Host as they pass from altar to altar, unconsciously following in the footsteps of their Pagan forefathers, and keeping green the memory of an immeasurably ancient custom. In Protestant countries the same impulse finds a less poetic outlet in the annual Sunday School excursion, with its waving banners, brazen music and merry romping in the open air. The high priest of this type of worship in Hebrew literature is David, the shepherd king of Israel, the royal minstrel of the ruddy locks and comely countenance, who slew the giant with sling and pebble, charmed the demon of melancholy away from the clouded mind of Saul, and scandalised his haughty consort Michal by personally taking part in the procession of singers and dancers who escorted the ark to the temple of the Lord. His psalms, in the original, probably form the most perfect examples of Leonian style in existence, and even in translation have served as models to many of our greatest writers. Among their special characteristics we may note the constant recurrence of the words Majesty and Glory, and their marvellous clearness and lucidity;—a clearness attained partly by simplicity of phrasing, and partly by careful repetition of important passages. Even where metaphor is employed the form is often that of direct statement. "The Lord is my Shepherd. . . . He leadeth me beside the still waters." In his darkest moments, when "out of the depths" the Psalmist cries unto his God, his agony, unlike that of the prophet, never urges him to elaborate or twist a phrase. "*My life is spent with grief, and my years with sighing. . . . I am like a broken vessel. . . . My heart faileth." Sorrow and suffering have never been more clearly and simply expressed. Curiously enough, these moods of deep despondency are characteristic of many Leonians. The forethoughtful outlook naturally suggests forebodings; and the lack of ability to deal with difficulties in detail leads, at times, to a state of helpless dejection that seems at first

* Psalms xxxi. and xxv. Contrast style of *Jer.* ix. 1. "Oh that my head were waters and mine eyes a fountain of tears that I might weep day and night for the slain of the daughter of my people" The anguish of the prophet is more intense, but the sorrow of the King gains in pathos and dignity by its childlike simplicity. It is probable that none of the elaborately built acrostic psalms (such as the cxix.) were by this Leonian hand.

sight to be absolutely incompatible with the normal bearing of the sign. This condition is generally associated with inefficient heart action—a frequent physical affliction of this type, and a very depressing one;—but it is also partly due to an entire absence of resentment, rancour, and bitterness. These feelings are vicious and objectionable in themselves, but they are active; and by encouraging a fight, they keep their victims from being flattened out and crushed by sorrow, as the Leonian is too apt to be. He cannot raise his head in his woe, and simply waits with resignation till that faith, which never altogether fails him, can gather strength enough to lift him out of the slough of despond once more. Greek tragedy echoes this mood, teaching absolute submission to the divine will. The misfortunes heaped upon its characters are always traced to their original cause in some act of disobedience to Divine law, and it was considered the chief duty of the dramatist to demonstrate clearly the relation between cause and effect. The children of Apollo in our day and generation content themselves with less worthy and more cynical theatrical fare; but they may sometimes feel a faint and far-off echo of the sensations which these marvellous dramas were meant to evoke, *e.g.*, when they stand uncovered at sight of some regal pageant designed to quicken the pulses of national life; or when in church or in concert hall they rise as one man to the glorious strains of Handel's great chorus, with its ringing Hallelujahs to the "King of Kings and Lord of Lords."

Primitive Type

Primitive Leonians are generally afflicted with an unquenchable thirst for personal glory, and a ridiculous ambition for positions of responsibility and authority, which they are quite incapable of filling with any degree of success. Many, especially those of the commanding, or masculine type, contrive to give themselves the illusion of kingship by assuming airs of self-importance and lording it over their inferiors and juniors. The gentler or more feminine type seeks, above all things, a comfortable throne—and a well-cushioned one at that; and asserts her queenship by betraying a marvellous skill in delegating disagreeable duties, a total incapacity for serving either herself or anyone else, together with a wondrous power of swallowing flattery. The lion seen through a diminishing glass is very much like the domestic cat—an animal attached to its home and, as far as in it lies, to those who are willing to stroke it the right way; but never much inclined to put itself out for anybody. Even at his best and grandest the King of Beasts is no warrior; and indeed some naturalists have stigmatised him as the greatest fraud that ever wore a crown. He attacks his prey from behind, selects the weakest antagonists, and strikes them at their most unguarded moments. It is good generalship—the wiliest of warfare; and when the arm extended to strike is no arm, but an army, and the object of all this manœuvring is the saving of bloodshed and the speedy conclusion of hostilities, the method is kingly though hardly heroic; but the monkey who makes use of the cat's paw to save his own skin shows the same tendency at a more elementary stage, and nobody finds his example inspiring. A talent for deputing work is first cousin to the habit of shirking it; and it behoves every son of Apollo to ask himself candidly where he draws the line. The pitiable state of muddle found in some Leonian kingdoms is due to the fact that the monarch has claimed the throne too soon, and is either inclined to fidget in it or to snooze. At this early stage the tolerant attitude is apt to suggest that nothing matters very much; and the comprehensive intellect tries to cover so large a field of activity that it loses the ability to estimate relative values, and for lack of a clear focus cannot distinguish mountains from molehills.

The vice of kings is favouritism; and exaggerated faith in humanity may lead to many a blunder in the choice of friends. Primitive Leonians are apt to select those who can make themselves useful, or who flatter them by showing a certain amount of abject dependence on their favour. Their love affairs develope along the same lines, and are apt to be numerous and unfortunate. They very often marry beneath them—possibly from a desire to make sure of at least one "subject,"—and not infrequently find that their judgment has been at fault, and that the submissive and devoted fiancée shows a tendency, after marriage, to usurp the throne

Physical Characteristics

Manifesting physically, this sign is most easily recognised by its commanding presence, stateliness of bearing, and deliberation in speech and movement. It is not easy to pass over a Leonian in a crowd, and even when he is so small as to be a mere pocket edition of the type, he generally makes his presence felt. The body is symmetrical, the limbs well proportioned, the step firm yet light, the stride longer than the average. Many of them excel in dancing, even when, as often happens, they are inclined to be stout. The features are marked, and in some cases rather heavy—either "Roman," or more or less feline in type—and generally show decided character. The hair is luxuriant—golden, brown or black; the eyebrows well arched and sometimes very finely pencilled. The eyes are large and round, and inclined to open wide, and to look directly and somewhat over-boldly at the interlocutor in conversation. Astrological Tradition declares that Italy—especially its capital—and also a large part of France, are much under the influence of Leo; and certainly the dignity of the typical Roman, and the importance of his native city as an organising centre, accord well with such a theory. Both countries have shone in the past, and still shine in the present, in the cultivation of literature, of science and of art, and both races are distinctly comely. The feminine edition of the Leonian has less solidity of build and pose, and more grace than her lord, and even when short in stature she can play the queen in Society right royally and fill her throne and reign over her own circle—small or great—in fitting style. Queen Victoria was born with the Sun rising, and showed many Leonian traits.

A couple of quaint caricatures of this type are to be found in *Alice Through the Looking-Glass*, where, in the Red and White Queen, the author has given us excellent sketches of the fussy Leonian and her more helpless sister;—fittingly evolving both from a previous "feline" existence as kittens! The Red Queen is a stickler for etiquette and always knows exactly what other people ought to do; is always ready with advice, order and reprimand, disdains circumlocution and is inclined to flat contradiction in conversation. The White Queen is gentle and helpless, is afflicted with dark forebodings—*e.g.*, when she is about to prick her finger—and is so absolutely without resource that she can only bewail her fate and await it, while after the accident she depends entirely upon Alice to adjust her shawl and fasten her brooch. Another burlesque is to be seen in the Frenchman of the English comic papers—fatuously vain and idiotically self-satisfied; placidly convinced that he is the centre of admiration wherever he goes and that no woman can possibly resist him or resent his attentions. He fights farcical duels, resulting in a pin's prick, and is constantly making himself conspicuous in all sorts of ridiculous ways, and always with the same object—"LA GLOIRE." Tartarin was of this brotherhood, and even his fellow countrymen appreciate the justice of his castigation; but many of the heroes held up to admiration by Alexandre Dumas *père*, impress the Saxon reader, as being only a little

In Fiction

Literary Style

less absurd. That author was born with the Sun rising in Leo, so is doubly Leonian, and shows the influence strongly, both in his choice of a field for his literary activity and in his method of treatment. Like Sir Walter Scott—also born with the Sun in Leo—he was extraordinarily prolific in the production of historical romances of considerable length, dealing largely with the fortunes of royal and princely personages, or with questions of chivalry, of honour and of glory. Both told their tales in a straightforward style, and both neglected the useful art of pruning; and that to such an extent that their novels have been published by enterprising firms in abridged editions. Another literary celebrity born with the Sun in Leo was Alfred, Lord Tennyson, the sweet singer of King Arthur and his table round.

Health

In the matter of health Leo rarely does things by halves, and the sons and daughters of this sign are generally either exceptionally strong—radiating vitality around them—or always more or less on the sick list. The dangers to health on the higher planes are discordant and inharmonious surroundings, and the sorrow that springs from misplaced or unrequited affection; to which may be added, in the case of primitive specimens, wounded vanity or lack of praise. Physically the trouble usually works out in some weakness or irregularity of the heart beat, affecting the circulation, and when this becomes marked, the characteristic energy of the type passes into abeyance, and the tendency to lean upon subordinates altogether swamps the desire to rule them. Acute rheumatism is sometimes an affliction also, and, if the attack is a sharp one, the fever may run dangerously high. Such fevers—or possibly the drugs prescribed to allay them—generally have as bad effect upon the heart as the unhappy love-affairs hinted at above, and the convalescence drags along somewhat drearily. The best remedies are love and peace and harmonious surroundings; to which should be added a short period of restful solitude daily, during which the patient should tune himself to his surroundings by silent meditation.

♍ VIRGO ♍

THE VIRGIN.

The Sign of the

CRAFTSMAN OR CRITIC

A mutable earthy sign.

Keynote—Purity.

Watchword—Service.

Ruler—Vulcan
(or the Negative side of Mercury ?)

☿

Mystical Gems—Pink Jasper, Hyacinth.

Colour—Yellow ?　　*Metal*—Quicksilver ?

Physical Manifestation—Crystallisation.

Mental Manifestation—Discrimination.

Who then is willing to consecrate his service this day unto the Lord?

And they with whom precious stones were found, gave them to the treasure of the house of the Lord . . . and David said . . . But who am I, and what is my people, that we should be able to offer so willingly after this sort? for all things come of Thee, and of Thine own have we given Thee.—I. CHRONICLES XXIX. 5.

So likewise ye, when ye shall have done all those things which are commanded you, say: "We are unprofitable servants: we have done that which was our duty to do."—ST. LUKE XVII. 10.

Be intent on My service; performing actions for My sake, thou shalt attain perfection. If even to do this, thou hast not strength, then, taking refuge in union with Me . . . renounce all fruit of action.

Thy business is with the action only, never with the fruits; so let not the fruit of action be thy motive, nor be thou to inaction attached.

On Renunciation followeth Peace.

THE SONG OF THE LORD OR BHAGAVAD GITA.

CHAPTER VI.

The Virginian Type

The ruler of Virgo is described in astrological tradition as "the negative side of Mercury," an expression which tells us that this aspect of deity cannot be positively connected with the power of any known planet. Some recent astrologers have put forward the theory that the true ruler is Vulcan, a planet whose existence is suspected by astronomers, and whose invisibility is accounted for by the smallness of its size and by its nearness to the Sun, whose radiance eclipses it; and turning to the key of classical mythology it will be found that the Smith of Olympus is, in truth, an excellent symbol of the form of energy most apparent in those who come under the Virgo influence. Vulcan is the craftsman, the artificer, the practical worker among the Gods. He forges their armour, fashions their ornaments, and builds their palaces. In serving them he obeys the essential impulse of his own nature, never drudging mechanically as a slave, even when working under orders, but always with some originality accepting commissions, but executing them according to his own designs. In fact he works as a great artist does, obeying the dictates of his patrons without troubling his head about why the order is given or whether it should have been given at all, and concentrating all his energy and intellect on the manner of its execution. His will is enough to set his great bellows in motion. His glowing furnace tries and tests and purifies the materials at his disposal, separating the true metal from the dross. He wields his hammer with power and might, and gold and silver and shining steel leave his hands fashioned into forms so fair, as well as so strong and lasting, that all Olympus marvels. His frame is powerful, his muscles firmly knit, his right arm is ever bared, and ready for work. As he stands at his forge he is a grand and

Ruler

* Astronomy of late has been inclined to shelve this theory Astrology clings to it yet.

impressive figure; but when he leaves it to join in the festivities of the Gods, and, true to his instinct for serving others attempts to carry round the cup of nectar, he does it so awkwardly that Olympus rings with laughter—for this strange, strong deity of the forge is lame. His "one-sided" tendency is also expressed by the poets in the legend that he had no Father, but sprang from Juno alone, the inner meaning of which becomes clear to the student if he calls to mind that Vulcan's wife (according to the *Iliad*) is Charis, or Love, the Mother of the Graces. The type of energy expressed by Virgo needs Grace to complete it. Service, to be perfect, must be loving service; otherwise it becomes uncouth, unwelcome, and even, at times, ridiculous. And note that Charis signifies love at its purest and most passionless; the self-sacrificing, self-effacing love expressed by the power of Pisces—the sign opposite to Virgo in the horoscope. In the *Odyssey* Vulcan is mated with Venus—unequally and unhappily mated, for she prefers Mars, and is false to her lord, who punishes her by turning upon her the ridicule of heaven; and the gods themselves amid their laughter, acknowledge that after all, the erring pair are well-matched. A strange and puzzling story to the student of mythology, but one pregnant with meaning to the astrologer; for Venus and Mars are the true wedded couple—Libra balancing Aries; and Virgo and Pisces, which complete and harmonise each other, expressing service with devotion, are both, in their highest human manifestation, celibate signs. The Vulcanalia, or chief festival of the lame god, was held in Rome on August 23rd, at which time the Sun is in Virgo—an interesting and suggestive coincidence. In Greek mythology Hephaestos corresponds to the Latin Vulcan, and both are closely related to the various Gods of the anvil or the furnace who are found in almost all religions. In Christianity this power is represented by St. Clement, the patron saint of blacksmiths, and finds another sympathetic saint in St. James, the apostle of good works, who is a special favourite with the serving orders of monks and nuns.

Evolved Type

The chief characteristic of the fully developed Virginian is his marvellous power of discrimination. He tries everything in the furnace of his criticism, separates, sifts, classifies and arranges his materials and his men, recognising at a glance the potential value of each, and organising the work entrusted to him so as to make the very best practical use of everyone and everything. Hand and brain generally work together in people of this type, especially in all matters in which accuracy and method are important. Their clear heads and thrifty ways make them excellent managers, enabling them to shine as public servants, and qualifying them to bear the burden of much anxious and responsible work in connection with large enterprises and important undertakings. An ideal staff of officials for any company, club or association would include a Leonian as President, a Cancerian and a Scorpionian as vice-presidents, a Taurean as treasurer, and a Virginian as secretary. The last-named generally does the hardest work and gets small thanks for it. If he fails in his duties, the Society he serves will probably go to pieces, but few realise that, and he is generally too much occupied by practical details to care greatly whether they do or not. His business is to carry on the activities of the concern with strict attention to the rules of a constitution which is framed and directed by others, and when he has done all that is his duty to do, he personally sets the example of regarding himself as an unprofitable servant, and the vote of thanks, by his own directions, goes to the chair. In this matter the Virginian is wise as usual. It is not his province to command, and when he attempts to issue orders in his own person, or to assume airs of authority he very frequently gives offence; but people will readily work with him and accept services from him; for he is splendidly capable, and very quick to see how a thing should be done, though disinclined to trouble his head about the why. "It is an order" is a sufficient reason for him, for Virgo, like Taurus, is one of the Earthy or "Service" signs. The above statement must not, however, be interpreted as signifying that the Virginian is always doomed to work without reward or appreciation from his fellow men. Untiring industry, practical ability, clear vision and critical acumen are bound to bring a man to the front sooner or later; and though it is often later —for this type generally seems to start handicapped in some way— many a son of Vulcan has inscribed his name on the Honours list in life, thanks to his Virgo qualities. Success has been achieved notably in the lines of criticism and literature, and also in art—especially painting. These people work best "at the forge"—*i.e.*, alone in studio, study or workshop—have small patience with underlings, assistants and apprentices, and no patience at all with the critics, unless their comments show exceptional discrimination and are practically helpful. Women born under this sign are usually skilled in needlework, and often achieve their greatest triumphs in that line when spurred by necessity and handicapped by limitations, finding a use for the most unlikely materials and showing great judgment in their adaptation, and ornamentation. When well off they generally dress with care and taste—never showily or ostentatiously, and sometimes even with a certain puritanical sobriety, but always suitably, and with a reasonable attention to health, common-sense and the practical durability of their garments. If not compelled to the use of the needle, they often take it up for pleasure, or pursue some form of handicraft—wood-carving, design, embroidery, lace-work, etc. Those who do not, have something of a masculine turn about them, are keenly intellectual, and somewhat critical both of themselves and of others—an unhappy condition of mind. Even at its brightest this type tends to be a grave one, for it has few illusions, and little buoyancy; but when Vulcan is " wedded to Charis," *i.e.*, when this influence is properly blended with one of the gentler and more loving signs, nothing can exceed its charm. The pointed speech then becomes extremely witty, and the clear eyes are always wide open to whatsoever things are pure and lovely and of good report. If there is any virtue, life's keen critic will point it out, and if there is any praise he will utter it; and though his native penetration refuses to leave him in ignorance of the shortcomings of frail humanity, his healthiness of mind will prevent his dwelling upon them or indulging in morbid analysis of anything that is objectionable or unclean.

Certain astrologers have declared that this is a selfish sign, and for some time the writer was at a loss to account for such an assertion; for the type of selfishness that demands and exacts assistance and attentions from others is the very last accusation that could be brought up against Virginians, many of whom dedicate their whole lives to the service of their fellow-creatures, toiling unremittingly, often for very inadequate pay—and always finding far more satisfaction in helping others than in working for their own benefit. They give freely and ungrudgingly of their time and strength and ability up to the very measure of their natural forces, and sometimes beyond them; but nevertheless there is a limit to their generosity, and when demands are excessive and unreasonable they know how to say no, and to stick to it. In addition to this they are rarely lavish in their affections, never prodigal of praise, and usually very prudent in the expenditure of their income, which is often a narrow one—possibly because when souls are meant to evolve through a life of labour they are guided into an environment which gives them ample opportunity for it. An inevitable accompaniment of this love of giving active service is an intense dislike to the idea of accepting it, and a horror of dependence in old age, which naturally leads to the careful husbanding of their pecuniary resources, and makes many of them live very simply and frugally; but when ample wealth is placed at their disposal, and they have no need to worry about the future, they spend wisely and well, generally receiving full value for their money.

Love and Friendship

The Virginian heart, like the steel of Vulcan, is true metal, and not easily melted; but when once it finds itself in love's furnace it glows with a pure white heat, and takes a long time to cool. His love affairs are few, and when, as often happens, they are unfortunate, he takes refuge in his one panacea of hard work, and is apt to shrink from the society of his fellow-men. The sign is unfavourable for progeny; *i.e.*, the women only attain motherhood with much suffering and difficulty if they attain it at all, and many of the men are sterile. Neither sex seems to crave much for children though the members of both make very careful and conscientious parents. When highly developed they accept celibacy easily and are fruitful in good works, caring little for posterity so long as they can serve their own day and generation. They have the instinct of chastity and turn with special repulsion from literature dealing with sex problems, especially if there is anything morbid or unwholesome in the treatment of the subject. Students may smile over such an assertion, remembering that among men born with Virgo strongly accentuated are several notable examples whose lives have been far from ideal in the matter of purity. In accounting for such exceptions the horoscope must of course be examined in detail, special note being taken of the position of Venus. If it is in a susceptible or fickle sign, the Virgo influence will be to some extent counteracted; and environment must also be considered. Thus in the case of Charles II., the planet of love is found in Taurus—the most amorous sign—and the low ideals of his corrupt generation, as shown in the life and literature of the time, will account for his responding more easily to the vibrations of Venus than to the sterner call of Vulcan. Perhaps if the Merry Monarch had ever experienced the white heat of a true Virginian affection, the history of his court might have been different. It should be noted that his children were few and his marriage sterile, and also that he was one of the wittiest men of his day.

Religion Taurus lays the foundations of the temple of the Lord, and sees that its walls are solidly built. Libra gives grace to their proportions, and balances arch against arch and curve against curve, tapering the spire, and raising the dome. Virgo tries and tests the materials and provides the cunning workman in brass and silver and gold, the fashioners and broiderers of tapestry and vestment, the carvers in wood and stone who fill in the details and find out the best practical methods of carrying out the design of the architect. The humbler members of this brotherhood will cleanse and purify the building, sweeping, scouring, dusting, polishing, repairing and replacing with untiring industry and exhaustless energy. The holy water is their fitting symbol; baptism—the first and lowliest of the sacraments—the only one that seems to them of any importance. To enter the service of the Master is the chief event in their religious life; to bring to that service clean hands and a pure heart, a sound mind and a healthy body seems to them all that is really essential. Elaborate ritual strikes the average Virginian as a waste of time; theological debate as a wearisome repetition of meaningless phrases. He gives his sanction to the preaching of the word, because it stimulates energy and conduces to good works; but it must be brief and to the point, and he is seldom roused to enthusiasm by it. He never seeks for praise or thanks himself, therefore it does not occur to him to render either to his Maker, Whom he conceives as above both, and consequently—though this does not necessarily follow—indifferent to them. After he has asked for a blessing on past work, and for strength to labour in the future, his petitions are done, and with regard to every other form of religious observance he is inclined to ask his recurrent and characteristic question, "What is the use of it?" When reference is made in his presence to the rapture of the Mystic, the ecstasy of the Saint and the inspiration of the prophet, he shrugs his shoulders. If others talk of the faith that removes mountains, he shakes his head. "Show me your faith without your works, and I by my works will show you my faith," he says; for, from his point of view, "True religion and undefiled before God and the Father is this; to visit the fatherless and widows in their affliction, and to keep himself unspotted from the world." A successful ship-builder on the banks of the river Clyde was once questioned as to his beliefs. "It is my religion," he replied, "to build good ships." He was probably a Virginian; and though his reply will shock many, it has its impressive side for all that. "*To build good ships*"; *i.e.*, to fulfil one's contracts faithfully, even at the risk of losing by them; to give honest workmanship and sound timber and true steel; to tolerate no shams, no pretences, no hypocrisies in commercial life. The cause of true religion would gain and not lose, if more of our business-men would follow such an example.

Astrological tradition associates this sign of Virgo with the Holy Hermits of old, and though such an idea seems to contradict the above, the two forms of religion are not really irreconcilable, for the hermitage is generally associated with the closing years of a life that has been full of activity. Saints of this type were generally believed to have played their part in the world before leaving it, and were, not infrequently, reputed to have suffered much through the affections. Elderly Virginians will generally own that the descriptions of these pure and peaceful lives appeal to them very strongly. The rocky cave for shelter, the limpid stream for the daily bath, the simple diet of nuts and fruits, with the milk of the hind—emblem of purity—for all luxury. The practice of such austerities hardly smiles upon us in our northern clime; but in far-away forest and desert and cave many a Virginian follows the calling still, and lives out his declining years in the lap of nature, resting after labour, and learning, who can say how many lessons in the process.

Literary Style

Literary men, born under this sign, excel in the mastery of detail and are exceedingly industrious and prolific, adapting their genius to the demands and necessities of their day, and usually finding their market in consequence. Dickens, who gave the hour of his birth to an American inquirer as 7.50 a.m. and so must have been born when Virgo was rising, is an excellent example of this type. He never spared himself—died, in fact, of overwork, and published in rapid succession a large number of novels, in most of which the side characters and detailed description are of much more importance to the reader than the heroes and heroines or the main outlines of the plot. His gallery of clear and definite portraits is something extraordinary. In Bleak House alone there are over eighty distinct and living characters—all real breathing people capable of interesting the reader in their various personalities and concerns; and although his work in life was that of a writer of light fiction, and he used his Virgo wit to keep his audiences thoroughly well entertained, his real aims and ideals were utilitarian. His great ambition was to better the physical condition of the poor, and to interest the men and women of his generation in such questions as workmen's dwellings, prison reform and poor-law relief. In spite of his great kindliness and charming personality, his attitude of mind was always intensely critical, and his portraits of his fellow creatures far from flattering. In fact, when he attempts to idealise, as in the case of such a character as little Nell, he fails to produce a convincing portrait, and his most lovable characters are full of weaknesses and intensely human. Among significant facts, for the astrological student, are to be noted his failure to find happiness in marriage, and his resentment of criticism.

The average Virginian, instead of mastering detail, allows detail to master him, and if he takes up literature at all is more likely to succeed as a critic of other men's work than in any field demanding creative power. His style, though concise and clear, is somewhat formal, and best suited to the framing of business notices. He will draw up an index or a catalogue, compile a dictionary, or lend a hand in the production of an encyclopædia. Hard work never daunts him, and to express himself with neatness and precision is a real joy; but apart from criticism his pen seldom runs freely, and his letters are usually the driest of the dry.

Primitive Type

It has been neatly said, and the saying is often quoted, that the critics are those who have failed. It might be said with greater charity and fuller truth that the critics are those who are not yet sufficiently evolved to succeed; and of these critics, the most captious, and aggravating and impossible to please are the undeveloped Virginians. The advanced type, bringing its clear vision and fine discrimination to bear upon the work entrusted to it, sees at a glance all the practical possibilities and opportunities for usefulness involved. The primitive type only sees the impossibilities and the flaws; and it finds them, by preference, in work done or schemes drawn up by others. The developed specimen never asks for praise; the primitive specimen never gives it. The former will conquer adverse circumstances, and make his very handicaps contribute to his success. The latter quarrels with every condition imposed upon him, resents his limitations, and invariably blames circumstances for his failures. His ambition to achieve something practical and his inability to do so are apt to result in impatience, nervous irritability, and ill-humour; and sometimes in chronic discontent. If hampered by ill-health or in any way restricted in his activities, he takes it cantankerously, sometimes working on till dead-beat in defiance of the doctor, and meeting all the kindly remonstrances of his friends with a snap and a growl. Even at this rudimentary stage he has very little laziness about him, and if he is under wise guidance and control will make an admirable servant, loyal to his master's interests, and rigidly faithful to his orders; but these orders must be clear and precise, and the reversal of one of them, especially if sudden and unexpected, will upset the Virginian's temper completely, and make him, for the time being, a very disagreeable companion. His horizon is bounded by the circle of his own duties, and by dint of concentrating his attention solely on the details immediately under his own nose, he loses sight of the larger outlines and consequently cannot adapt himself to changes which spring from causes beyond his ken. His views are not merely limited, they are microscopic, and he is apt to make mountains out of molehills on every possible occasion. He is the kind of man who is capable of surveying some Masterpiece of art in a stony silence that chills the blood of any real art lover in his company, and who, before turning away, will point out mercilessly some trifling error in the darkest corner of the background, some tiny flaw in the construction of the frame. In fact, at his worst, he exercises a most depressing and deadening effect upon his fellow creatures, killing enterprise, enthusiasm and hope, and nipping youthful ardour ruthlessly in the bud. Virginians who find themselves prone to such habits of thought and speech should strive earnestly to cultivate the appreciative faculties and force themselves to enter kindly and sympathetically into family and social life; otherwise they will develop into mere machines, spending their days in a dreary round of drudgery, and allowing love and friendship to slip away from them or pass them by, till they realise, too late, that they have developed into crusty old bachelors or lonely old maids, with absolutely no ties binding them to the rising generation. Marriage, if resorted to in time, is a remedy, but it is surprising how "old-maidish" these people—men and women alike—can contrive to be, even in the bonds of holy wedlock; and there is always a danger of matrimonial shipwreck for them unless great care is taken to avoid the failings of their type. The male Virginian allows business to absorb him to such an extent that all outward signs and tokens of his affection tend to disappear; and his wife, becoming convinced of his indifference, looks outside the limits of her home for sympathy and companionship, and if at all vain or weak, is tempted to accept the admiration and attentions of others. The women of this Virgo type make idols of their household gods—their carpets and their curtains, their crockery, furniture and plenishings generally; and are so much absorbed in their upholstery and their house-cleaning, that they can scarcely lay aside their needles or their dusters to give their wearied husbands a kindly welcome home. Consequently they too, pave the way for their rivals, and especially for such jovial and genial rivals as the club and the public-house.

Physical Characteristics

Manifesting physically, the Virgo type is associated with a somewhat wiry build, generally strong and muscular, and capable of enduring long hours of steady work, and much physical fatigue. The hair is usually dark brown or black, the eyes very clear and often hazel or grey; but colour varies, as always, with race and climate. The mouth is small, the nose rather long, the expression always intelligent and sometimes keenly critical. The type at its best is exceedingly handsome, but there is apt to be a "faultily faultless, icily regular' flavour about it. The beauty depends on regularity of feature and fineness of form, and lacks plastic grace, unless one of the softer and more loving elements in the horoscope—Libra, Venus, Pisces, etc.—is strongly emphasised, in which case there is great personal charm ready repartee and a sparkling wit. Even at its gentlest this type is always critically alive to the faults and failings of those around it—its dearest friends included. Though France and her children generally are ruled by Leo, the city of Paris is said to be specially under the influence of Virgo. It is certainly a city of detail, the home of encyclopædists and the centre of an organisation of the most finicking type: The French Government dictates the very hours of the children's lessons with such precision that the little scholars in the

East of France have to attend their classes by Parisian time, rising winter and summer an hour earlier by the Sun than their contemporaries in the West. The Parisian is generally handsome and always tastefully and suitably dressed, has few illusions and no cherished beliefs; is sceptical, practical, makes an excellent craftesman, and is very often exceedingly witty. There is more Leonian tolerance than Virginian purity associated with the life of the gay city; but it is an oft repeated assertion that the foreign elements of the population are responsible for its doubtful reputation, and not the native-born Parisians, who are usually hard-working, frugal and temperate. The irritable bachelor uncle of the comic papers is a burlesque of this type, and another is the Angular Spinster of the caricaturist, with her sharp speech, dislike of children and weakness for cats,—which animals are traditionally said to be ruled by Virgo.

Health

A curious fact which, so far as the writer is aware, has not been noted by any other astrologer has pressed itself on her notice while this article has been in course of preparation. Among the people personally known to her whose horoscopes she has collected, all those who are lame come under this Virginian influence in one way or another—suggesting a further tie between them and the power of Vulcan. It would be instructive to gather statistics at some hospital for cripples, and find out whether the rule is invariable; and the result might settle various matters of dispute among astrologers—*e.g.*, whether Byron and Sir Walter Scott were born with Virgo as ascendant Inquirers would have to bear in mind the probability that Vulcan, in or near the ascending degree, would have the same effect as an accentuated Virgo influence; and it is interesting to note that in some cases where there is a strong Virgo element visible in the life, and nothing to account for it in the horoscope, the ascension of Vulcan is a possible explanation.

Virgo is an extraordinarily healthy sign and more capable than any other of incessant and unremitting labour. In fact, the chief dangers to health are overwork and absorption in purely practical matters, leading to a certain sceptical and unsympathetic attitude of mind—a kind of dryness and barrenness in the life—a total absence of the spontaneity and joy which ought to accompany the exercise of the faculties. There is seldom any serious illness; but occasional functional derangements appear, and diet is often a difficulty, for certain foods which other types can eat with impunity are apt to prove poisonous to Virginians. Many of them are seriously upset by preparations of fruits and vegetables such as tomatoes, rhubarb or prunes, and cannot touch dishes which are highly spiced or seasoned—pickles, chutney, curries and so forth causing disagreeable eruptions and other disturbances. Virginians are consequently inclined to be fastidious and fussy about their food, and especially about its purity and the manner in which it is prepared and served. Some of the specimens whose horoscopes have been collected, have suffered from internal abscesses and ulcerations, difficult to treat successfully, and in these cases some weakness or curvature of the spine is usually perceptible, the removal of which —by careful remedial gymnastics—is the best prescription for the other afflictions. As has already been said, a notable percentage of Virginians are lame and the lameness is often due to an accident in very early childhood.

Virginians I have known are tidy and orderly about their possessions, and can often help those who are apt to lose or mislay theirs, by an intuitive knowledge of where to look for the lost article, which may be of any kind, from a live kitten to missing jewellery. It is possible that those who are gifted in "dowsing" for veins of metal are born under this sign.

♎ LIBRA ♎

THE BALANCE.

The Sign of the

STATESMAN OR MANAGER

A cardinal airy sign.

Keynote—Beauty.

Wetchword—Harmony.

Ruler—Venus.

♀

Mystical Gems—Diamond, Opal.

Colour—Indigo Blue. *Metal*—Copper.

Physical Manifestation—Equilibrium.

Mental Manifestation—Balance.

The woman's cause is man's ; they rise or sink
Together, dwarf'd or god-like, bond or free :
For she that out of Lethe scales with man
The shining steps of Nature, shares with man
His nights, his days, moves with him to one goal.
. . . . *But work no more alone !*
For woman is not undevelopt man,
But diverse : could we make her as the man,
Sweet Love were slain . his dearest bond is this
Not like to like, but like in difference.
Yet in the long years liker must they grow ,
The man be more of woman, she of man ;
He gain in sweetness and in moral height,
Nor lose the wrestling thews that throw the world ;
She mental breadth, nor fail in childward care,
Nor lose the child-like in the larger mind ;
Till at the last she set herself to man,
Like perfect music unto noble words.
Self-reverent each and reverencing each,
But like each other even as those who love.

TENNYSON.

CHAPTER VII.

THE LIBRAN TYPE

APHRODITE, the Greek representative of the Latin Venus, the laughter-loving goddess of love and beauty, is said by the old poets to have been born from the foam of the sea; and the sea, mystically interpreted, is the emotional, psychic, or astral plane. It is a wide expanse, this great realm of Neptune, and hides in its bosom many possibilities; but here it is only the foam which concerns us—the shining crest that crowns its curling waves when the winds of heaven breathe upon them. For foam is air imprisoned in water, and speaks to us of the union of two mighty elements; of interaction and of interchange—and also of something whose chief beauty lies in its constant variety of form, in its power to adapt itself to ever changing conditions; in short, of the "Eternal Feminine," the female element in the Divine Nature, the "*Ewig Weibliche*," which draws us onwards and upwards to Perfection. Fiery Mars, the essentially masculine force, is represented on the physical plane by action; Venus by reaction. She gives the pendulum its swing back to the starting point, and represents the power of response in all its manifestations. She completes the arch of the temple, and balances line against line and curve against curve; and is said by an old writer to be "the cause of all harmony and analogy in the universe, and of the union of form and matter." **Ruler**

A man or woman is generally driven to seek a mate by a feeling of loneliness and incompletion, by some sensation of superfluity or of deficiency, by the desire to adjust the life through giving, receiving, or interchanging affection; and consequently, everything connected with the attraction of one sex for another comes under the sway of Venus. When the ancient forms of faith in Greece and Rome fell to pieces the devotees of this deity forgot her higher aspect and broke the sacred laws of love in her name; but the earlier ceremonial of her temple was probably pure as well as beautiful. The gentle dove was her symbol, spring and summer blossoms her votive offerings, and no blood of slaughtered beasts ever smoked upon her altars. The fragrant incense and the joyous sound of happy chanting alone rose into the air, and youths and maidens whose hearts were stirred by the tenderest and most sacred emotions of their lives came to crave her blessing on their new-found happiness. The typical music of Venus is the soft chiming of the wedding bells; her most fitting ceremonial the holy rite that joins two hearts and lives together, crowning their days here below with the best gifts this world can give. The creation of the curious myth of Psyche, that "loveliest and latest born of all the gods," who was said to rival Venus in beauty and was wedded to her son, was probably inspired by the decay and degradation of the Venus worship, and the necessity of reaffirming the higher aspect of that deity. Other representatives of this influence are found all over the world, in various forms, and with different attributes, the one recognisable characteristic being intense femininity; but modern Christianity is singularly lacking in a right understanding and true reverence for this particular expression of Divine life. Possibly our Western worship of Mars—*i.e.*, of specialised energy in all its branches—has made us too prone to undervalue Libra, which is exactly opposite to his sign of Aries in the Zodiac. We thirst too much for immediate results, for something to show; we like to see what is active, forceful, masculine in character, even in our women. But after all, the specialist, in spite of his apparent progress, is only growing lopsided, and must call a halt and balance up some day, or else become a mere monomaniac. There has been too much exaltation of the limited life, running strictly in one groove and "going far"; too many souls cramped by artificial restrictions and limitations. The hard and fast line sometimes drawn between the sacred and the secular is absurd, illogical, and extremely mischievous; for everything is, in its inner essence, sacred, if only we have the heart to understand it. The Christ's command is not that one shall be pure, and another wise, and another loving, but that all shall be everything—perfect, even as the Father in heaven is perfect; and the symbol of perfection is not the scourge of the ascetic, but the golden circle of Hymen. Marriage is no longer considered a sacrament in our Protestant communities, and though it is nominally so for Roman Catholics their catechism practically cancels the teaching by inserting a clause which declares that the state of celibacy is more pleasing to God. Consequently, those of their persuasion who dedicate themselves particularly to His service are expected to acknowledge this peculiarity of the great Creator of both sexes, by renouncing the love that is one of

His most wonderful and inspiring gifts to men, and living and dying unwed. Outside the Church as well as in it there is much false doctrine taught upon this subject. The wholesome natural discipline of marriage, with its power of saving men from egotism and women from hysteria, is spoken of as hampering the stronger sex and limiting the weaker; and artificial conditions of life, or man-made forms of discipline designed to favour growth in one direction only, are pressed upon those for whom they are not only unsuited but positively harmful. On no point does Astrology give a clearer and more helpful verdict than upon this; for only two of the twelve types are suited to celibacy—those under Virgo and Pisces, and not even these, unless they are extremely far advanced in evolution. Average Virginians grow cantankerous, and Piscarians over-emotional, if they remain unwed, unless the former are unselfish enough to dedicate the *whole* of their energy to the service of humanity, and the latter sufficiently well-developed to substitute for earthly happiness the mystic marriage of the higher planes. In both cases, naturally, the celibacy must be a reality and not a hypocritical lie. Of the representatives of the other ten signs it may be emphatically said in the words of the Scripture that it is not good for them to be alone, and this list includes the three signs that are best adapted to guide and control the father confessor or parish priest: *viz.*, Capricorn, Leo and Sagittarius. It is significant and regrettable that the saint who is generally considered to have taken the place of Venus at the time when Christianity was substituted for the earlier religion of Italy, is Mary Magdalene, the protector and consoler of the frail, and that the chief gift she has to offer to her devotees is the gift of penitence.

In seeking to understand the Libran type of humanity, we must begin by laying firm hold of the essential difference between the sexes, and the difference has been recently defined for us by the sanest of men—the natural historians. A man's strength lies in his power of concentration, his intensity of application, and capacity for sustained effort. He works in splendid spurts, followed by periods of complete relaxation, during which he usually declines to use any of his faculties whatever unless urgently required to do so. He feels perfectly satisfied lounging in an armchair and smoking a cigarette; and when he has rested long enough, and no longer, he rises and goes at his task again with the same indomitable energy as before. That is the normal healthy average man, in the fulness of his powers—say from 30 to 40—and if he is succeeding in life, he is generally in one way or another a specialist. A woman of the same age who has followed her natural vocation and accepted the profession of wife and mother, dare not allow herself to specialise in anything. If she has a hobby dear to her heart, which absorbs all her faculties and engrosses her attention, she must renounce it—at any rate until her children are old enough to look after themselves, when it will probably be too late to make very much of it. She may cook, but she must not aspire to such cookery as requires constant watching and a high degree of skill, for she may be called from her pots and pans at any moment. She may sew, but her sewing must be taken up and laid down again at odd minutes, and her stitches will never compare with those of the tailor round the corner who does nothing else. She has probably to keep the household books, but it is very unlikely that her accuracy will ever rival that of the banker's clerk. She must be alert and alive and resourceful and ready for every emergency all day long; turning herself quickly and adroitly from one thing to another, answering the incessant demands of half-a-dozen little creatures, all of diverse dispositions and temperaments, and all at different stages of development. She must exercise endless tact and diplomacy, keep her temper, never show weariness, impatience, or irritation; and welcome the tired husband at the end of the long day with the bright smile and the loving word that repays him for his arduous toil. After the children have gone to bed, she is expected to be his sympathetic and responsive companion; and when she goes to bed herself, she must be careful not to sleep too soundly, or she will not hear the little voice from the cot demanding nourishment or soothing in the small hours of the morning. It is the kind of life that would kill a man or drive him crazy in six months; but the "weaker vessel" will keep it up bravely for twelve or fifteen years without a break, and survive, and keep sane; and the power that gives her most assistance in her task is the power associated with Libra and the planet Venus. Happy are the women who are born under their gentle influence! Loving and beloved, centres of peace and happiness and quiet content, they can fill their days with what are called the little things of life, that is to say with constant petty items of self-sacrifice of the kind that no one notices or realises;—and they can do it cheerfully and without repining.

This sharply defined description of the difference between the sexes, must not, however, lead us astray. Roughly speaking, when souls are incarnated as men they are intended to do specialised and concentrated work; if they are born as women, their task is all-round development, and to the reincarnationist who believes that these experiences alternate pretty regularly for all of us, there is naturally nothing to grumble about in the arrangement. But the above is only a rough statement and we need the key of Astrology with its further classification of men and women into masculine and feminine types, to explain the existence of numerous exceptions to the rule. It is not merely the mannish women and the effeminate men who are accounted for in this way. There are womanly women with sufficient strength and concentration to do a man's work in the world, and do it well—and these of course we must look for under specialist signs like Aries and Scorpio; and manly men, so extraordinarily gifted with all-round efficiency, that they can fill posts in which the ordinary specialised worker would be useless; and that is the sort of man that we naturally expect to find under the influence of Venus and of Libra. They are as many-sided as the Leonians, and sometimes share their difficulty in choosing a profession, often making a false start, and then changing; but they have not the Leonian tendency to depute their duties to others, however competent. In most cases their desire for perfection makes them exceedingly painstaking and patient, and particularly careful about detail; so that they rarely have to undo anything they have done; and though they may lack brilliance, there is rarely anything meretricious, showy or slapdash in their methods; they are immensely popular, both with men and women, and generally safe men for promotion; for owing to their gentle manners, tact, courtesy, and genuine appreciation of what is admirable in others, they have very few enemies. They are scrupulously honourable in money matters, and do well in various branches of government service, especially in spheres in which ready tact, social charm or all-round ability tell; they are, however, seldom attracted to the medical branch of the service, for the sight of suffering and weakness gives them much pain. Some build up an excellent practice at the bar, but those who choose this sphere will be wise not to fix their hopes on sailing into success through some brilliant piece of oratory or striking achievement in the detective line; for the preliminary up-hill grind will have to be gone through, and unless influence comes to the rescue—as it very possibly may—they will have to wait for fortune to smile upon them. After that point is reached, the fickle goddess will probably not desert them again, and their judicial minds may find a congenial field of activity in the highest of positions—on the bench, or even, perhaps, on the woolsack. The innate strength of this type consists in a certain sane and wholesome and well-balanced element that runs through the whole nature, moral, mental and physical. These people hate injustice and unfairness and everything ill-proportioned and ugly in life, and also dislike exaggeration and all feelings that are morbid, depressing, hysterical or strained, turning from them resolutely and refusing to dwell upon them. Their healthy, normal and natural form of expression is music in all its branches, and vocal music especially is a rest and a refreshment to them—their relaxation when they are wearied, their remedy when they are sick and sad, the offering they personally are likely to lay upon the altar of their god.

Religion And this gives us the keynote to the religious life of the Libran—which is harmony. There must be no harsh notes, no discordant element in his worship. The wrangling of the theologians, the petty persecutions of one sect by another, the bickerings and jealousies and narrownesses too often associated with our religious observances, have turned many people of this type away in disgust; for if they cannot find beauty and concord in their cult, they will content themselves with striving after beauty of life, and leave rites and ceremonies alone. They tend to live a good deal in the present, letting the dead past bury its dead, and are seldom introspective, self-analytical, or inclined to worry over the slowness of their progress or their probable fate in the future. The religious life of Burmah—a country which, tradition tells us, is specially under the influence of this sign,—shows us many Libran tendencies, and the absence of ceremonial observance is one of them. There is no Burmese priesthood, set apart for God's service as distinct from man's. Any man may for a time become a monk, live a frugal, celibate and self-denying life, study the scriptures, teach, pray, and give special time to meditation; but that is merely part of his general training and development, and when this period of discipline is over, he generally returns to active life, marries, and becomes the father of a family. Another characteristically Libran trait is the Burmese treatment of the departing soul. When a man is known to be dying there is no thought of reminding him of his past misdeeds, failures and mistakes, of urging him to dwell upon them, or to confess, or to repent. His time of striving is assumed to be over. He is going to have another life and a fresh start by and bye; but in the mean time the important thing is to cheer him up and make him realise how much progress he has made this time, and how much he—and his friends through him—have to be thankful for. So one of the kindliest of his old cronies comes and sits by his couch and recalls to his failing consciousness the memory of his good deeds. And indeed this gentle and comforting procedure is very frequently followed by clergymen in our own churches, not a few of whom are peace-loving Librans. The Anglican Church especially seems to attract this type into its ministry, probably by the possibilities it offers for a life of refinement and quiet leisure, and the cultivation of many delightful hobbies—including music. The English country parson leads a life retired yet sociable, enjoys ample time for study, a peaceful atmosphere, permission to marry, and the *entrée* into the best society of the neighbourhood. His chief duty is that of intoning musically from time to time a beautiful and dignified liturgy, or of deciding just how much beauty it is safe and tactful and judicious to introduce into the service. In such a post our Libran will give every satisfaction. His eloquence will be gently persuasive, his little homilies carefully considered and neatly rounded, sometimes perhaps tending to truism, platitude and mild pedantry, but warranted free from all startling eccentricities or disturbing originalities of thought or style. In due time he will find preferment, and possibly a bishopric, in which sphere he will be immensely popular and a real ornament to his profession. In short he will do all that England expects or desires of her parish clergyman; for John Bull dislikes the typical priest on account of his arrogance, and distrusts the prophet—because he neglects to cut his hair. The Libran is a safe man, who can be warranted free from either vice, and any astrologer who doubts the strength of this influence in the episcopal body has only to scan the church advertisement column of the London papers any Saturday morning, and note the tremendous importance given to the choice and rendering of the music. Perhaps it is as well for the Anglo-Saxon race that so prominent a place is assigned to this wholesome and harmonising influence; for its quiet sanity is certainly needed to counteract the fanaticism and exaggeration of the idolatry of Mars—*i.e.*, of specialised energy—shown by the nation in all its favourite forms of activity; and particularly in what has been described as the real religious ceremonial of England—the solemn celebration of the game of cricket.

Literary Style

Of Libran style it is difficult to speak; partly because there is nothing striking about it, but still more because few Librans specialise in literature or in anything else to such an extent as to take a position in the first rank. We may best understand its good points by remembering that the only branch of literature in which women undoubtedly do easily excel men is ordinary everyday letter-writing to intimate friends and relatives. The Libran is a capital hand at jotting down the annals of the present day, and can make even trifling details interesting and important. The style is chatty and informal, free from all roughnesses, eccentricities and obscurities, simple in construction, easily read—and sometimes as easily forgotten, for it is apt to be a little tame. Whenever an astrologer finds a man whose letters are as good as any woman's—as is the case with Edward FitzGerald and Chas. Lamb—he is justified in expecting to find a Venus strain in the horoscope, and there are many charming volumes of more or less gossipy reminiscences that betray this element. Mary Anderson, the famous American actress, was born under the sign of Libra, and her short book of Memoirs displays much of its natural feminine charm. It is instructive biographically also, as betraying many typically Libran tendencies in her methods of work and ideals. The reasons given for her withdrawal from stage life may be summed up as a fear of growing lop-sided, and it is interesting to compare them with similar reasons for the same step given by the famous singer Jenny Lind,* whose lovely voice, sweetness of disposition, and well-balanced nature are very suggestive of the same sign. It is giving way to temptation to hazard further guessing in this direction; but it is perhaps pardonable to suggest the addition of Jane Austen to this sisterhood.

Love and Friendship

To the typical Libran, love affairs are naturally among the most

* Jenny Lind's horoscope has been drawn out with Scorpio ascending, but it surely ought to have been rectified by some minutes to bring her under this gentler sign, for Scorpio in connection with her personality is unthinkable

important events in life, and even in old age the subject never loses its interest. The well-developed specimen chooses his mate early, marries as soon as he can afford to do so, and makes an excellent husband, tender, affectionate, and very easy to live with. The only danger he runs is that of a too youthful engagement, for love-making comes easy to him, and is generally crowned with success. He may consequently be tempted to propose to the first pretty girl who smiles upon him, and live to regret his precipitation; but his innate refinement and somewhat fastidious taste will probably save him from any danger of a low connection; and a well-balanced mind and dislike of emotional excitement will keep him from rash proceedings and discreditable entanglements. His sister Libran runs the same dangers, and shares the same protections. She is generally immensely popular with the opposite sex, because of her gentle uncritical attitude and frank admiration for the manly qualities. She hates to hurt anyone's feelings, so finds it almost impossible to say a decided no, and sometimes needs to have it pointed out to her that too much hesitation on that point is only prolonging the agony, and is consequently a very mistaken form of kindness. She makes the orthodox ideal wife, her whole being revolving round her husband, who is sometimes idolised to such an extent that the children come in a bad second; for this sign, though intensely conjugal, is not particularly maternal. The writer has known two Libran brides, both of a high type, who refused to wear orange-blossom on the wedding day because it was the symbol of fruitfulness, frankly admitting that they thought children would be a great bother. When in due course the little ones arrived, nature asserted itself, and they found their welcome and were tenderly cared for; but both mothers admit that they find looking after them very tiring, and in both houses the husbands distinctly play lead. A physical peculiarity closely related to this element in Libran character, is that many mothers of this type are unable to nurse their children; whereas Taureans, who are much more truly maternal, rarely fail in that respect. This point is worth insisting on because of the muddle-headed treatment of this subject found in many modern novelists, especially in France. They try to glorify the "Venus" side of life—partly perhaps from a natural rebellion against the rigid teaching of the Church—and they not only fail to do so, but actually cheapen and depreciate it, by attempting to tack it on to the maternal instinct; and so blunder into mere sentimentality, excusing corrupt, degenerate and unwomanly actions by silly maunderings about yearnings for motherhood and Nature's loving care of the race. The impulse that makes a woman seek her mate, turning from all thoughts of pride and self-sufficiency and craving for the qualities which she can only find fully developed in the opposite sex, is a beautiful impulse, complete in itself, grounded on true humility, and requiring no excuse or justification whatever. We wrong our young people if we teach them to be ashamed of it. We wrong them still more if we fail to teach them that it is a sacred impulse, as such to be watched over and guarded—never to be followed selfishly, dishonourably or at the expense of others. For it is as strong as it is holy, and strength with ignorance spells danger. Astrologers will clear their minds on this subject by remembering that the sign of the chaste Diana has always been considered the maternal sign. The yearning and craving for the care and teaching of little children is found more strongly in Cancerians* than in any other class; and yet their manner to the opposite sex is often positively forbidding, from its shyness and reserve. Married people of this type often reverse the Libra principle, making the progeny play lead and looking upon the helpmeet as one whose chief claim to consideration is that he or she is the father—or mother—of the bairns.

Primitive Type

People with Venus against them in their horoscope are handicapped instead of helped in their career by their all-round tendencies, and primitive Librans suffer in this way to such an extent that their parents and guardians are sometimes in despair over their start in life. Their partiality for equal development is apt to make dabblers of them, and they take up one thing after another, to throw it aside in favour of something else. The rudimentary desire for perfection has also its drawbacks, making them potter and trifle over their work, wasting time in weighing straws and splitting hairs; and they are apt to become confused and bewildered if they are called to order and

* Among the castles in the air built by juvenile Cancerians at a remarkably early age, the writer has had occasion to note the following specimens: to be head of a kindergarten or school; to be matron or nurse in a sick-children's hospital; to have a big house and a lovely garden in which to receive little Anglo-Indian children while they are separated from their parents; or to marry a widower with a very large family and help all his neglected motherless children to grow up strong and happy;—the point about this kind of marriage being that the family would be an absolute certainty.

asked to make a decision or hurry up. Sometimes they will prevaricate and temporise, and hedge in the most annoying way, when a straightforward and energetic policy is called for. Tact and diplomacy run to seed are uncommonly like insincerity and moral cowardice, and when contemplating the sons and daughters of Aphrodite at this stage of development we are often reminded that foam is only another name for froth, and that one of its characteristics is that it spreads itself very lightly over the surface and is never found at the greatest depths.

This tendency to trifle is naturally carried throughout, and is specially noticeable in the sphere of the affections. The natural impulse to seek the mate developes early, and is translated by these people into a tendency to regard every second member of the opposite sex they come across as the not impossible he—or she. They never break their hearts about anyone, for their memories are short; but there are frequent sprains and bruises, so to speak, and a great deal of waste energy, if nothing worse. The gentleness of the men is apt to make them soft and weak with women, and if they remain long unmarried, or are absent from home for any lengthy period, they may drift into the unmanly position of playing tame cat to the first energetic and unscrupulous woman with a desire to dominate, who is willing to take trouble enough to annex them. For women under this sign the peril is naturally graver, for though the power to appreciate what is good and beautiful in others is a great gift, the absence of the critical faculty is often a sad handicap. To be easily pleased and to please as easily; to be born attractive and comely, and with a craving for everything that is fair and lovely in life and a dislike of all that is ugly and sordid and mean: to be gentle and yielding and sweet-tempered, and incapable of saying "no"; to live habitually in the present and for the present, caring little for the ties forged by the past and less for the possibilities hidden in the future;—these in certain circumstances are dangers indeed, and parents and guardians of girls of this type cannot be too careful. Their very guilelessness and innocence is their worst enemy, for those in authority cannot bear to wound it by warning them. Thus their most gracious gifts unite to form the source of their deadliest peril, and their instinct for refinement and desire to rise to something better, is the most likely occasion of their fall. It is not a sensual or vicious* type, but the first false step is fatally easy, and after it is taken the chances are that the erring one will be dragged or pushed or kicked along the downward path, till the only escape from a life her soul loathes is—suicide. There is something rotten in the principles and practice of a society where such things are possible, but it is no use pretending that they are not. Perhaps some remedy will be found when we begin as a nation, and not merely as isolated units, to ask ourselves what Christianity really means, and to strive whole-heartedly to follow the Master, who said of the sorrowing Magdalen —the woman who had sunk so low and yet was so quick to recognise and reverence Perfection when she met it!—that to her "much was to be forgiven, because she loved much."

Physical Characteristics

An old writer describes those born under Venus as "having a love dimple in the chin, a lovely mouth, cherry lips, and a right merrie countenance." The hair is generally plentiful, smooth and glossy, the eyes bright; and the whole personality breathes forth an atmosphere of kindliness, and gives an impression of comeliness, contentment, and fair proportions. The stature is often short, especially in women; the skin healthy, and the complexion good. They appear well-nourished and are inclined to plumpness, dimples, curves, and rounded contours generally, though not to excessive fat. They have often a sweet voice, and a bright ringing laugh, and though not as a rule witty (unless Virgo or Vulcan is accentuated in the horoscope) are intensely appreciative of fun in others. In fact they are so charming that it is difficult to suggest a caricature of the type, though perhaps the lady-like curate and the stage bishop might serve the purpose. Browning's poem, "A Fair Woman," touches the Libran weaknesses with a delicate hand, and Shakespeare's picture of Cressida—so sweet and lovable and responsive—so hopelessly incapable of lasting love and loyalty—is a graver and more bitter description of what this type is like before intellect and memory have awakened. The same master-hand has shown us, in the character of

* These papers only profess to deal with normal types, and the lowest depths of degradation connected with the step-daughters of Venus are associated with mental deficiency The majority of women of this class are incapable of sufficient mental control and concentration to earn a decent livelihood in any way whatever, and if the recommendations of the recent Royal Commission (July, 1908) on mental inefficiency are carried out, these unfortunate creatures will be put under proper control, for their own safety and that of the nation.

Desdemona, how tenderly devoted and absolutely pure in heart a well-developed Libran can be, and how wofully her gracious ways to men, and gentle compassion for the unfortunate, may be misconstrued by the husband whose judgment has become perverted by the insidious poison of jealousy.

Health The Libran type has an instinct for health and sanity, and generally manages to keep the balance true and avoid serious break-down of any kind, but if circumstances push it too far in the direction of concentrated specialisation, or if it gives way to excessive emotion, and especially if the sense of justice and fair play is outraged in any way, the constitution will suffer. The most frequent symptoms of overstrain are usually connected with the kidneys and bladder, which organs are curiously sensitive. When below par in any way the sons and daughters of Venus will find their best remedy in rest and retirement, with careful diet and due development of the apprecia-tive faculties connected with all that is best and most beautiful in music, poetry, or art—especially music.

Then, welcome each rebuff
That turns earth's smoothness rough,
Each sting that bids nor sit nor stand but go!
Be our joys three-parts pain!
Strive, and hold cheap the strain;
Learn, nor account the pang; dare, never grudge the throe!

BROWNING.

♏ SCORPIO ♏

THE SCORPION.

The Sign of the

GOVERNOR OR INSPECTOR

A fixed watery sign.

Keynote—Justice.

Watchword—Power.

Ruler—Pluto
(or the Negative side of Mars?)

♇

Mystical Gems—Topaz, Malachite.

Colour— ? *Metal*—Steel.

Physical Manifestation—Combustion.

Mental Manifestation—Determination.

KARMA.

VENGEANCE IS MINE; I WILL REPAY, SAITH THE LORD.
ROMANS xii. 19.

Be not deceived, God is not mocked; for whatsoever a man soweth, that shall he also reap. For he that soweth to his flesh shall of the flesh reap corruption; but he that soweth to the Spirit shall of the Spirit reap life everlasting.—GALATIANS vi. 7.

If any man hath an ear, let him hear! He that leadeth into captivity, shall go into captivity: he that killeth with the sword must be killed with the sword.—REVELATION xiii. 9.

With what judgment ye judge, ye shall be judged: and with what measure ye mete, it shall be measured to you again.
ST. MATTHEW vii. 2.

EVERY MAN SHALL BEAR HIS OWN BURDEN.—GALATIANS vi. 5.

And he that overcometh, and keepeth my works unto the end, to him will I give POWER *over the nations; and he shall rule them with a rod of iron, as the vessels of a potter shall they be broken to shivers . . . and I will give him* THE MORNING STAR.—REVELATION ii. 26

CHAPTER VIII.

The Scorpionian Type

Astrological tradition describes the influence which rules this sign as "The negative side of Mars," which suggests that it cannot be *positively* associated with the god of war in his most familiar guise, though when he is looked upon in his sterner aspect, as destroyer and regenerator, we come near to the true spirit of Scorpio. It is possible that some planet as yet unknown represents this aspect of deity in our solar system, and if so, our ignorance of its position must be accountable for many an astrological blunder; for the strength of its vibrations, and their tendency to act very decidedly on the physical plane, must naturally have an enormous effect upon us. Careful analysis of the type associated with this Power carries our thoughts back a generation in the story of the Gods, and brings before our minds a statelier and sterner deity than Mars, *viz.*, Pluto, the god of the underworld, the brother of Neptune and of Jupiter. He is represented in ancient mythology as the just and incorruptible judge, dealing out the discipline which strengthens and purifies, and giving to each soul the sorrow and suffering that is its due. Because of his sphere of work, he is sometimes spoken of as the god of the infernal regions, and his counterpart is consequently to be sought in the Christian devil, especially as presented in the power called "Satan" in the book of Job; he who came among the other "Sons of God" to present himself before the throne, and report on his labours, and whose duty it was to go to and fro upon the face of the earth, testing and trying the children of men, by sending upon them sore calamity, suffering and loss. This destroying force is recognised in all religions **Ruler** and in some—notably in Zoroastrianism and in modern Christianity—has been unduly exaggerated, so that the devil is made a *rival* of the supreme deity; which is not only heresy, but a contradiction in terms. Problems of sin and temptation, of sorrow, suffering and death, are very insistent when forced upon our personal consideration, and often take gigantic proportions. Hence many earnest souls forget that only through the gates of death can we enter into the larger life, and that the great destroyer is a liberator and a regenerator as well. This doctrine is clearly brought out in Brahminism, where the destroyer Siva is given an extremely important place as one of the three persons of the Trinity, and honoured accordingly. The wonderful myth of the dance of Siva, which has given to Indian artists one of their finest subjects, illustrates his regenerating power very clearly and beautifully. It tells us how the evil forces in the world combined to attack him, and succeeded in forming a huge serpent. But when it approached he twisted it around his own neck and transformed its shining coils into a glorious necklace. Again uniting, they formed a cruel tiger, which became in the hands of the god a lovely mantle to clothe him. Lastly, they moulded a hideous mis-shapen dwarf, hateful and hating, but Siva, lightly stepping on his neck, broke the twisted spine, and crushing the creature to death made of his body a platform whereon to dance. And it is through the growth of this power that we attain such moral force as enables us to choose the good from the evil, to break the bands that bind us, to die to sin, and arise to newness of life, converting low cunning into wondrous wisdom, and cruelty into strength; trampling hideous hate under foot and making of it a stepping-stone whereby we may rise into the realms of love and joy and beauty.

Not only spiritual regeneration but physical reincarnation is associated with this sign, and this deity is therefore also reverenced as one of the Lords of fertility and specially as representing the male element in the generation of physical life upon earth. In Greek mythology Pluto is wedded to Proserpine, who symbolises the seed, which remains in his dark kingdom underground during the long winter months, and, being fertilised, issues forth with the blossoms of spring that gladden the heart of Demeter. He is consequently spoken of as the god of riches, and the symbols given into his hand are the horn of plenty and the sceptre of power. Serapis in Egypt shares these attributes, and this double function—that of the deity of reproduction as well as the deity of death—is also given to Siva. Serpent-worship is connected with this line of theology, that creature being naturally accepted as an emblem of successive births and deaths in countries where the doctrine of reincarnation flourishes; for it sloughs its old skin annually—emerging in fresh beauty after its long sleep, the same serpent transformed by a new garment; and so is a fitting symbol of the immortal ego, persisting through all its transformations and transmigrations.

Evolved Type

The kingdom to which the son of Scorpio is called is a kingdom of power, and his highest achievement is the manifestation of that power in the most gigantic of tasks—absolute self-mastery. The destruction of egotism, the domination of desire, the abolition of everything that can retard his moral, mental and physical regeneration; the attainment of complete control over the will, the intellect, the passions, the emotions, the bodily activities and the psychic faculties;—these are, or ought to be, his ambitions, and very frequently he makes—in spite of false starts, failures and shortcomings—very considerable progress on the way to realising them. Further, he not only desires rapid progress on the upward path for himself; he craves it also for others, and gives freely of his own magnificent vitality—moral, mental and physical—in order to hasten their development, and bring them into better conditions. It is this characteristic that draws so many sons and daughters* of Scorpio into the medical profession, and makes astrologers refer to it as pre-eminently the physician's sign.

When the ideal doctor—who may stand very well for the ideal Scorpionian—enters the sick-room, the first impression he gives is that of power—quiet, resolute strength; capacity, will, and determination to wrestle with and overcome suffering, disease and death. The anxious nurse gives a sigh of relief, and the restless invalid stops moaning and lies still. Such a man can impress his will on the most fractious and rebellious of patients, sometimes even dominating delirium and insanity. The writer has known one who temporarily cured a nervous head-shake, which had persisted for years, by one

* The superstition that the study of medicine makes women unwomanly, is based on the fact that it is generally women born under this virile sign who enter the medical profession

steady look and the quiet command to "stop that"—such treatment being, of course, of the hypnotic order, and closely allied to many so-called *miracles* of healing.

Scorpionians are generally more or less psychic, but often fail to realise it, because they make such exceptionally good use of their sense perceptions—sight, hearing, etc.—that they attribute their achievements in rapid diagnosis and other kinds of detective work entirely to quickness and accuracy of observation, in which they know that they excel the majority of men. As a rule, too, their psychism is of a very healthy and normal type, and allows its possessors to sense their finer impressions intuitively and without effort, rarely disturbing them by disconcerting and incomprehensible glimpses into the unseen world. Doctors who feel inclined to disclaim such powers should ask themselves candidly how often they have diagnosed a difficult case correctly before definite and recognisable symptoms have appeared at all, or how often they have had premonitions of a sudden summons to cases which, as far as outward knowledge went, seemed independent of their aid; or even been impelled to go to them just in the very nick of time. They are also gifted telepathically, but the gift is sometimes a lopsided one; *i.e.*, they can transfer their own thoughts to others more easily than they receive them from without.

Besides striving to conquer death and disease, Scorpionians find intense satisfaction in dominating the forces of nature—in taming the torrent, harnessing the lightning, enslaving the steam, for the use and benefit of mankind. As practical engineers they excel, and long before they have learnt to show patience and forbearance to frail humanity, will display these qualities to an admirable extent when called upon to deal with a refractory piece of machinery. Though rarely quite original in their work, they are clever in utilising ideas flung off by others of a more daringly inventive turn, apparently finding stimulus and inspiration in the very difficulties that had checkmated their predecessors. Anything that calls for strenuous effort and heroic endurance is congenial to them, and the breaking down of opposition and obstacles is the very breath of their life. Their analytical methods and power of destructive criticism stand them in good stead in many walks of life, and some do brilliantly at the bar, usually making their way to the front by their success in dealing with criminal cases.

The intense virility of this type naturally makes it somewhat difficult for women born under it to accept the limitations and restrictions imposed by their sex, and most of them openly regret that they were not born men; but when highly developed they accept their conditions and make the best of them, finding happiness in the mothering—or rather the *management*—of what is usually a very large family, and very often in the extra labour involved in the successful rearing of twins. Such an one has an intense and very natural scorn for the type of woman who shirks matrimony and motherhood from physical cowardice, and if cut off from these possibilities herself, is often at a loss as to how to employ her energies. Superfluous sister or younger daughter at home is the very last *rôle* for which she is fit; for her love of power and desire to dominate cannot be altogether held in check, and her tendency to grasp at the reins is apt to be resented by her seniors and make difficulties with domestics, who object to serving two mistresses. Her disciplinary powers are well adapted for the heavier appointments at large schools; but she sometimes fails in teaching, through lack of sympathy and imagination, and her selection of subjects is frequently limited. The power of concentrating on whatever work is taken up, makes Scorpionian women the best housekeepers and cooks of all. Every hole and corner in their domain is kept speckless and spotless. Their dinners are served to the minute, piping hot, and nothing is ever presented burnt, or underdone, or otherwise spoilt by careless cookery. Their spring-cleaning is their annual holiday and a heavy removal gives them something nearly akin to enjoyment, putting, as it does, a tremendous strain on their power of endurance, and calling into requisition all their special gifts—including that form of destructive criticism which demands the burning or distributing of rubbish and lumber. The writer has known an excellent specimen of this type whose prowess at such times earned for her the title of "The Destroying Angel," and who was the recognised stand-by of all the wearied and overworked mothers in her large connection, whenever a domestic crisis arose. The harder the task, the more these people seem to rise to it, and the necessity for sleep or food or reasonable rest quite escapes their memory; for which foolhardy enthusiasm they naturally pay dearly when the rush is over.

Love and Friendship

In love and friendship Scorpionians tend to be very intense, and distinctly exclusive, and they are prone to sudden and violent antipathies and likings—due possibly to psychic intuition, or connected with the slumbering memories of past lives. They despise gush and sentimentality, dislike demonstration of all kinds; and often find much difficulty in expressing their inner thoughts and feelings even when they desire to do so—which is very rarely, for they are taciturn and laconic by nature, and exceedingly reserved. When very deeply moved, however, their feelings do find utterance, and they are then apt to say more than the occasion warrants; for the Scorpion has a sting to its tail. Sometimes, though more or less tongue-tied, they have their pens well under control, and write delightful letters—terse, pungent, full of suggestive detail, and abounding in satirical humour. The style of Jane Welsh Carlyle suggests this influence, and many of her other characteristics confirm the impression that she belonged to this type. The difficulties of her married life—though grossly exaggerated by Mr. Froude, as has been proved by recent publications—were nevertheless existent, and were largely due to her intensity of temperament, and her heroic—and sometimes unnecessary—endeavours to work beyond her strength. And this brings us to the question of marriage in general. Scorpionians—especially the women—are not easily mated, and are apt to prove exacting and difficult to live with. Strong and efficient themselves, it is almost impossible for them to make full allowance for the weakness and incapacity of others, or to understand why and how natures, dispositions, temperaments and ideals should differ so widely. Geminians are especially trying to their nerves, and many of the other types are, from their point of view, aggravating and incomprehensible. They mate best among* themselves, or with Cancerians, who resemble them in intensity, and excel them in sympathy and imagination; for in spite of their passionate tendencies, Scorpionians can be unrelentingly and coldly stern, especially where principle is involved. Although Siva is the deity of generation as well as of re-generation, the old myth asserts that one glance of his eye can reduce the god of love to cinders, and the marvellous self-command of the highly-developed men and women of this type corresponds well with this assertion. They attain purity

* This is perhaps misleading, for two people with Scorpio *rising* are often at a deadlock from reserve; but a Scorpionian should choose a mate with Scorpio or Cancer accentuated somewhere—by Sun or Moon or position at Zenith

of life, not, as the Virginians do, through coldness of temperament, but through sheer force of character, passing through the strait gate and along the narrow way with erect heads and unfaltering step. Consequently they are in little danger of shipwrecking their lives through rash engagements or hasty and ill-considered marriages; and though their personal magnetism may attract many, and especially those of a weak or vacillating character, they will probably find no difficulty in administering the rebuff which is, in such cases, the truest kindness. They very often recognise the future husband or wife at first sight and seldom waver or vacillate in the matter, till the wooing is brought to a successful conclusion—though they rarely confide their hopes or intentions to friends or relatives till everything is practically arranged.

The great masters and founders of religion have ever been healers, and in olden times the offices of priest and physician were one. It is often an eminently devout impulse that carries the Scorpionian into the medical profession, and even when out of tune with the particular ceremonial and dogma of his day, he is seldom or never an irreligious man—though his uncompromising tendency may make him shock orthodoxy by claiming to be considered so. Further, though he often shakes off the shackles of his childhood's faith, he rarely gets quite out of touch with ideas impressed upon him by the teachers and thinkers he reverenced most during the plastic period of his early manhood, and in his later years will surprise the younger generation by the extraordinary rigidity of his beliefs; for the tendency of this force is to go far rather than to spread itself over a wide field, and the Scorpionian resembles his beloved steam-engine in running its best and farthest on lines already laid down. His chief demand upon dogma is that there should be no sickly sentimentality about it. He prefers it bracing and virile in quality; such teaching as makes some definite call upon his strength and manliness, and possibly also upon his powers of belief. Sir Thomas Browne, who was of this type, gloried in orthodox church teaching *because* it was difficult to accept; and wished it were more so, that he might show more faith—a peculiarity possibly to be accounted for by the fact that, consciously or unconsciously, the really advanced Scorpionian is almost as much at home upon the psychic plane as upon the physical, and therefore realises that it is absurd to settle religious questions without reference to our intuition and other superphysical faculties. When he preaches to his fellow- **Religion** men—as the healer is frequently called upon to do—his sermons are forcibly expressed and very often effective for reformation. "By what things a man sinneth, by these he is punished." "Whatsoever a man soweth, that shall he also reap." These are favourite texts, and are regarded as no mere empty sayings, but as stimulating facts, to be acted upon. His views on heredity are grave, his code of morals high and somewhat stern. He realises that the sins of the fathers *are* visited upon the children unto the third and fourth generation, and that the law of individual Karma is the law upon which he must take his stand. It was, in all probability, a Scorpionian who drew up the Commination Service, which is not, as many are inclined to think, a calling down of curses on sinners, but a solemn reminder, very plainly and severely expressed, of an indubitable fact, *viz.*, that sin brings its own punishment. "Cursed *is* he" that breaks the law; and it is the Scorpio element in us that has sufficient fortitude to answer "Amen." There is, of course, a danger of over-severity and a tendency to relapse into the callous "serve him right" attitude, if these truths are pondered to the exclusion of the gentler elements of mercy and love; and the best corrective to exaggeration in such matters is the acceptance of the idea of the gradual evolution of the soul through repeated reincarnation; a doctrine which always tends to develope patience and serenity, and to some extent humility, in its believers, who feel that having climbed upwards from the lowliest stages themselves they are not in a position to disdain those who are following in their footsteps. Without this teaching, the theology of the Scorpionian—particularly if he belongs to the primitive type—may become not only stern but fanatical and cruel, and it is men and women born under this sign who find a morbid and gloomy satisfaction in contemplating the possibility of innumerable souls—including those of unchristened babes—undergoing an eternity of torture because their circumstances and stage of development have made it impossible for them to obtain certain privileges, either actual or ceremonial, while here on earth. The light that lightens the pathway at this stage is a very lurid one, and, especially in later years, these people resent the attempts of the more enlightened to throw any brighter ray upon the way in which they have chosen to tread; for they enjoy the idea that there is much to endure in the next world as well as in this. They generally, it is true, expect that other people will do the enduring, for they are confident of their own salvation; and if they are sufficiently devoid of imagination to accept such a theory with serenity, it does comparatively little harm; but there are others with more humility about them, whose lives are terribly warped by such teaching. Carried away by the strength of their passions till their own stern judgment condemns them as "lost," they feel that they may "as well be hanged for a sheep as a lamb," and become absolutely reckless, callous and indifferent. The evil done to children by these horrible misrepresentations of Divine Justice is incalculable, and adds enormously to the difficulties of those who have to face the task of bringing up little ones in whom this Scorpio element is as well marked as it must have been in the case of the small boy who, after some childish misdemeanour, answered his nursemaid's threats of everlasting punishment with the defiant words: "God may burn me if He likes; but He'll *never* make me cry."

In Real Life

The list of Scorpionians who have distinguished themselves in literature is too long to be adequately discussed here, and their "hall-mark"—the strength and virility of their style—has already been touched upon. One of their characteristics is courage in tackling difficult and disagreeable subjects; *e.g.*, those connected with public and private morality, or with questions of heredity, of degeneration, and disease. Certain* writers in whom this influence is strong have dragged into light, dwelt upon, and analysed some of the darkest and most disgusting elements in human nature and in the history of our modern civilisation. Thus, Sir Richard Burton gave years of study to problems connected with sensuality. But it is notoriety rather than fame that is attained through a taste for rummaging among the dustbins of life, and the chief glory of the sons of Scorpio has been won on larger fields of speculation and research—fields so vast that even the names of those who have dared to explore them inspire us with an admiration akin to awe.

Goethe†, Milton, and Victor Hugo are three of the intellectual giants born under this sign; and Martin Luther, a great "destroyer and regenerator," was strongly under its influence, his horoscope showing it strikingly emphasised by the Sun, Mars, Jupiter, Mercury and Saturn—all in the ninth House, and so suggesting *Religion*.

* Zola has Jupiter, the planet denoting the mental activity, in Scorpio; as also Henrik Ibsen.

† In his own words Goethe tells us he was born apparently dead, but care and skill induced him to breathe; and if the process took a while, it may be that Pluto was rising in Sagittarius, with Scorpio at the zenith. Pluto is well aspected to the Sun, but square to the Moon.

Goethe has recorded his exact hour for us—noon—on the authority of his father; so we know that the 17th degree of Scorpio* was rising. Milton was born "between six and seven in the morning." Our choice consequently lies between Scorpio and Sagittarius, and although his biographer thinks that the "half an hour after six" mentioned by our contemporary is "probably correct," the astrologer is impelled to place the event some minutes earlier; for no gleam of true Sagittarian sunshine brightens the pages that describe Milton's† personality. "The prevailing tone, the characteristic mood and disposition of Milton's mind, even in early youth, consisted," we are told, "in a deep and habitual seriousness." His striking qualities were austerity, self-command, and a stoic scorn of temptation. In his earliest poems he chose death for his theme, and in the amusements of his college companions he took little or no part. Of their prowess in University theatricals he remarks cuttingly: "They thought themselves gallant men. I thought them fools." And we find an echo of the same severity years later, in his biting reply to the young daughters who begged him to teach them to understand the Greek and Latin which it was their dull duty to read aloud to him hour after hour; "One tongue is enough for a woman." It is impossible to admit the stern old puritan to the "Jovial" circle of the sons of Jupiter after that, and the treatment of his chosen‡ theme, "Paradise Lost" is in the true Scorpionian vein. He gives to Lucifer—the real hero of the poem—a regal dignity and a tragic beauty, and his oft-quoted exclamation:

"*Better to reign in Hell than serve in Heaven,*"

is echoed by many a son of this sign. We look in vain through this epic for the self-effacing love, the sweet humility, and the tender grace of the Christianity he sought to praise, and the finest passages in all his works—even in Lycidas, which is a lament for a dear friend of his youth—are denunciations of the sternest and most uncompromising type.

Martin Luther, in his efforts to reform the Church, swept away the doctrine of purgatory—the mediæval substitute for the doctrine of grad-

---

* Modified by Saturn two degrees above the horizon.

† Milton died of suppressed gout accompanied by high fever, a *Scorpio* illness.

‡ Note that the theme of "Paradise Regained" was suggested to him, not chosen, and is unsuccessfully treated as compared with its predecessor.

ual evolution through repeated incarnation—and put nothing in its place, leaving the trembling soul to choose between the immediate bliss of heaven or the horrors of hell; and inferring that the vast majority would be doomed to the latter. Goethe takes his hero through sin and suffering to regions of the blest, and in his case also, it is the earlier passages of the poem that are most eagerly and frequently read. Mephistopheles is a more living and quite as famous a creation as Faust himself, and one of the poet's best-known utterances is of the very essence of Scorpio Philosophy, "*Entbehren** *sollst du; sollst entbehren*,"—a line in which the poet tells us that in this world we must do without—and endure.

It always requires some effort to turn from the pleasant duty of dwelling on the fine qualities of a sign to the ungracious labour of cataloguing its weaknesses and defects. In the case of Scorpio the task is peculiarly unwelcome and disagreeable, and before embarking on it, it is perhaps judicious to remind the reader that although for purposes of study the twelve strands, of which our complex human nature is woven are here separated out and sharply differentiated one from another, in reality a *pure* type—*i.e.*, a man or woman born exclusively under any one influence—does not exist. All the signs in turn, and often several at once, bring their various forces to bear upon us, so that no one can really congratulate himself on being free from all danger of the special failings attributed to any particular one. Whatever we possess in the way of self-control and moral backbone—of ability to stand on our own feet and exercise our own will—we owe to the power of Scorpio manifesting in us; and the better we are able to answer to his call for strength, the more we must be on guard against abusing it; for the sin of Scorpio is the sin of the fallen angels; the desire to share in the Power of the Lord of Hosts without sharing, in the same degree, in His Wisdom and His Love. After which preamble it is well to state the worst at once and get it over; and that worst is just as bad as it can be.

Primitive Type

The primitive Scorpionian is not merely wicked; he is fiendish. Not content with his own reckless defiance of the laws of God and man, he takes a devilish delight in inciting or betraying others into breaking them also. He will lead youth and innocence along the

* *Entbehren* is sometimes incorrectly translated as *renounce*; but it has none of the joy of true renunciation There is no exact English equivalent. perhaps *forego* expresses the idea best.

downward path to the very brink of the precipice, and with his own hand give the push that sends him over. He will hold out the glass to the trembling hand of the hopeless drunkard, and watch him totter to his fall with a sardonic smile; and the words that rise to his lips are those so sternly and strongly forbidden to all the followers of the MASTER, Who told us that whosoever shall say unto his brother "Thou Fool," stands in danger of the fires of hell. All the terrible dangers which surround those born under this sign may ultimately be traced to this attitude of contempt for their fellow-men, and to the desire to exalt and glorify themselves at their expense.

This type, as has already been said, never wavers or wobbles, and whatsoever the Scorpionian's hand findeth to do is done with energy and might. Therefore, when he is bad he is thoroughly bad, and no mistake about it. Experiences which arouse in other types feelings of mild discontent or half-formed dislike, awaken in his breast anger and resentment, fierce rebellion, mad jealousy and vindictive hate. His passions are ten times stronger than other men's, his courage never fails him, and his will is iron. If he fails to find his way into his true kingdom—that of self-mastery—he may make fearful havoc and shipwreck of his life, developing into the reckless gambler, the insatiable drinker, or the heartless profligate. Nevertheless, the strength of the type is such, that even at the lowest depths of degradation there is always hope, and it is among those under the influence of this regenerating power, that we find startling and almost incredible instances of complete conversion which knows no relapse.

At the same time it is hardly to be expected that they should become absolute saints of love and tenderness and patience all at once; and apart from the terrible type of Scorpionian sketched above, we find many who are undeniably on the straight road, and doing their level best to keep to it, who yet have a far heavier burden of aggressive and unlovable faults to struggle against, than falls to the share of others. It is practically impossible for them to take the second place graciously and contentedly, even when they are sufficiently developed to acknowledge their own unfitness for the first; and their vigilant outlook makes them abnormally and disagreeably quick in detecting the backslidings of their fellow-creatures. To discover that others are weaker, more forgetful, or more self-indulgent than themselves, feeds their self-esteem—always considerable—and the exposure of an erring brother's failure or lapse is consequently hailed with an evident satisfaction that is extremely aggravating to witness, and very galling to the victim of the moment. A tendency to enjoy seeing their friends and intimates waste their time and energy, leads Scorpionian humour to express itself in unkind practical jokes which upset the dignity and wound the self-respect of those who suffer from them, and are the more irritating because it is almost impossible to catch their perpetrators napping, and pay them out in their own coin.

Even at this half-developed stage the sons of Scorpio are often attracted into its chosen priesthood, the medical profession, though their motives for entering it are rather mixed, and frequently include a morbid desire to know the worst that can be known of frail and diseased humanity. Drugs, and especially poisons, have a curious fascination for them, and they are always in favour of strong measures and drastic treatment. Hence the number of medical men who kill or disable a large percentage of their patients; doctors who, for example, will permanently weaken a patient's heart while dosing him free of rheumatism, and then ruin his digestion by administering dangerous stimulants to prevent—or rather delay—collapse; and continue to feel perfectly well satisfied with themselves, however many may succumb to their heroic remedies, because they have always followed out the instructions given to them in their college days, and followed them out *thoroughly*.

It will be readily understood that it is almost impossible for primitive female specimens born under this sign to adjust themselves to the conditions and limitations imposed on them by their sex, especially in the lower classes and in ill-educated communities. They carry out their allotted tasks carefully enough, working, scrubbing, scouring and setting in order with fierce energy, and are often held up to admiration by outsiders as model wives and mothers—a verdict which they themselves heartily endorse; but when they have overworked themselves into their graves, their bereaved husbands will probably heave a sigh of relief, and if they find courage to venture on matrimony again will very likely select some kindly slattern as a partner—or at any rate someone who will allow them to rest when they are tired, smoke where they please, invite such friends as they choose to share their hospitality, and feel that they are at least part owners of the income they have earned. Not only the husbands but the children also are apt to suffer from the joyless atmosphere created by mothers of this type. Their budding individuality is crushed and warped; innocent pleasures and harmless recreations, and all those pleasant hours of quiet relaxation and idleness and chit-chat which tend to weld the separate units of a family into one harmonious whole, are looked upon as a sheer waste of time, little short of criminal; and the young people, driven from task to task, with never a chance to blossom out, and grow natural, and beautiful and happy, turn sullen and sour—or take the earliest opportunity of escaping from the maternal nest. One of the peculiar traits that adds much to the difficulty of home life under a Scorpionian's sway is that she—or he—dislikes to acknowledge any inferiority by asking questions, and, is, nevertheless, deeply hurt if left in ignorance of any trivial facts known to the other members of the household.

Physical Characteristics

Manifesting physically, this type is said to give a powerful, muscular, and somewhat thick-set frame, strong and rather heavy features, dark grey eyes, a swarthy complexion and plentiful dark hair, usually crisp and curling. The writer knows a few Scorpionians who answer fairly well to that description, but the majority she has come across are slender rather than thick set, and most of them are strikingly handsome—some, even, very beautiful. Dante's profile is repeated by several, and as a rule they are very dark; but among the Scottish specimens a goodly number are exquisitely fair in complexion, with beautiful blue or grey eyes, and blond or golden hair. Milton had red curls, and was so delicate in feature and complexion that his Cambridge nickname was "The Lady of Christ's." Sir Richard Burton, on the other hand, passed easily for an oriental. He could assume without difficulty the oriental impassivity—*the* trait by which this type is most easily recognised. Scorpionians are generally proud of this absolute command of feature and immobility of expression, and rarely give themselves away by flushing, wincing or starting, however deeply their emotions may be stirred. Their aim is to read everybody else like an open book, and remain inscrutable themselves, and their intense reserve—which amounts to secrecy in the primitive specimens—together with their psychic intuition, make such an ambition easy of attainment. They usually carry themselves well, with something of a soldierly bearing, but are often a little heavy of foot, and averse to dancing, running and any other forms of light exercise which they are apt to deem undignified. Their exaggerated ideal of self-control makes them peculiarly sensitive to awkward gestures, nervous twitches, restlessness and other signs of weakness in others, and they often attempt to excuse their violent antipathies for certain people on the ground that they wriggle or fidget.

The marvellous fineness of sense perception in the sons of Scorpio is probably responsible for one of their most unlovely and unlovable traits; *viz.*, their fussiness about their food. When highly developed they can, of course, subdue the natural man and force themselves to partake of plain and wholesome dishes without grumbling, even if they are not particularly tempting; but the vagaries of many of this fraternity are such as pass the wit of man to account for, and the patience of woman to gratify. The following is a list of articles of diet rejected by various Scorpionians—most of them people of culture and common-sense;—and rejected, at times, with such contumely and scorn as inferred that *no* human being should be asked to eat anything so outrageously disgusting. Milk, and milk puddings; rice, macaroni, and eggs; butter, olive oil, or fat in any form; fresh fruits, and boiled vegetables! At the same time, even when out of health and inclined to nausea, their palate craves for strong sensations, and some of them revel recklessly in chutneys, curries, pickles, kippered salmon, juicy meats, rich gravies and strongly seasoned savouries of every description even when the digestion is quite out of order! On the other hand, many of them are capable of senseless heroism in the way of going without food—and sleep—for unnatural periods in order to "get through" some piece of work; and many have ruined magnificent constitutions in this way.

One of the countries which according to tradition is markedly affected by the power of this sign is Norway, the land of taciturnity, of self-reliance, of forceful character, and of psychic intuition. Ibsen shows its influence so very strongly, that possibly he was born under it. The place he gives to the power of thought transference and other psychic faculties is as characteristic as his very pronounced views on heredity, and his love of denunciation. His hero *Brand* shows this type run to seed, and his castigation of "*Peer Gynt*" betrays the Scorpionian's rooted aversion to the primitive sons of Mercury, with their overweening egotism and tendency to evasion in action and speech. These tendencies are, however, perhaps sufficiently explained by the fact that, like Zola, Ibsen had Jupiter in Scorpio; and he has left it on record that he was his own model as far as *Peer Gynt* was concerned. His photograph suggests the Cancerian type—and so does his dramatic style, full of metaphor and illustration, as also the somewhat morbid and pessimistic moods suggested by some of his writings.

In Drama and Fiction

Shakespeare's arch villains Iago, Edmund and Iachimo will occur to readers of the above as primitive examples of the type under discussion, and he has also contributed some striking cases of sudden conversion, *e.g.*, Orlando's eldest brother and Rosalind's uncle. Some of Byron's melodramatic heroes—and especially Don Juan, with his callous indifference to the fate of the victims he has hypnotised—stand half-way between Iago and the conventional stage villain—sinister and handsome, dealing in daring crimes and twisting all the weaker characters round his little finger. The heartless coquette of the modern novelist—the mere hunter of scalps, who feeds her egotism by exacting homage from men to whose affection she is utterly and superbly indifferent, has a Scorpio strain in her; and the beautiful she-devil who lures impressionable youth to his destruction, and is always most dangerous when spurred by the prospect of eclipsing a rival, is a more definite and lurid example. The burlesque editions of the above are shown in the Wicked Fairy and Demon King of the Christmas pantomime.

Health

The ideal Scorpionian has a magnificent physique and phenomenal powers of endurance, and, as has already been said, he is frequently tempted to defy the laws of health in consequence, indulging in prolonged spurts of excessive over-work that would kill any man of ordinary capacity, and taking a pride in the fact that he can go on to the end of his task without rest, food or sleep, when all those around him are breaking down. If this is carried to excess he finds the sleep he has flouted difficult to capture again, and is sometimes tempted to force it by having recourse to opiates, which he substitutes for proper nourishment. At the primitive stage worse temptations still assail him, and he may possibly indulge in wild bouts of alcoholic and other forms of excess which bring their own terrible forms of retribution physically. Evil passions—envy, suspicion, hatred, jealousy, resentment and pride—are also apt to poison the vitality, and if cherished, will result in very severe suffering of one kind or another. When he is ill the Scorpionian is thoroughly ill, indulging in high fevers and dangerous attacks of gout, rheumatism, and other ailments, besides such illnesses as typhoid and malaria. These troubles sometimes take the form described by physicians as *suppressed*, or bring about rigid conditions of the body which cripple the energy and call for great endurance. There is also a possibility of mysterious internal complaints of a painful or inflammatory nature, very hard to diagnose and difficult to treat. Rest cure and wise living are the Scorpionian's best remedies, giving the magnificent power of recuperation, always associated with this sign, a chance to assert itself; but he loves heroic remedies and is seldom content to let well alone and trust to nature. Especially is he prone to use—and abuse—powerful and dangerous poisons in the shape of drugs and tonics—which usually only serve to make matters worse. The desire to dominate and to endure ought to find sufficient outlet in the heroic effort after patience and sweetness and self-control which severe suffering and prostration demand of an invalid or convalescent; but it does not always do so, and this is, in many cases, a very difficult sign to nurse, because these under its influence know—or think they know—just exactly what the nurse ought to do; and have no hesitation about allowing her to feel that she has failed in her duty.

Note—Since the final revision of the proof-sheets of the foregoing, I have been told by "Kymry," an astrologer who is very accurate in his work, that the horoscope quoted by me in my reference to Milton was inexact, as 6 30 a.m. on the day of his birth works out with 7° ♐ rising, so that a rectification of three-quarters of an hour is necessary before he can be classed among the sons of Scorpio. Another student who has worked at astrology both in the East and in the West for over twenty years assures me that he has met a Sagittarian as grave and stern and "superior" as Milton is said to have been. I can find nothing in the poet but his red hair suited to that type; but naturally feel bound to respect the opinion of more experienced astrologers. Still it may be pointed out that the hour given in his bible at the British Museum was not set down on his birthday, but years after—for it is in his own handwriting, and consequently may only represent the time as *recollected* by one of his parents; and I have often found on looking up a birth certificate that parents who *thought* they remembered correctly were two or even three hours wrong. Sun rising does steady and dignify Sagittarius, giving it weight. A Scorpio zenith and a strong Pluto would emphasise that sign.

It's wiser being good than bad;
It's safer being meek than fierce:
It's fitter being sane than mad.
My own hope is, a sun will pierce
The thickest cloud earth ever stretched;
That, after Last, returns the First,
Though a wide compass round be fetched;
That what began best, can't end worst,
Nor what God blessed once, prove accurst.

BROWNING.

♐ # SAGITTARIUS ♐

THE ARCHER.

The Sign of the

SAGE OR COUNSELLOR

A mutable fiery sign.

Keynote—Wisdom.

Watchwords—Law and Liberty.

Ruler—Jupiter.

♃

Mystical Gems—Carbuncle, Turquoise.

Colour—Light Blue. *Metal*—Tin.

Physical Manifestation—Rotation.

Mental Manifestation—Creative Thought.

When I was yet young, or ever I went abroad, I desired WISDOM *openly in my prayer. I prayed for her before the temple and will seek her out even to the end. Even from the flower till the grape was ripe hath my heart delighted in her. . . From my youth up sought I after her. . . My soul hath wrestled with her. . . I stretched forth my hands to the heaven above. . . I directed my soul unto her, and I found her in pureness; I have had my heart joined with her from the beginning, therefore shall I not be forsaken.*

ECCLESIASTICUS li. 13.

CHAPTER IX.

THE SAGITTARIAN TYPE

Ruler

THE planetary power or ruler associated with Sagittarius is Jupiter, the younger brother of Pluto and of Neptune; and these three deities must be studied in relation to one another if we are to understand them aright. They are the sons of Saturn; a deity described in modern parlance as "*Old Father Time*," and a brief consideration of this latter title, which resembles the Greek *Chronos*, will give us some clue to the comprehension of the particular myth we have now to disentangle. Time swallows all things; and therefore Chronos is said to have devoured his children until the birth of his youngest, Jupiter, who united with his brothers Neptune and Pluto* in dethroning their parent, after which the Kingdom was divided among the three. Pluto accepted the Under-world, the realm of Action, and consequently stands in this version of the Trinity for DIVINE POWER, which manifests most fully and definitely on the Physical Plane. Neptune is associated with the realm of Emotion, and so, viewed from the highest standpoint, represents DIVINE LOVE, and rules the vibrations of the Astral or Psychic Plane, symbolised by the Sea. Jupiter himself took the Sceptre of the Upper-world, the realm of Thought, and so rules the Mental Plane and stands for DIVINE WISDOM. These three, united, represent the whole range of the activities of the present, which, so far as we are concerned, is constantly dethroning the past and concentrating our attention upon itself; for "*Now* is the accepted time," and the old order ever changes, yielding place to new; God fulfilling Himself not in one way alone, but in many.

A point to be carefully noted in the above story is the danger that threatens the childhood of Jupiter. This element is almost invariably represented in the innumerable versions of the tale which

* It was Themis, "one of the Oceanides," who liberated Neptune and Pluto by administering a potion to Saturn which made him disgorge all his children The interpretation may be that a vibration of desire—one of the waves of the ocean —must *precede* the awakening of mind and memory

the student of mythology finds all over the world. Sometimes there are three daughters instead of three sons. Sometimes it is a step-mother or step-father that persecutes; occasionally the older generation is ignored and we are only told that the two elder children are jealous of the wit or beauty of the youngest. In every case the tale ends by the triumph of the latter, to whom is given dignity and power and responsibility far above all former rivals. In this old myth, world-wide in its range, undying in its vitality, we have the germ of countless popular tales and dramas of every conceivable form—from the tragedy of King Lear* to such nursery favourites as Puss in Boots and dear old Cinderella; and the reason of their popularity and insistence and recurrence is that they either veil or unveil a tremendous truth. The three brethren, Thought, Emotion, and Action—or Wisdom, Love, and Power—must always dwell together in unity, if harmony is to reign in the hearts and lives of men; and of the three, it is *Thought* or *Wisdom*—ever the latest born—that should take precedence, ruling and regulating the emotions, and through them guiding the actions aright. This precedence is of course, in a sense, illusory, for the planes are not really set one above the other; they interpenetrate and interact. It is, in fact, heretical to exalt one Person of the Trinity over the others, but which of us is free from a taint of heresy of some kind? and if any choice is to be made, better to err by worshipping Divine Wisdom to excess, than by devoting all one's energies to the service of either Passion or Power. If Paris had handed the Apple of Discord to Athene instead of to Aphrodite, the result would certainly have been disaster in some form; but the Trojan War, with its terrible record of lust, anger and bloodshed, would never have taken place.

Jupiter is thus the ruling representative of the *Divine Mind* in the mythology of classic times, and is consequently hailed as *Optimus Maximus*. His Greek counterpart is spoken of with equal reverence; for the Zeus of Homer is the Greatest and the Best, and the most to be revered of all the deities; the God of Light, of Justice, and of Truth; the Father of Gods and of men. He dominates all the planes, because his thought comprehends all things. One vibration of his

* Lear is Ler or Lyr, an old Celtic deity, and in the original story, as handed down by Geoffrey of Monmouth, the youngest daughter is triumphant in the end. It is a curious proof of the power and vitality of this theme, that for 150 years the public accepted and enjoyed a poor adaptation of Shakespeare's masterpiece because it ended in the orthodox way, Cordelia surviving, victorious over Goneril and Regan.

mighty will makes the whole universe tremble. One movement of his eyebrow shakes high Olympus, and the very gods upon their thrones. Princes and rulers are appointed by his divine decree, according to the deserts of the nations; and when he has bowed his head, his decision is irrevocable, and cannot be altered. Above all things he is beneficent, benevolent and kindly—ever ready to hear the prayers of his children, and to grant their requests. The ancient Greek hymns addressed to him, besides acknowledging his goodness and greatness, begged of him such boons as rain after drought, healthful breezes, and favourable weather generally. The mountain peaks are his sacred places, and in his sterner aspect he is the God of lightning, of tempest, and of cloud. He holds the thunderbolt as well as the sceptre, and beside his golden throne stand two brimming cups, from which he pours out, according to his divine will, good and evil for the sons of men. It is he who appoints the judges of the infernal regions, and the condemned criminal was regarded as a suitable sacrifice upon his altar.

The Divine Mind is intimately connected with every part of the Universe, and gives rise to innumerable forms of activity. Therefore Jupiter is said to have seven wives* and many children. His first mate is Themis, and his union with her is so close that he is described as not merely wedding, but *devouring* her also; and from this strange marriage springs pure Wisdom, in the person of Pallas Athene or Minerva, ready armed for constant warfare against ignorance and vice. Another spouse is Latona, famed for the accuracy of her oracles, and consequently a representative of Truth or *enlightenment*, and the mother of the Sun and Moon—Apollo† and Diana. Another is Mnemosyne or Memory, the mother of the Nine Muses; but the most important and best known is Juno, who stands—somewhat severely—for law and order, and is the mother of health and of enterprise in the persons of Hebe and of Mars. The decadent poets of later days added to the mystic histories of the seven symbolical wives innumerable lighter tales of mortal maidens who temporarily enjoyed the favour of the God; but the student will easily appreciate these legends at their true value, remembering that the "children of

* Corresponding to the seven planes of Hindoo cosmology?

† Apollo is the leader of the muses and the patron of Science and Art; Diana, astrologically, gives sympathy and imagination.

Jupiter" in the astrological* sense are many, and are generally well qualified to arouse the interest and attention of their fellow-men.

The Person corresponding to Jupiter in the Christian Trinity is the Father, to whom we are taught to direct our prayers, leaving the issue to His Divine Wisdom. The heretical tendency in the West is to doubt and deny that wisdom, and to conceive of deity as a mere blind force, manifesting unconsciously; a tendency which leads many, even among those who consider themselves orthodox, to exalt *Power* unduly, and to worship it to the exclusion of the other attributes—"Co-equal and Co-eternal"—of *Wisdom* and of *Love*.† Among the twelve apostles of the Christian Church, St. Peter stands out as the characteristic representative of the Sagittarian element; ever the first to speak, and often the first to act; eager to learn, impetuous in faith, and yet prone to sudden attacks of wavering and scepticism, which paralyse his spiritual energy, and actually make him deny his Lord; and, with it all, the Rock on which the Church is built; for Christianity in its original purity satisfies the *Mind*—*i.e.*, the Jupiterian element in man—as well as the heart.

Evolved Type

The chief characteristic of the fully developed Sagittarian is his extraordinary power of mental activity. He brings his reason to bear upon every phenomenon that comes under his observation, and finds his most congenial occupation in getting to the bottom of things in general—facing the facts of life fair and square, and reducing its problems to their simplest terms. His curiosity is insatiable, his mental energy never flags. He interests himself intensely—and often succeeds in interesting others—in the relation of cause to effect and effect to cause. If his nature is well balanced, and his environment helpful and congenial, he not only makes very rapid progress in evolution himself, but is a great centre of helpfulness and illumination for others; for he comes readily into touch with his fellow men, takes an eager interest in their true welfare, and especially in their education. He is sometimes a very successful teacher of the Socratic type, going straight to the goal and awakening the minds of his students, teaching them to observe and reason and think for themselves. He is con-

* *E.g.*, Alexander the Great was described as a Son of Jupiter. It was probably through his conquests in the West that astrological tradition was first popularised in Greece and Italy.

† *Love* is revealed in the Person of the Son; *Power* in the "working," or manifested *Action*, of the Holy Spirit.

sequently better adapted for the training of older pupils than for beginners who have not yet attained proper control of intellectual expression; for he encourages and enjoys argument and discussion to such an extent that it is easy for those under his tuition to lead him away from the subject in hand, and juvenile scholars naturally take advantage of this propensity on occasions when close questioning would betray the fact that preparation has been shirked. The Sagittarian's skill in dialectic, however, puts some check on such nefarious practices; for he is a formidable antagonist, and foolish objections and suggestions will meet with small mercy from him. The thunderbolts of Jupiter were forged by Vulcan, and are generally effectual; and the "Archer" aims well, showing an intuitive knowledge of the weak places in the armour of his adversary, and seldom missing the mark. This tendency naturally makes the legal profession, and especially the bar, a suitable field of activity; but literature and journalism also claim their share of devotees among the sons of this sign, and the teaching of philosophy or religion, either by the pen or by practical discourse and example, is the most congenial occupation of all. The study of medicine is more rarely taken up, but some Sagittarian doctors do brilliantly as brain specialists and heads of lunatic asylums.

Sagittarians are almost all keen sportsmen of one kind or another—excellent shots, enthusiastic fishermen, golfers, wrestlers, hockey players, etc.—and show a special predilection for outdoor work, such as geological research and difficult explorations, and for all such professions as keep them moving over rough and mountainous country, and are connected with the training and exercise of horses and of dogs—the animals which respond most quickly to the mental vibrations of their owners. This type fairly revels in the open air, and cannot endure the stale atmosphere of stuffy rooms. Glorying in the breezy uplands and snow-clad peaks themselves, they have an immense sympathy for those doomed to a life of confinement in workshop, or factory, or mine; and are often keen social reformers as regards the limiting of hours of labour for the working classes, and the bettering of the conditions in which they are compelled to work.

If these points are taken up by Sagittarians, they will spare no pains to collect the necessary information, and show much practical common sense in suggesting remedies; for their theories are not drawn up in the study from books alone, but from actual contact with suffering, toiling humanity. Snobbery is impossible for them. They are willing to fraternise with all sorts and conditions of men, and to learn from anyone whatever he has to teach. At the same time they are much too clear-headed to be carried away either by anarchist doctrines, or by socialism of the sentimental type; for in spite of their tendency to regard mankind as one great family, they realise that in the matter of understanding, at any rate, we are not all "free and equal," but that many of us are bounded and limited to a pitiable extent. Therefore, they consider it the duty of the fathers and elders to enlighten the babes—of the wise men to legislate for the fools; and the problem of problems consequently becomes how best to establish wisdom in the seats of the mighty. Sagittarian interest in this subject is sometimes accompanied by an inclination to question whether hereditary rights, custom or tradition should be consulted in the matter at all; and occasionally even advanced souls of this type are seized with a wildly rebellious longing to upset the whole existing order of things, and start fresh.

The man who looks with friendly eyes on humanity, and comes very easily into touch with his fellow creatures at large, naturally feels less need of family life than do those whose geniality is not always available, and who are less quick to understand the position, mental attitude, and essential characteristics of the men and women they meet. Sagittarians are often extraordinarily detached from their kindred. If they happen to find their immediate relations congenial, well and good; they add them to the list of their friends, and treat them as such; if not, they point out their faults and foibles with unfailing frankness, and will publicly discuss and comment upon them with a freedom that makes more reserved types gasp. Parental authority is treated as a subject for inquiry and investigation; and though the juvenile Jupiterian may be open to conviction on the question of obedience due, and is ready to submit if parental wisdom can be demonstrated to him, he tests that wisdom in ways peculiar to himself, and woe to the father or mother who fails to pass his tests. The best way to deal with the small examiner is to meet him fair and square on his own ground—the mental plane; to answer his questions honestly and without prevarication; to administer discipline after the manner of Herbert Spencer, reasonably and logically, and, above all, to admit ignorance and even error where it exists. At the same time it is prudent to safeguard the health and sanity of the child's tutors and guardians by suggesting the propriety of his thinking out as many of his conundrums as possible for himself, and only bringing what proves insoluble to the busy grown-up people, whose work cannot always be interrupted and who have plenty of problems of their own to decide; for the influence of this sign produces the kind of small boy who, when he has driven his seniors to the last stage of despair by his questions, and has been told that he must on no account dare to say "*Why?*" for the next half-hour, looks up with redoubled interest and eagerly demands, "*Why not?*" This trait is frequently noticeable, up to the seventh year or beyond it, in those born with the Moon in Sagittarius; for the Moon recalls the past, and often seems to give the key to the methods and habits of the preceding life.

While carefully guiding the growing mind of the youthful Sagittarian, and providing for its constant exercise and ample nourishment, his parents should never forget that, in order to maintain his balance and make a complete man of him, the emotional side must also be developed and given its proper place. Otherwise there will be a tendency to a kind of self-examination which kills all sentiment by handling it too roughly at the early stages, and there is also some danger that the feelings of others may be treated with the same disregard, the insatiable inquirer looking upon them as fair game for experimental cross-questioning and light-hearted chaff. The delightfully wide-awake youngster develops first into an *enfant terrible* and later into a tiresome tease, and among those strongly under Sagittarian influence we find those whose outspoken comments spare nothing and nobody, and who take—and show—positive delight in the discovery that they can compel some unfortunate individual to give himself—or herself—away by losing self-control. Especially is this pursuit considered "sport" if the victim is of the opposite sex; and although listeners and onlookers may chuckle and be vastly amused by the game, it can be rather a cruel one, and is quite insufficiently atoned for by the whole-hearted and concerned apology which sometimes follows the realisation of the mischief done; for sensitive types who aim at self-command are often very deeply humiliated by being forced into a sudden betrayal of emotion or display of temper.

Love and Friendship

The same frankness and outspoken sincerity which characterises the many friendships of this type, and adds so much to their value, is also to be found in connection with its love affairs. But in that field of activity there is generally more chance of breeziness blowing up the clouds than of its dispelling them. The man who prefaces his proposal by an honest admission that he has loved before, or explains clearly and logically exactly why he has been led to take this step, and what makes him think it may prove advantageous to him in the long run, may possibly find favour with a woman who has learnt by bitter experience just how little the typical lover's sigh may prove worth; but he will make small speed in the wooing of the average romantic young girl. What leads the Sagittarian wooer into blunders of this kind is a misunderstanding of his own type. He ought to choose his wife on the mental plane; *i.e.*, putting mental response and mutual understanding first; though without ignoring questions of temperament, character and outlook, which are always of enormous importance. Instead, he is very apt to choose by logic alone, and to argue himself into a condition in which he is ready to decide for or against the momentous step without fully comprehending what he is doing. A girl may be everything that can be *reasonably* demanded—healthy and handsome and capable, and clever with her fingers; unstained in reputation, extremely popular, suitably endowed with this world's goods—without being gifted with a single quality of heart or mind that will make a suitable mate for him; and yet in a great many cases the youthful son of Jupiter will go light-heartedly forward, beginning as a rule with a so-called friendship which is merely a thinly disguised flirtation, and too often ending in a precipitate engagement which he finds it impossible to fulfil; for this is the type of man that absolutely refuses to go to the altar with a lie on his lips, and tie himself to what he feels to be impossible conditions. In consequence, broken engagements, with all the accompanying pain and humiliation and loss of self-respect, are not uncommon among the sons of Jupiter. The more fortunate escape with a refusal, which serves the same purpose of pulling them up and making them think; and either experience, taken the right way, may be a blessing in disguise; but primitive specimens are apt to take such blows badly, and develop a touch of cynicism, for they have little or no idealism to help them along, and romance too often dies early in consequence.

"Once bitten, twice shy"; and our sportsman developes a self-protective prudence and caution to a rather unlovely extent—shuns the innocent-hearted *ingénue*, and hovers around the married women, or seeks the society of his seniors, who are capable of giving his somewhat precocious mind the companionship for which it craves, and who are less likely to be misled by his manner and mode of address. Not infrequently a friendship formed in this way ends in matrimonial felicity, but there is a danger that this inclination to dominate the emotions and be guided by common-sense may produce a tendency to evade the possibility of matrimony altogether, and the Sagittarian may end as a bachelor, an experience always to be regretted in his case, for his nature demands emotional exercise to complete it, and will never blossom and bear fruit as it might, if shorn of the glory of fatherhood. If, on the other hand, he succeeds in finding his true mate—a woman who really understands, loves and trusts him—his whole nature expands, he reaches his highest possibilities, and makes an enthusiastic and very devoted husband, proud of his wife and of all her achievements, grateful for her affection, and very quick to make allowance for shortcomings due to physical infirmity or fatigue.

He mates best with his own wideawake type, or with the daughters of Aries, whose energies he likes to dominate and direct. But the other fiery sign, Leo, is also capable of yielding him a suitable partner, and its characteristic qualities of faith, tolerance and magnanimity are sometimes extremely necessary. The sons of Jupiter demand freedom in their choice of companions—of both sexes—as in all other fields; and the jealous, mistrustful wife, of narrow sympathies, who fancies that she can have her Sagittarian husband "all to herself" by shutting him off from exchange of ideas with anyone else, will have a very poor time of it. He may shrug his shoulders and submit to her whims, for he is eminently practical as regards conduct, and always inclined to make the best of any situation his own blunders have brought him into; but his thunderbolts of sarcasm will be hurled with increasing frequency, and the marriage, though outwardly decorous, will be no true union, but merely an ill-assorted partnership on the physical plane.

The women of this type run the same dangers as the men, and their bright frank ways with the opposite sex are very often misconstrued—friendship being mistaken for love, and love for friendship by a mystified mankind, which looks for, and very often prefers, uncertainty and evasiveness in a woman. When a tragedy of misunderstanding has occurred, pride generally comes to the rescue, and the heart-ache is carried off with a laugh and a brave front; or possibly by such a divertingly burlesque account of the whole affair as leaves the listeners with an impression that it was all a joke from beginning to end—an impression they are usually quite ready to spread by announcing that "she never really cared for him at all"; which naturally puts an end to any prospect of matters straightening themselves out happily. After such an experience the Sagittarian maiden, like her brother, cultivates self-control, and finds great difficulty in letting herself go beyond the safe limits of a pleasant friendship with just a spice of flirtation to flavour it, so may easily acquire a reputation as a shallow-hearted coquette, unable to take either herself or anybody else sériously. This state of affairs frequently leads to spinsterhood, and to the consequent loss of many beautiful opportunities of development; but there is no fear of her degenerating into the sour or embittered type of old maid.

Primitive Type

At the primitive stage the Sagittarian tendencies naturally take a more accentuated and less desirable form. Matrimony is frankly decried by both sexes as an intolerable burden, a tie and a bore. The men safeguard their personal liberty by cultivating a blunt and boorish discourtesy with women who are their equals, and only permit themselves to relax into easy-going familiarity with those that no one can expect them to marry. The women often allow their breezy unconventionality to degenerate into casual, and careless, and free-and-easy ways with men, openly admitting that they "prefer twenty shillings to one sovereign," and, especially if they have an inclination for sport, imitating the tricks and manners of their male comrades and chums, in gait and speech and forcible phrase. Both sexes at this stage tend to become inherently selfish and inconsiderate, in spite of a certain rough kindliness of manner; because this is a type which lives in the present and is consequently apt to lack loyalty and sympathy—qualities which demand memory of the past for their development. They rarely allow their emotions to carry them away, and are seldom inclined to be vicious. Yet their unconventional disregard of public opinion may make them fit subjects for scandal-mongers' tales; for they are careless of reputation, both for themselves and others, to an extent that argues a real want of consideration, and, as far as the men are concerned, a total lack of chivalry. This last failing is due to the fact that although they usually hold strong views—based on the dictates of reason—on the essential difference between the sexes, and are even inclined to dogmatise on the subject, they are nevertheless generally able to see that a woman may be different from a man without being his inferior; and when that point is reached a crude logic sometimes suggests that since she is his equal she can surely fend for herself and fight for her own hand. Women who do so successfully very often win Sagittarian respect, while the more appealing and helpless and emotional types merely irritate and annoy.

Ancient astrologers tell us that the faults of this type are "such as are easily pardoned." And this is just as well; for they certainly tend to come to the surface, and are very easily seen. There is, in fact, a curiously child-like transparency about these people—probably due to the absence of complex emotions, such as jealousy or vindictiveness—which makes them very easy to understand, and ensures speedy detection if they attempt to go off their own straightforward line and dabble in deceit. Sagittarian theft is invariably exposed, and the comparatively harmless fibs in which many of this type indulge when convenient are rarely believed, even for five minutes. They cannot lie or cheat successfully; and will do wisely, even from the low standpoint of immediate self-interest, never to make the attempt.

Religion

In religious matters, the Sagittarian is very often something of a sceptic, because his activity of mind compels him to examine and reason upon the faith that is in him; and if the teaching provided by his race and environment is illogical and unsatisfactory, he cannot help seeing its fallacies and shortcomings, and is generally very outspoken in pointing them out. At this juncture, however, his practical common sense frequently comes to his aid, reminding him that no system of theology devised by the mind of man is likely to represent accurately and adequately the whole truth about the nature of Deity, and that some sort of working hypothesis is nevertheless necessary. Selecting and accepting certain premises as foregone conclusions, he may succeed in silencing his own doubts, and in arguing both himself and others into a fairly orthodox position, after the fashion of Bishop Blougram in Browning's well-known poem; and many men of this type make excellent clergymen—breezy, unconventional and energetic, and usually much beloved by their flock, in whose mental, moral and physical welfare they take a keen and almost gossipy interest. They often take an active part in movements for the better housing of the poor, country holiday funds, open-air spaces, etc., and throw themselves heart and soul into the recreations of the country side; sometimes, indeed, spending too much energy in that direction. The sporting parson of a bygone day, who rode straight to hounds, must have belonged to this type. Their ministrations are always free from any touch of pharisaism or snobbery; and they may even, at times, scandalise the aggressively righteous members of their congregation by their sympathy for sinners and tenderness in dealing with them; for the true Sagittarian realises that all crime is the outcome of ignorance, and he is consequently far more eager to enlighten than to chastise.

Among the unceasing, ever-varying creative energies of the mental plane we find a marvellous range of activities that go to the building and moulding of what are sometimes called thought forms, *i.e.*, the shapes or designs moulded by mental vibrations out of the subtle matter—*mind stuff*—on which all such vibrations act. The dream of the sculptor appears in the thought world, white and glorious, long before his chisel shapes it in the marble. The drama of the playwright is acted there, long before the manuscript is ready to be submitted to the manager. All our dreams, ideals and aspirations are at home on this higher plane, and consequently Prayers are said by Homer—very beautifully—to be "the children of Zeus." Therefore Prayer in its most familiar guise—the simple childlike demand for daily bread and other boons—is the form of religious expression most natural to this type. "Ask and it shall be given you," is its motto; and when fully developed, the Sagittarian realises the tremendous responsibility involved in the fact that "Everyone that asketh receiveth," and learns to take heed how and what he asks. All really advanced souls, capable of strong concentration and clear and definite purpose, are familiar with the experience of having their wishes and aspirations—even when not sifted and hallowed by being cast in the form of prayer—literally and suddenly fulfilled; and many of them have had to acknowledge that had they foreseen the manner of such fulfilment, their demand would have been less insistent, or guarded by the graces of patience and humility expressed in the memorable "Not my will, but Thine be done" of the Master; but fortunately for us, our own restless cravings and shifting ideals often prevent the crystallisation and consequent fulfilment of the desires which chase each other in contradictory succession through our half-developed minds, hindering progress by an endless process of cancelling; and, luckily for us, ending in smoke. It is only the single-minded and simple-hearted—those of an absolutely child-like trust in God that can ask in faith "*nothing wavering*," and receive the promised reward; whereas "He that wavereth is like a wave of the sea, driven of the wind and tossed;" and as the apostle warns us, is doomed to disappointment, "For let not that man think that he shall receive anything of the Lord."*

Whatever is highest and best in the teaching of mental scientists, Christian scientists and others of similar tenets, is to be classed as to some extent belonging to the field of Sagittarian activity; and it is well that our attention should be called to the subject at the present day. The absurd ignorance and incoherence† of some of the exponents of these systems ought not to blind us to what is valuable in them; namely, the resolute turning of the mind away from morbid, depressing and unhealthy thoughts; and the whole-hearted directing of our energies towards a right understanding of the Divine Mind and our own filial connection therewith.

In Real Life

The Sagittarian's love of argument, and enjoyment of active encounters with antagonistic thought, leads him to make free use of dialogue form when he turns to literary expression, and not infrequently sends his energies in the direction of drama. His handicaps in that field spring from his mentality. He exalts mind and its activities to such an extent that the physical plane escapes his attention at times, and though his personages may be intensely interesting, his plot usually leaves much to be desired, and the action is out of all proportion to the length of the speeches. There is also a tendency to discursive and tangential talk, and the needless and heedless introduction of extraneous matter—possibly very entertaining, for the Sagittarian never lacks humour—but too unexpected to be harmonious or

* *James* i. 6 and 7

† The misguided enthusiasts who travesty the teaching are generally Geminians; a fact betrayed by their ceaseless iteration of the first personal pronoun, and constant dwelling on their own personal experiences and achievements. Their activity is intellectual, not mental, and they have failed to grasp the essence of the truth they try to explain, and represent themselves as ruling the Deity, instead of obeying His laws

artistic. A congenial field of activity is also found in writing books of travel, which generally make very pleasant reading; for the sons of Jupiter are keen observers of the ways and doings of their fellow-men and though very outspoken in their criticism are rarely harsh or contemptuous in expression. Unfortunately few famous specimens have been accurately recorded so far; but the characteristics of the type are so unmistakable, and so easily recognised, that any astrologer personally acquainted with a dozen well-developed specimens can point their brethren out in history and literature with a fair amount of confidence.* And the first name that presents itself is, naturally, the sage of sages,—Socrates. Everything recorded of him proclaims the Sagittarian; his conversational method of learning and teaching; his mental activity, his utter lack of pose and readiness to consort with all sorts and conditions of men; his warfare against ignorance and self-satisfaction; his uncompromising attitude and defiance of public opinion; the geniality which endeared him to his friends, and made him ever a welcome guest at other men's tables; the quaint homeliness of his similes and illustrations, condemned as inelegant and uncouth by the fastidious scholars of the day; his indifference to family life, and startling theories about marriage; and last, but not least, his own blunder in selecting a mate,—a terrible warning truly! —for this great philosopher, one of the wisest men this world has ever seen, called upon logic instead of love to send him a wife; and, cold and pitiless, it responded by giving him—Xantippe. No doubt, when he chose her she was everything that reason could approve, but in all the intangible essential ways that really count, the marriage was a hopeless misfit. Who can measure the ineffable scorn with which the high-spirited and probably ambitious woman must have looked down upon the ugly, undignified little husband who spent his idle days in what must have seemed to her profitless and unremunerative chatter among men with whom she had no ideas in common, and

* It is necessary, when classifying by characteristics alone, to guard against a certain surface similarity between Sagittarians and Geminians *when both are highly developed* The writer has erred more than once, confusing the two; but there is a difference between the man of mind and the man of intellect, and in all the primitive stages the two have little in common excepting physical restlessness Rebellion is very like lawlessness, and an irrepressible temperament closely resembles an excitable one; but they are not identical. Geminians are rarely or never sportsmen —often positively disliking sport; and Sagittarians, though they may be fairly versatile, are seldom variable, hysterical or nervous By their faults ye shall know them; but discrimination is necessary.

women for whom she had no respect? She cleaned his house for him all the same; but when she had finished—unless tradition belie her—she emptied her slop-pail over his head.

A brighter picture comes before us in the life-story of another great son of Jupiter (?), the poet-philosopher, Robert Browning, whose works show the defects as well as the qualities of Sagittarian style—homely ruggedness and lack of finish, along with exceptional vigour and vitality. He was first attracted to his wife on the mental plane—through her books; and proposed to her after one interview, the temperaments having proved congenial. Possibly only a Sagittarian could have carried such a love affair through to a successful issue; for the bridegroom had need of vitality enough for two. Elizabeth Barrett was not only some years his senior, but a bed-ridden invalid besides: and so could not "reasonably" be expected to make an ideal wife. Yet, in defiance of logic, and in spite of all the inevitable drawbacks—the displeasure of her father and the amazement of all their friends—the two poets made of this madcap marriage a triumphant success, and together lived a more exquisite poem than any either ever wrote.

As will easily be understood this type is pre-eminently fitted to provide humanity with those who are called upon to play the part of popular rulers over alien or mixed races, especially if they have to come into close personal contact with all sorts and conditions of men. The task of establishing peace and welding together the huge empire built up during the reign of Queen Victoria was rendered much easier for her son, King Edward VII., by the fact that he was a typical Sagittarian. His son-in-law, King Haakon of Norway, is another son of Jupiter, and lost no time in winning the confidence of his somewhat critical and reserved Norwegian subjects. Astrologers recognise in ex-President Roosevelt, politician and sportsman, another of the same genial brotherhood. The diplomacy of all three is of the most effectual type—absolutely straightforward.

The poet Shelley was born with Sagittarius rising, unmodified by any planet,* and gives us a notable example of how this "benign" influence may handicap a man if its tendencies are carried to extremes.

* Shelley hated cruelty and blood sports. I expected to find him a Mercurial with Gemini rising and an Aquarian zenith, and feel doubtful about his hour, though it was "recorded". Pluto and the Moon in Aquarius emphasise that humane sign, but I feel it ought to be at the Zenith. See page 223 on "misfits".

Shelley was so utterly devoid of family feeling that he used to entertain and horrify his school fellows by cursing his own father; and so incapable of understanding what the average Englishman means by the marriage tie, that he invited the wife he had forsaken to join him on a tour abroad along with the girl with whom he had eloped. A very strong Leo accentuation smoothed out the Sagittarian "kinks" in many of his verses, but there are plenty of obscure and irregular passages in them, and his attitude of flat rebellion against the existing order of things, and of scepticism in matters of dogma and doctrine are extremely characteristic of the type when lop-sided. His active eager mind was ready to contest and argue every point, and in spite of his interesting personality, wonderful gifts, and many admirable qualities, he was a most fatiguing member of the home circle both during his boyhood and after his marriage.

Physical Characteristics

Manifesting physically Sagittarius generally gives a well-shaped head, breadth of forehead, a frank and open countenance, quick movements and an inclination to vigorous gesture—expressive, but sometimes far from graceful. The eyes are generally blue or grey, bright and observant, and often of the type that twinkles or dances with fun. The eyebrows are clearly marked, the nose usually well formed, but sometimes insignificant in the plainer specimens. The hair is traditionally chestnut; but the writer has seen every variety in Scotland, from rich dark brown to sunny blond. The women usually have masses of it, but it has a tendency to fall out early, and many of the men are bald. The ideal Jupiterian model is the grand old marble Jove in the Vatican; and the type at its plainest is seen in the bust of Socrates. Shelley* was of the snub-nosed variety, and lacked the self-control and personal dignity which characterises the properly balanced specimens, and prevents their originality from degenerating into mere eccentricity. Many of this type are short, broad-shouldered and rather thick set, growing positively fat in old age; but others are tall and athletic, and somewhat commanding in stature and bearing, though much too genial to be terrifying, except, at times, to evil-doers. As is the case with most of the signs, the primitives are more easily recognised than their elder brethren,—though the accentuated types also declare themselves clearly, even when well advanced in evolution.

* His authentic portraits were mere amateur attempts and do not correspond to the personal description given by those who knew him.

They are generally extremely restless—absolutely unable to sit still or remain in the same posture for five minutes together, even on a public platform; and their disregard of convention, bright self-confidence, and readiness to come to the front on every occasion, makes them conspicuous wherever they are, though in some cases this is held in check by an affliction which, so far as the writer is aware, has not been recorded by other students; *viz.*, a difficulty in speech, varying from a slight hesitation, or interjected syllable, to a most lamentable stammer. The Leonian is sometimes* tongue-tied, and the Taurean is inclined to drawl; but the Sagittarian is harder hit by his handicap than these others can be; for he is generally far more burdened by thoughts which he is willing and eager to express; and is often full of good stories, which he knows exactly how to tell—if only his treacherous and rebellious tongue will let him. In some cases, after the stuttering stage is conquered, the little hesitation that remains actually adds piquancy and point to the anecdote. A notable percentage of "specimens" collected, suffer from a nervous blink or twitch of the eyelid; and some of their most characteristic movements suggest the shying of a restive horse. Other students declare that many Sagittarians actually look like their beloved equine friends, facially; but the writer has failed to note any animal traits in her specimens; excepting the ears of the more pugnacious among them, which are often of the elephantine variety; resembling those of the American humorist, who found his ears very convenient when camping out, as "he could sleep on one, and cover himself with the other."

The country traditionally associated with the influence of Sagittarius is Spain; and Spaniards certainly have much of the Sagittarian pride and independence, as well as something of its sunshine and buoyancy in them. They are often keen mountaineers, good shots, and excellent horsemen, and though it is curious, at first sight, to find the bull-fight preferred as a national pastime by a people under so genial a sign, sport is never really merciful, and the Archer is always inclined to enjoy a successful hit, on all the planes. An intense interest in religion and devout belief in the efficacy of prayer characterises a large percentage of the people; while those whose minds are dissatisfied with the ceremonial and theology offered to them are not indifferent, but keenly sceptical, militant in argument and debate.

* Literally tongue-tied—born so; but there are also Leonians who seem to be possessed by a kind of a "dumb devil," which makes it impossible for them to speak out, even though the organs of speech are physically perfect

In Drama and Fiction

This type occurs very frequently in literature, and Shakespeare gives us specimens at all stages of development, among them two delightful characters—*Benedick*, who will "still be talking" though "nobody marks" him; and *Rosalind*, whose candid admission "When I think I must speak," betrays the same tendency. The former's diatribes against marriage are particularly characteristic, and his list of the virtues and graces he personally intends to exact in a wife has been echoed, time and again, by his astrological brethren;—most of whom, however, have had to content themselves with somewhat less of a paragon when the time came. The characteristically Sagittarian touches about Rosalind are her buoyancy and playfulness; the frankness with which she owns her love for Orlando to her cousin and confidant, and the wilful waywardness which makes her disguise it from him and play at indifference till the last possible moment. *Petruchio*, in "The Taming of the Shrew," is a more primitive and much less lovable specimen of the tribe; full of energy and of practical common sense; too full of vitality—and too thick-skinned—to object to "ructions" in his own home, and well able to keep his head in a tussle with a hot-tempered daughter of Aries. Had Katharine been born under Scorpio, the story would have had a different ending, and her light-hearted suitor would have found himself in a rueful plight—under the domination of an iron will that his primitive starvation methods would certainly have left absolutely untouched. Bottom the weaver and Sancho Panza were also of this brotherhood; and belonging to a different stage of evolution, that prince of philosophers, and prizeman among irrepressibles, the immortal Samuel Weller. Caricatures of the type have been presented by Aristophanes in his comedy of *The Clouds*, in which Socrates and his school are depicted as engaged in serious argument over the measurements of the hind-leg of a flea and its power of leaping; by Mr. Rudyard Kipling in his delightful description of the *Elephant's* Child* in the "*Just So*" *Stories*, and—at a much more primitive stage—by Mr. George Grossmith in his portrait of "*The Noisy Johnnie*," whose friends and relatives are martyrised by his jovial theory,

> "What's very bad form in other men,
> Is very good form in me."

* An appropriate animal to choose Ganesha, the God of Wisdom in India, has an elephant's head; chosen as the symbol of practical wisdom because the hand—the trunk—and brain are in close connection.

The success of Sagittarians such as H. M. Stanley, Cecil Rhodes, and Sven Hedin, in the field of exploration is largely due to their quick observation, splendid physique and power of establishing friendly relations with the most uncivilised, mistrustful and impossible of their fellow men. Sagittarius at the zenith often gives something of the same bright optimism and child-like confidence in others, and the Moon in Sagittarius also confers popularity as a rule. The Sun in the sign seems rather to increase the longing for wisdom and understanding, and its effect may be seen in the later writings of Thomas Carlyle—the Sage of Chelsea—and in the music of Beethoven, wisest of musicians.

Health Almost the only dangers that threaten the health of the typical Sagittarian arise from his over-activity of mind and body. He has too many schemes and projects on hand to attend to all of them satisfactorily: and there is, in consequence, a continuous depletion of the life forces through unnecessary scattering of energy. Rapidity of movement, reckless cross-country riding, and other rough forms of exercise, such as mountaineering, are responsible for a larger percentage of sprains and fractures, than falls to the share of any other type; and carelessness in the matter of over-heating and exposure to cold is accountable for the attacks of acute bronchitis which afflict some sons and daughters of the sign, and which, if not watched, may lead to a permanent weakening of the lungs and the development of consumption, especially in early youth. This is a type, however, which has sufficient vitality to throw off even that deadly disease—if only it can be persuaded to take reasonable care of itself. If the Sagittarian escapes this danger, and survives his allowance of accidents and falls, he will probably live on to a good old age, retaining his faculties to the last, and dying in harness from heart-failure due to over-work or bronchitis or both. Sometimes, however, there is trouble mentally, due to restlessness of body and brain. It takes the form of considerable eccentricity and lack of self-control during the last few years of life; especially if the energetic hunt for the unattainable has run on false lines, and the prize sought has been position—or happiness—instead of wisdom, and if the natural affections have been smothered by the genial selfishness of the sign.

Stern daughter of the Voice of God!
O Duty! if that name thou love
Who art a light to guide, a rod
To check the erring, and reprove;

* * * *

Stern Lawgiver! yet thou dost wear
The Godhead's most benignant grace;
Nor know we anything so fair
As is the smile upon thy face:

* * * *

Give unto me, made lowly wise,
The spirit of self-sacrifice;
The confidence of reason give;
And in the light of truth thy bondman let me live.

WORDSWORTH.

♑ CAPRICORN ♑

THE GOAT.

The Sign of the

PRIEST OR AMBASSADOR

A cardinal earthy sign.

Keynote—Reverence.

Watchword—Excelsior.

Ruler—Saturn.

♄

Mystical Gems—White Onyx, Moonstone.

Colour—Green. *Metal*—Lead.

Physical Manifestation—Vibration.

Mental Manifestation— { Concentration.
Relaxation.

One thing have I desired of the Lord, that will I seek after; that I may dwell in the house of the Lord all the days of my life, to behold the beauty of the Lord, and to enquire in His temple. For in the time of trouble He shall hide me in His pavilion, in the secret of His tabernacle shall He hide me; . . . therefore will I offer in His tabernacle sacrifices of joy, yea I will sing praises unto the Lord. . . . Evening and morning and at noon will I pray and cry aloud; and He shall hear my voice.—FROM THE PSALMS.

CHAPTER X.

The Capricornian Type

The ruler of Capricorn is Saturn or Chronos; a deity who is said by the classical writers to have reigned during the Golden Age, a period described as the happiest this world has ever known; when men lived like gods, free from toil and care, and from all the weaknesses of old age; when death came kindly and gently, like a sleep, and the earth brought forth abundantly without cultivation;—a description suggesting the early chapters of the book of Genesis. The end of this reign is associated with the rebellion of the three sons of Chronos, who are said to have divided his kingdom among them as told in the preceding chapter; but it should be carefully noted that this ancient God is not spoken of as dead and gone, but as reigning still—in the background—dwelling, some say, in Tartarus; but, according to others, in the Islands of the Blest, where he assists Rhadamanthus in deciding the fate of departed heroes; for Time tries all men. His temples were few and his worship simple and severe in character. In some places human sacrifices were offered by his priests, but in later days various animals were substituted. The worship of Chronos was never widespread or popular in Greece; but in Italy his representative, Saturn, had special honours paid to him—notably at the time of the Saturnalia, when the woollen bands which bound the feet of his image were undone, and seven days were passed in feasting and jollification. Every man offered up a sacrifice in honour of the God. The schools were closed, and gifts were bestowed, especially in the form of playthings for the children. Caste distinctions were temporarily abolished. The slaves sat at table with their masters. No punishments were ever inflicted, and freedom of speech was unchecked. All of which things, be it noted, were associated with the *setting free* of Saturn from his normal condition of bondage, typified by the woollen bands aforesaid. This festival was held in December, at the time when the Sun enters the sign of

Ruler

Capricorn; and has been retained by the Christian Church in a modified form as the festival of Christmastide, when Peace and Good-will are the watchwords of all. The place of Saturn has largely been taken by St. Nicholas or Santa Klaus, the "Father Christmas" beloved of the little folks; and another modern representative of this deity is Old Father Time, whose scythe recalls the sickle of the elder God, but whose wings and hour-glass are a recent addition. All great religions personify or define this form of energy in one way or another. The Hebrew definition of the Lord as "The Ancient of Days" suggests this aspect of deity; and the invariable association of the idea of the flight of time with this power should be noted. The patient investigations of modern science are ever bringing to light facts which prove to us that there is nothing new under the Sun, that every phenomenon is recurrent and that the Universe is well and truly built *on numbers.* Vibration, which seems to be the essential characteristic of many familiar forms of energy—such as heat, light, and sound—consists of repeated impulse. This wonderful Cosmos is one harmonious whole, and all its activities are rhythmic, and have been so since Time began. Hence the truth of the assertion that although Saturn belongs to a past generation he still continues to reign.

Evolved Type

The typical Capricornian takes life earnestly and is generally an enthusiastic upholder of tradition and authority. When fully developed he has a fine historic sense which gives him a keen interest in the events of the past, and a profound understanding of the problems of the present. He frequently treads the path of scholarship, does well at the University, very often shines in diplomacy or in some kind of work which involves acting as an intermediary between those whose interests or theories clash, and generally enjoys life. Social legislation may claim a large share of his attention and he usually has the welfare of the community very strongly at heart. This is not an easy type to analyse, and it is consequently difficult to sum up its characteristics briefly; but two main elements are always to be found in connection with its highest manifestation in humanity, namely noble ambition, and an extraordinary power of adaptability to environment. The first of these qualities results in abnormal industry, and the second makes the son or daughter of Capricorn peculiarly fitted to take part in the activities associated with city life, and with the guidance or government of large communities. Where civilised human beings most do congregate, it is necessary that the will of the majority should prevail if life is to run smoothly at all, and Capricornians not only acknowledge but proclaim that fact. They can accept conventions and traditional customs more easily than any other type, partly because historical values appeal to them, and partly because they possess an instinctive understanding of ordinary average humanity—its possibilities, its trials, its temptations and its shortcomings, and are therefore ready to admit the necessity of some kind of restraint.

Chains are an inevitable accompaniment of bondage, and as long as a man is a slave to his own passions, the fetters of the law must be worn. Wherefore our Capricornian, fully understanding the position, assumes them easily, and even wears them with a certain dignity and grace. He has usually a strong sense of the desirability of fixed standards of conduct, in social as well as in political and municipal life; and accepting these readily himself, is inclined to insist upon their acceptance by others; but at the same time such insistence is of the diplomatic and persuasive order, for his ambition is not of the type that sweeps obstacles out of the way, regardless of the interests or feelings of his fellow men.

The symbol of the sign—the Goat ascending the mountain—is a very appropriate one; for it is always depicted as *steadily following the upward path.* Every experienced climber knows that the beaten track is the safest road for those who desire to travel far, and that the attractive short cut is generally a snare and a delusion. Our Capricornian climber scarcely gives the latter a glance; and his reverence and admiration for those who have preceded him, and have already attained the heights on which his own soul is set, is tremendous. At times he may pause for a breathing space and look backwards, remembering with gratitude the resting-places and the guidance given in the earlier part of his journey, but the climbing is speedily resumed, and continued till the goal is reached; after which the ambition simply becomes more inclusive, and embracing the careers of others, finds more and more scope as the years of the long full life go on. And those who feel critical of such methods of attainment and are inclined to reserve their appreciation for work that is daring, experimental and original, should remember that experiment may be carried too far. The tendency of some people to use the words "traditional" and "conventional" as terms of abuse, is wholly unjustifiable. If a conventional method happens to be a good one, it is folly to reject it; and to abolish all tradition and start afresh in any department of human activity—in building, engineering and in all technical handicrafts, as well as in poetry, music, philosophy, art and religion—would involve a colossal waste of time and energy. He who cannot learn from his predecessors is awanting in intelligence; and psychologists and brain specialists are all agreed as to the enormous advantage that accrues to man from the fact that he can acquire habits by repeating actions until they become mechanical. The unfortunate individual who cannot do so is hopelessly handicapped in the battle of life, and in extreme cases must be classed as an imbecile; so that without some power of responding to the regularising influence of Saturn, not one of us could establish a claim to sanity.

While we shall probably look in vain for the sons of this sign among those pioneers of humanity who face heavy odds and break absolutely fresh ground against strong opposition, we shall find that many of them shew to advantage at later stages of the work of reform. The crest of the wave rather than its first advance is the place for them, and none are quicker to feel the heart-beat of their own generation and to respond to it. Their enthusiasm is slow to awaken, but it is of the kind that grows and gathers force through coming into touch with the enthusiasm of the masses of their fellow-men and women, and they not infrequently throw themselves into the task of guiding a popular movement—which has passed through its initial difficulties—to a successful issue; winning great praise and much esteem by their ability, especially in particular crises which require the exercise of tact and *finesse*.

Primitive Type

Here we have described the Capricornian at his very best and most successful; but there is naturally another side to the picture; for until the complete and well-balanced development of the whole nature—mental, emotional and physical—has been attained, boundless ambition is often a source of worry and torment rather than of happiness. Even at the early stages it is a splendid spur or goad to activity, but to the eyes of the onlookers it is often only recognisable in the form of gloomy discontent with present circumstances. That other source of Capricornian strength, adaptability, has also its unlovely side. To be all things to all men *may* be a splendid achievement, for constant courtesy and consideration for others means constant self-control; but if the nature is ignoble and the ambitions despicable, such pliancy may take very undesirable forms; and reverence for superiors at its lowest level tempts a man to cringe before them in servile ways. There is also a danger in this "earthy" type, with its keen realisation of the use and value of experiences on the physical plane, that worldly success may be given a disproportionately large place, and that the methods by which wealth and position can be attained will not be too closely scanned. Typical Capricornian employments, as has already been remarked, are those associated with mediatorial work; and a perfectly legitimate and useful form of that work—at least in the present condition of our commerce—is that of the middleman or broker; but what a man does is always less important than why and how he does it; and if we follow that line of employment down to the sweater's den and the resetters' pawnshop, we are conscious of a strong sense of repugnance and disgust. How much lower this type can sink may best be indicated by reminding readers that there are men and women so debased—so lost to all sense of humanity and brotherhood—that they are willing to draw a comfortable income from the worst vices of their fellow creatures. The go-between who will do any kind of errand, however base, if it can be made to pay, is, in fact, a kind of "ambassador" in his own way. The Capricornian has none of the innate cruelty of the Scorpionian at the early stages; but his ambition to make his way in the world makes him unscrupulous in his use of the tool and the catspaw; and although he does not rejoice that others are weaker than himself he acquiesces in the fact and uses it. "*It is impossible but that occasions of stumbling should come*" is a thought that is often present to his mind, and he is apt to think that it is quite legitimate to take advantage of the fact, forgetting that the Master finished the sentence with the stern warning: "*But woe unto him, through whom they come.*" And verily it shall be woe! For "*It were well for him that a millstone were hanged about his neck and he were thrown into the sea, rather than that he should cause one of these little ones to stumble.*"

The Capricornian's relations to his fellow-men have already been touched upon, but the importance of this element in the lives of people of this type can hardly be exaggerated, and both in a public and in a private capacity, the interest is focussed on the past and present achievements of humanity, considered—according to temperament and training—racially, politically, historically or individually. It is in the regulation of their relations with their fellow creatures that the majority of the sons and daughters of this type find most satisfaction, especially in what they themselves would possibly describe as their leisure hours. They have an intense desire to influence others—to manage them, mother them, direct, protect, persuade, convert, pervert, wheedle, attract or meddle with them in one way or another. This tendency is of course apt to prove somewhat irritating to their friends and relatives at times—especially when they are quite young; but as they advance in years and grow in wisdom, they learn to control it, and are naturally listened to with more deference and respect when they do speak. In fact the longer they live, the better they are able to exercise their particular gifts, and to see them at their very best, one should pay them a visit on the golden wedding day, or at the festival of Christmas tide, when they gather together their family and friends and dependents, and show the kindliest sympathy in the cares of the seniors, the love affairs of the juniors and the games of the little ones. They like to remember and observe dates and anniversaries, and to make much of special occasions of social re-union, for they are excellent hosts and hostesses, and generally popular in that capacity, besides making charmingly adaptable guests. In later life they are generally looked up to as authorities on matters of dress and deportment, and often consulted on questions of precedence or social procedure, and some of the less developed give an exaggerated importance to such matters, burdening themselves with all the worry and expense that hamper the devotees of *Madame la Mode*. It is in fact a real affliction for these people to have to appear anywhere in unbecoming or unsuitable or old-fashioned garments, and they rarely grudge the time and trouble given to preparation for great occasions, inclining to the magnificent in their own attire, if their means will allow, and doing marvels in the way of making a brave show even at a considerable sacrifice of personal comfort.

Love and Friendship

This tendency to give importance to externals, affects their friendships to some extent, for it makes them inclined to cultivate people of superior social position;—to pay undue attention to those who are *in the running*, and too little to those who fall by the way, until, indeed, these latter have fallen so low that it is possible to patronise them from a safe distance without the embarrassing chance of being treated by them as equals. In short, one of the vices of this type is snobbery; and it should be remembered that it is a vice which appears and re-appears in many strange guises, long after its victim fancies it has been overcome. At his worst the snob grovels before rank and wealth and scorns poverty and obscurity; but when he has got over that weakness, and has carried his social ambitions into literary or artistic or political—or even into religious—circles, his snobbery remains snobbery still, so long as he worships at the shrine of popular success, and turns his back upon failure.

The Capricornian's interest in love affairs—his own and those of other people!—is so very strong a characteristic of the type that it ought to have a chapter to itself. The consciousness of sex difference is very strong and at the primitive stage it is almost impossible for these people to be easy and natural and altogether free from excitement in the presence of any member of the opposite sex. Their constant desire to breathe forth some sort of a challenge provokes many encounters of wit—not always of the most desirable type, for it is full of innuendo; and most of the sons and daughters of this sign are, in early youth, and sometimes much later too, incorrigible flirts; a weakness not always overcome even at a fairly advanced stage of development. In the men the protective tendency—passing sometimes into patronage—is accentuated; and in the women there is usually a distinct craving for protection, which results in a manner that is often charmingly appealing and confiding. Roughly speaking, ambition is the preponderating quality in the masculine type, while adaptability is so markedly present in the feminine variety that it sometimes fairly runs to seed, depriving its owner of the power of concentration or specialisation altogether; but if that is the case it will generally be found that ambition is not really absent, but merely vicarious, and that the woman who at first sight seems only bent upon making herself agreeable all round, is in reality on the road to distinct social success, and that when once her own welcome is assured she will spare no pains and leave no stone unturned for the advancement of husband or brother or parent or child. Especially is she in her element if she can forward a promising love affair, likely to result in what she terms a *suitable* marriage. Luckily she is far too loving a parent to sell her children into uncongenial slavery, and her policy is more in the direction of weeding out detrimentals and giving to a choice of pleasing eligibles a fair field and a judicious amount of favour, than of actually forcing matters forward against the victim's will. Having disposed of her own sons and daughters successfully, she is generally more than ready to turn her attention to the children of her friends and relatives; for love and marriage have usually played so very important a *rôle* in her own life that she simply cannot understand that for some types single blessedness is no tragedy but rather a relief, and that interest and interference, however kindly meant, may prove unwelcome and distasteful to those who are naturally sensitive and reserved. In default of this matrimonial agency work, the patching up of broken friendships and starting of new ones, the removal of misunderstandings and the smoothing out of troublesome tangles in family life are all congenial occupations. In the primitive type such a tendency naturally manifests in an irresistible inclination to have a finger in every pie.

Literary Style

The literary style of the Capricornian, like everything else about him, has two aspects. It is stately, sonorous, ornate, rolling on into long periods and imposing paragraphs; sometimes rhythmic, always weighty and impressive, frequently veiling rather than revealing its meaning by its wealth of heaped-up metaphor or over-elaboration of phrase; or else it is pithy and sententious and laconic, taking shape most readily in the maxim and the popular saying, and sometimes degenerating into the trite, the commonplace, and even the vulgar, after the fashion of our homelier proverbs. Specimens of both styles may be found alternating in that strange and interesting expression of typically Capricornian thought and feeling, the book of Ecclesiastes. Its third chapter begins with a hymn of times and seasons that might have been dedicated to Chronos himself:

> "To every thing there is a season,
> And a time to every purpose under the heaven.
> A time to be born, and a time to die,
> A time to plant, and a time to pluck up,"

and so on with rhythmic recurrence through the times to weep and to laugh, and to mourn and to dance; to kill and to heal, and to love and to hate. Nothing could possibly be more characteristic; and having established so much as an axiom, the preacher goes on to discourse very sagely and wisely on the value of wealth and the legitimacy of enjoying a reasonable amount of worldly possessions and creature comforts; showing a characteristic preference for length of days and a somewhat morbid shrinking from death as, apparently, the end of everything worth having—such exaltation of physical experiences being distinctly typical of this *earthy* sign. Then the style changes again, rising in certain wonderful passages to great heights of stately and sonorous descriptive writing—still on the same subject—and picturing for us with marvellous beauty and pathos the quiet ending of a long full life; when "man goeth to his long home, and the mourners go about the streets"; after which the writer relapses into prose again and ends somewhat abruptly with sundry sage reflections on the futility of embarking on abstruse literary and philosophical endeavour, and the wisdom of cultivating an attitude of reverence, and simply accepting and obeying the Law as handed down to us by the Fathers:—"*Fear God, and keep His commandments: for this is the whole duty of man.*"

Religion

The religious life of the advanced Capricornian is the strongest and most important element in his nature, for ambition when it comes to its height is transmuted into aspiration, and this type is peculiarly suited to the office of the priesthood. The handing on of tradition, the right and reverent rendering of ritual and the dutiful observance of all kinds of ceremonial, are thoroughly congenial to the son of Saturn. He is, further, the ideal father-confessor, and in churches where the official practice of confession is disapproved, he still inclines to claim and hold the office informally, visiting the sick and admonishing the sinners with great assiduity, and striving to guide their steps in the way they should go, through frequent personal intercourse. Full of wise saws and modern instances, this practical adviser and disciplinarian, who is at the same time a man of the world, is well able to direct others, speaking as one who has received authority and never losing sight of the fact that to whom much is given from him shall much be required;—a saying which he accepts very literally as applying to possessions, as well as metaphorically, as applying to the greater gifts of wisdom, love and power. His religious teaching and ministrations are generally adapted to the needs of ordinary average humanity, and he is consequently apt to find himself rather at a loss when brought face to face with exceptions and minorities, his general solution being a dictum that they ought to ease the situation by conforming to custom, however uncongenial or difficult it may be for them to do so. He also holds very strong convictions as to the value of all outward and visible signs of inward and spiritual grace, insisting on the reverent posture, the regular attendance on feast day and holy day and also—in many cases—on the methodical use of set forms of praise and prayer. The fact that these forms are antiquated and no longer understood by the majority of the people, in no way detracts from their value in his eyes. They belong to a great past and are therefore venerable for him.

The Jewish race, and also the Hindoos are said traditionally to be ruled by Capricorn; and students who wish to follow out this line of thought should analyse the ritual of both nations and compare their customs, giving special attention to the monotonous repetition of prayers and sacred invocations in an unknown tongue which is insisted upon as having a definite value apart from all question of intelligent comprehension on the part of the worshipper.

Rhythmic methods of counting prayers and invocations, such as the Hindoo and Roman Catholic use of the rosary, or the turning of the praying wheel by the worshipper in Thibet, are always suggestive of the influence of Saturn and are, of course, to be found all over the world, among Christians as well as among people of other faiths; and although to some of us, and especially to those brought up in Protestant countries, such practices may seem unnecessary and even ridiculous, we should think well before uttering a condemnation which, as far as we are concerned, is probably just as traditional and conventional as the custom we condemn. Granted the possibility of the mind dulled to apathy by monotonous exercise, the fact remains that routine and regularity have their value in matters religious just as in other fields of activity; and rhythmic chanting or repetition of invocation and of praise, even when it is "vain" as far as the intellect is concerned, does calm the physical body and steady the mind and attune the soul, thus preparing the whole man to respond fully and freely to the vibrations of the higher planes. This is in fact one of the functions of good music in general and of what is called sacred music in particular. It depends upon race and temperament and the circumstances of the moment whether the music that is appropriate and effectual be the pipe of Pan or the Gregorian chant of the cathedral choir, or the swinging chorus of the Glory Song beloved of the revivalist; and it is part of the priest's duty to know how and when to use this special key to that wonderful Kingdom of Heaven—the Spiritual Universe—which is within and around us all. Religious ceremonial, if it is to be really efficient, ought to set up an accord or correspondence between our higher and lower vehicles, and should tranquillise all the coarser vibrations, or forms of activity which go on in our normal consciousness, so lifting up the everlasting doors that the King of Glory may come in. With these ideas of public and private worship before us it is interesting to recall the words in which the Master Jesus Christ reminds His disciples—the first priests of the religion He founded—that the keys of the Kingdom of Heaven are committed to their charge. By the use of these keys, *whatsoever they bind on earth shall be bound in heaven.* That is to say that all the discordant jarring of the lower vehicle, or purely physical nature, will be tranquillised or *bound*, so that no disturbing element that might drag the soul down to earth again will be allowed to intrude upon the consciousness during the hours of devotion; and *whatsoever they loose on earth shall be loosed in heaven;* for there are forms of earthly activity that are in closest sympathy with the vibrations of the spiritual regions, and which, if given freedom in the right way, may actually enrich the Heavenly harmonies by adding to them the harmonies of the lower planes. Blundering generations have interpreted the passage in their own peculiar way, many people actually wresting the beautiful words so as to make our Lord assert that *whomsoever* any ignorant priest shall excommunicate and condemn upon earth, here and now, shall remain bound—and in torment—to all eternity!

The endeavour to establish the laws of the Kingdom of Heaven upon earth is the aim of every true son of this sign when he has attained to its heights; but it is the *earth* life he is mainly concerned with and responsible for, and it is consequently the secular priest rather than the hermit or the monk that we find under the sway of Saturn. The recluse and the mystic are ill-fitted to cope with the problems of social life in a big city parish, but there our Capricornian finds himself very much at home, and as it is desirable that he should share the experiences of his flock as far as possible, he ought to be a married man. The Greek Church insists upon the marriage of its clergy, giving weight to the apostolic declaration that the Bishop should be the "husband of one wife." The old Hebrew Law was equally emphatic on this point, and the officiating priest whose duty it is to come and go among his people and concern himself intimately with their affairs is, in nearly all the great religions, drawn from the ranks of the married, and not from the celibate orders. The instinct for home and family life is extremely strong in this type, and will find an outlet, so that the Church which forbids its secular priests to marry must either dispense with the valuable services of the Capricornian, or be content to have recurrent scandals in the lives of a section of its clergy, as is only too frequently seen even at the present day, especially among the Latin races.

Apart from the sacrifice of these home affections and relations, the Capricornian enters into the idea of giving to the Gods with great enthusiasm, and can tithe mint and anise and cumin with the best, the usual characteristics of the type coming out strongly in connection with his distribution of the offerings; for quite as much importance is given by him to the duty of giving generously to the upkeep of the dignity of the Temple and its officials, as to that of providing sustenance for the poor. The idea that "He that giveth to the poor, lendeth to the Lord" is not sufficient for him; for he holds that reverence and devotion should also be shown by the gift of cherished possessions to those who minister in holy things. Therefore the ceremonial that interests him most, is that of sacrifice. The Capricornian preachers of the Christian church dwell much upon the death of Jesus, the so-called wrath of God, and the Atoning Sacrifice associated by theologians with the Crucifixion; and are too often inclined to neglect the importance of the life and ministry of our Lord, which it should be remembered was as Self-sacrificing as His death. Perhaps that is why some of the more degenerate sons of Saturn who drift into the priesthood through impulses connected with temperament and heredity, without having any true vocation for the sacred office, are rather apt to neglect the active following of the great Example in their own personal lives, drugging their consciences to sleep with the comfortable but dangerous doctrine that everything necessary has already been done for them by the Saviour of the world and forgetting the clear and unmistakable teaching of the New Testament that a man must bear his own burden and work out his own salvation, and that he always reaps exactly what he has sown.

A characteristic part of the Hindoo social system which is strongly associated with the religious teaching given to the race is the very definite division of the people into different castes, a different ideal and standard of conduct being placed before each of the four great classes—the labourer, the merchant, the soldier or ruler, and the priest or teacher. These four have been sub-divided and made rigid to an extent that is excessively cumbrous and inconvenient, but the fact that all nations have to some extent a tendency to classify and to mark off boundaries and divisions is worthy of note. To marry out of one's own caste, or to take a mate of alien race and faith, is always regarded as a perilous venture, and generally results in suffering of some kind; and our standards of conduct vary according to a man's rank in life. Thus, a druggist may advertise; a doctor who does so is turned out of his profession: and, without precise definition of what is allowable in the conduct of public or private affairs, there is a healthy conviction on the part of most people that a particularly high standard should be achieved by men who hold government or church appointments and live constantly in the public eye. Such a theory is perfectly justifiable, and even inevitable in countries where the doctrine of evolution through reincarnation is accepted. For the elder brethren ought to be able to live by stricter rule than their juniors.

It is not always realised here that in our own Christian Scriptures this inequality of development is frankly admitted, although at the same time the essential brotherhood of the race is recognised; and that the apostles divide the community definitely and unmistakably into four great classes on this scientific basis of difference in the degree of moral, mental, and spiritual evolution; yet this is certainly the case. There are first of all the *Babes* or *little children* who are to be fed with the *milk of the Gospel* and only given the very simplest and most easily digested of teaching—so that they may grow in grace and find no occasion of perplexity or stumbling. Then come the *Brethren*, who are to be mutually helpful, diligent in the right conduct of their affairs, serving the Lord, and paying due reverence to the *Fathers or Elders*—the next caste—who are to hold offices of responsibility, and guide and admonish and direct the juniors. Finally come the *Saints*, or those made perfect through suffering, whose duty it is to teach by example and precept the precious doctrines concerning the laws of that spiritual universe of whose existence and great glory their own inner vision can tell them. Through all these stages the Christian convert must pass; and though some may fall by the way, and even—like Hymenæus and Alexander—be handed over to the Devil for a time "*that they may learn*," there is no mistaking the bright confidence of St. Paul that, in days to come, even the Babes shall attain to the fulness of the measure of the stature of the Christ. How then has that hope been lost by so many Christians? The answer is—*simply through the loss of the doctrine of re-incarnation*, which was held of old by the learned among the Jews* as well as among the Hindoos, and which is distinctly referred to by Jesus Christ Himself on more than one occasion, notably when He identified John the Baptist with the prophet Elijah.

In Real Life

A strikingly typical son of Capricorn may be studied in the person of William Ewart Gladstone, born with the Sun and Mercury rising in that sign; and those who wish to understand its peculiarities should read the pages of his biography with care. His style in writing is of the ornate and elaborate Capricornian type, abounding in Latin constructions and very scholarly in diction. He was amazingly fluent of tongue, so much so that both in conversation and in public oratory he was apt, as his contemporary Disraeli remarked, to be carried away "by the exuberance of his own verbosity." He was interested in ceremonial observances, and conformed easily to social customs and conventions, observing the etiquette of his generation so strictly in his youthful days that he often made twelve or fourteen calls in the course of an afternoon. He had serious thoughts of entering the priesthood, and was always an ardent believer in the value of prescribed forms, interesting himself very early in the origin and purposes of the Occasional Offices of the Prayer Book and in the

* The Rabbis find many references to the teaching in Jewish tradition The Talmud and Kabbalah both refer to it. The passage in Psalm xc, "Thou turnest man to destruction and sayest 'Return, ye children of men,'" is interpreted by learned commentators as a reference to reincarnation. When Jesus asked His disciples, "Whom say men that I the Son of Man am?" they answered, "Some John the Baptist, some Elias, some Jeremias, or one of the prophets," showing that the doctrine was current then. Certain early Church Fathers uphold the idea of pre-existence, and reincarnation was not definitely set aside by the Church till about the 6th century, and then only condemned in the form "taught by Plato," which included transmigration into animal bodies

doctrines expressed in article and creed. The Church of Rome both attracted and disappointed him, and his first visit to the Imperial city was a turning-point in his life, for there, on entering St. Peter's, he first realised the meaning of the ideal of the Unity of the Church, and began to long for its attainment. Further study in the same year (1832) presented Christianity to him under a new aspect. "Its ministry of symbols, its channels of grace, its ascending line of teachers joining from the Head" appeared to him, he says, as "a sublime construction, based throughout upon historic fact, uplifting the idea of the community in which we live and of the access which it enjoys through the new and living Way to the presence of the Most High."

We find a suggestion of the same feeling in Gladstone's own comment on the religious life of Eton in his time—a comment made more than forty years after leaving that school. "The actual teaching of Christianity was all but dead," he tells us, "*though luckily none of its forms had been surrendered.*" Such a sentiment would be exceedingly repugnant to many earnest and devout souls; and it is probably *only* a Capricornian who would take little or no harm from such a training. In some types it would induce insincerity and hypocrisy, and in others cynicism, scepticism and contempt for those who took part in what would simply appear to them as a piece of "useless humbug"; witness the fact that many of the bitterest atheists in France have been bred in the schools of the Jesuits, and in other monastic institutions in which the value of the outward form has been insisted upon *ad nauseam*.

Another great Englishman whose career, and style, and conversational abilities might well suggest that Capricorn was rising at the time of his birth, was Lord Macaulay, politician, historian, essayist and poet; a remarkably brilliant example of the type. That he had one of its weaknesses—excessive volubility—is suggested by Sidney Smith's quaint comment on the change visible in him in his later years: "Macaulay is distinctly improving. Yesterday he had some brilliant flashes of silence." His hour is however unknown.

Perhaps it is somewhat unfair to bracket with these two great men another whose name—in England at least—has become a byeword for indirect and evasive methods—namely Macchiavelli the famous Florentine. But his more recent biographers assure us that less than justice is done to him by popular opinion, that his patriotism was sincere, and that his principles, though adaptable—to put it mildly—had nevertheless a certain amount of back-bone in them. He took a delight in studying and teaching the most effective methods of diplomacy, and shared Gladstone's theory that the will of the people as a whole should invariably be carried out. It is interesting to note that a favourite pursuit of both statesmen was the thinning of the plantations on their country estates, the Italian statesman superintending the hewing-down of superfluous trees, and the Englishman carrying out the work with his own hands. Possibly the pursuit was typical of their firm belief that it was necessary for the healthy growth of the whole state that the minority should be sacrificed!

Physical Characteristics

Manifesting physically, Capricornians are even more difficult to describe and classify than they are mentally and emotionally, the specimens collected by the writer showing every variety of size and shape. The majority of them are distinctly well-favoured and the word Saturnine as used by the present generation is entirely inapplicable to every one of them. Some of the old books insist much on the serious aspect of the Capricornian, his tendency to gloom and despondency, leaden looks, swarthy complexion, sleek, lank, black hair and sparse little beard. Most of those on the writer's list are fair, especially in the Scottish contingent. The men are all comely and the women extremely attractive—some even beautiful. Most of them have lovely fair hair, soft and curling, and the traditional resemblance to a goat is only represented in a few by a slightly long face with a retreating chin, and by the clear sparkling amber lights in the eyes. As a rule they are exceedingly lively and talkative—voluble in fact—although only one or two are inclined to be silent and absorbed in serious thought when in the society of their home people. Of this fair type there are three diminutive, which is sometimes said to be a characteristic trait; and of these three, two are men. The others are all well grown, some over six feet high and strongly built. As usual the division into masculine and feminine types does not coincide with the actual division of sex; for one of the men could easily pass for a woman, and one of the women who had an exceptionally brilliant university career—taking, like Gladstone, a double first,—and has since played a prominent part in the suffrage movement, shows striking business ability and organising power, and a capacity for hard work that many a man might be disposed to envy. She is tall and dark, with masses of beautiful hair. Nearly all of these persons belong to the professional and upper middle classes, and it may be that a collection taken from the lower ranks would show more of the discontent and gloom and unloveliness associated traditionally with the sign. Also, naturally, the tendency of the talkative specimens to repeat and recapitulate must become very wearisome if the talker is lacking in intelligence and merely dealing with trifling items of gossip about his or her neighbours; and while the ambitions are limited to the mere out-shining of the said neighbours in the matter of possessions and "gentility," the society of the ambitious one can hardly be considered either cheerful or inspiring.

In Drama and Fiction

Some of the statelier priests and politicians of Elizabethan drama suggest this Capricornian type—notably Cardinal Wolsey, with his splendour and his pride and the soaring ambition which, by running entirely in worldly channels, brought about his downfall in the end. The oft-quoted passage beginning—

> "Had I but served my God with half the zeal
> I served my king"—

strikingly illustrates the change from lower ideals to higher; the ambition itself lives on, though ennobled and elevated. A less dignified specimen is easily recognised in the person of Polonius in "Hamlet"; and also, at a lower social level in the garrulous and kindly old nurse in "Romeo and Juliet." The darker side of Capricornian nature is represented by Dickens' portrait of Fagin, the Jew who lives on the dishonesty of others, and whose terror of death is a very characteristic touch.

Health

Father Time and Father Christmas are both represented as vigorous old men, and the sons and daughters of Saturn follow their ruler in being associated very specially with length of days. Capricornians are said to attain their best period between the ages of fifty-six and seventy, a much longer and older prime than is enjoyed by any other type. Many of them live to well over eighty, some remaining hale and hearty and retaining the use of their various faculties till the century is in sight or overpast. Possibly the rhythmic tendency of the type gives them a stronger and more regular heart beat than their fellows, and their ambition may prevent them from over-indulgence in the matter of eating or drinking at a critical time, when the constitution is forming; for although they attain to the heights on which their heart is set they generally have a bit of a struggle in early youth. The chief danger to health is thwarted ambition, inducing discontent and gloom, which may bring on bilious attacks and other derangements of the digestive organs. Later on in life, when prosperity is reached, there may be a tendency to gouty troubles: or, if the prosperity is overdue and still tarries, and the limited outlook and cramping conditions show no signs of giving way, gloom and despondency may turn to melancholia. The best remedies are hope and cheerful society. A change of air is beneficial and even essential in some cases, but it should not be a change to solitude, and no scenery is likely to be so much appreciated as the scenery associated with city pleasure grounds such as Hyde Park or the Bois de Boulogne. Capricornians always patronise the fashionable Spa in preference to the rural cot or the moorland and mountain, and no type is more keenly interested in the exchange of facts or surmises concerning the various celebrities and nobodies who haunt such favoured resorts. The best and most comfortable hotel that their means will allow is chosen on such occasions, and the skill of the *chef* is often considered an important point; for the Capricornian palate is sensitive and its owner not infrequently gives considerable time and attention to its cultivation.

♒ AQUARIUS ♒

THE WATER-BEARER.

The Sign of the

TRUTHSEEKER OR SCIENTIST

A fixed airy sign.

Keynote—Truth.

Watchword—Investigation.

Ruler—Uranus.

♅

Mystical Gems—Sapphire, Opal.

Colour— ? *Metal*—Aluminium ?

Physical Manifestation—Absorption.

Mental Manifestation—Curiosity.

These reflections ought always to be at hand.—To consider well the nature of the Universe and mine own nature, together with the relation betwixt them, and what kind of part it is, of what kind of whole; and that no mortal can hinder me from acting and speaking conformably to the Being of which I am a part

* * * *

The Philosopher Sextus . . . also bade me make nature and reason my rule to live by . . . and helped to draw up a true, intelligible, and methodical scheme for life and manners; and never to show the least sign of anger, but to be perfectly calm . . yet tender-hearted. He let me see in himself that a man might show his goodwill significantly enough, without noise and display; and likewise possess great knowledge, without vanity and ostentation.

* * * *

As for those that were philosophers in earnest, he (Antoninus Pius) had a great regard for them; but without reproaching those that were otherwise.—MARCUS AURELIUS.

CHAPTER XI.

The Aquarian Type

The ruler of Aquarius is Uranus, the deity who is described by classical writers as the father of Saturn, the grandfather of Jupiter and his brethren, and the great-grandfather of the lesser gods. He is thus identified as a Power concerned with the very beginning of manifestation, with the laying down of the general principles on which the Cosmos is built. The impression left upon the mind of the student after meditating on the myths through which the poets seek to indicate the place of this deity in the celestial hierarchy, is of something remote, far-off, immeasurably vast, indescribable and indefinable. He is concerned with fundamental truths too great for us to grasp. In those distant days when only his kingdom had come into existence, the reign of chaos was just over, and even the earliest beginnings of the separative or classifying tendencies had not yet emerged into actual activity. Hence we are told that while Uranus reigned his children remained imprisoned in the darkness of their mother Titheia, who is described as "the Earth," and probably stands for the feminine principle of the Universe—matter. Later they conspired to dethrone Uranus, Saturn taking the reins of government after mutilating his father. We have already identified Saturn with the form of energy manifesting in vibration or rhythm; and the myth is easily comprehensible if we realise that it is an assertion that Time sets limits and marks off boundaries. Through this action of his rebellious son, Uranus is thenceforth deprived of the power of generation, which passes on or "falls" into the vast ocean of Neptune, whose realm is ever the symbol of the astral plane. Hence the birth of Aphrodite, and contemporaneously the starting of an entirely new order of activities and energies, resulting in the evolution of the Cosmos out of what had been the Kingdom of Chaos. Ruler

The Hebrew scriptures tell the same story in another way in the first chapter of Genesis, beginning also with the mere potential existence of the Heavens and the Earth, which are "without form and void" until the Spirit of God has moved upon the face of the *Waters;* after which the "dry land—" the physical plane—can appear, and the vibrations of light have full play. The creation of energies is the work of the older Gods; the creation of activities comes next, and the evolution of types and of forms completes the story as far as the work of separation and differentiation is concerned. The poetic description of Uranus as "God of the Highest Heavens" seems to lift him to a region so remote that any conception of his function is beyond us. And yet, after all, this wonderful realm over which He presides is not really distant or foreign in any way. That the Kingdom of Heaven is within us, is a mystic saying profoundly true; and it is equally true that we are in the Kingdom of Heaven. Its influences surround us on every side, and even on the material plane the words are significant and full of meaning, for our Mother Earth shines with as tender and lovely a radiance as any of her planetary brothers and sisters. She is as much a part of the glorious firmament as they are, and if we define this Power of Uranus as the God of all Space, we shall realise that everything that exists must bear a certain relation to Him and come within the sphere of His influence. That the ancients regarded Him with peculiar veneration we may gather from the fact that no attempt to represent Him has been discovered anywhere in classic art; although Saturn and his children are frequently seen. It is probable that we altogether under-estimate the reverence of the worshippers whose teachers evolved all this complicated mythology; and we who talk somewhat glibly of the Eternal and the Infinite might take lessons in humility from those who felt that the best a man could do was to learn to understand some of His aspects and attributes, and to bow the head before them. The idea that the thoughtful Greek had no conception of God higher than Zeus, is quite erroneous. Of Zeus he felt it possible to speak, and to Zeus he dared to pray; but behind Zeus stood Chronos, and behind Chronos, Ouranos, and behind Ouranos, Chaos; far behind Chaos, THAT of which no man spoke, the Great First Cause. The Eastern nations have the same conceptions and the same reserves, and probably no finer expression of reverence has ever been framed than the prayer of Sankaracarya, the Hindoo saint: "O Lord, pardon my three sins. I have in contemplation clothed in form Thyself, that hast no form; I have in praise described Thee, who dost transcend all qualities; and in visiting shrines, I have ignored thine Omnipresence." The growth of the spirit which led to such an utterance is helped rather than hindered by an endeavour to realise the greatness and magnitude of any one aspect of deity, so long as we refrain from the idolatry of regarding that aspect as the whole; and no thought concerning deity will be found more calculated to inspire awe than this marvellous conception of the Deity as the Lord of the Firmament, the source and origin of all the countless myriads of suns and planets that go to make up the heavenly host. His outstanding quality, which is reflected in humanity as Breadth of Vision, is sometimes gathered up into some striking symbol or phrase, especially by the poets of Northern lands. The idea of *The Silent Watcher* occurs in Scandinavian mythology, and *the All-seeing Eye* is a symbol familiar to all Free masons. The Hebrew psalmist in his wonderful word-painting has also many references to this essential quality. "Behold! he that keepeth Israel slumbers not nor sleeps ; naturally, for the alternations of day and night, summer and winter, Pralaya and Manvántara can have no effect on the activities of Him who existed before Time was.

Evolved Type

The chief characteristic of the typical Aquarian at the highly evolved stage is, as has already been said, his extraordinary breadth of vision. He is absolutely unbiassed and open-minded, and without taint of prejudice or superstition of any kind. Tradition and authority leave him untouched. When he finds himself face to face with them, he regards them with tranquillity and serenity, and possibly with a certain friendliness and interest; but no amount of natural courtesy towards them will make him veil his sight or refrain from turning on them the search-light of the truth seeker. His ways are neither militant nor aggressive. He can wait; and the longer he waits, the more clearly he realises the difficulty of attaining certainty about anything that is worth knowing, and the folly of condemning too hastily the theories of other truth seekers, who are just as likely to be in the right as he is. This results in an entire lack of pose, and perfect freedom from vanity and self-conceit as far as knowledge is concerned. He is willing to learn from anyone, even from a little child, for the only thing of which he is sure is that he does not know very much. If after patient enquiry and deep probing he realises that he has made a discovery or exposed a fallacy, he is generally eager to pass the information on to others as quickly as possible, even if in so doing he has to recant views he has formerly advocated, and abandon some of his favourite theories. He is, in fact, the finest possible type of scientist; not necessarily the practical scientist who utilises universal law on the physical plane, but simply the student of these laws, the truth seeker, patient, dispassionate and untiring, whose method is to take a comprehensive view of his subject, form his own hypothesis, and then marshal his facts, trying and testing his theories until they are proof against assault. In fact "What is the *truth* of the matter?" is his one concern, and the pet question of the prosaic craftsman—who so often advances a bogus claim to a scientific attitude of mind—"What is the *use* of it?" rarely enters into his calculations at all.

Primitive Type

The faults of the primitive Aquarian may be summed up in the one word *inefficiency*, for breadth of vision at the early stages seems to bewilder rather than to assist those who possess it, and a wide outlook is often accompanied by such deplorably short sight—figuratively speaking—that practical details are lost in a general haziness, so that, however conscious these people may be of an overpowering number of things they ought to be doing, they have great difficulty in deciding just where and when to begin. They are consequently inclined to fritter away a good deal of their time and energy, often missing their best opportunities by vacillating and wavering over very trifling decisions, and showing a lamentable lack of the practical common sense which realises how to adapt available means to the end in view, and so to obtain the best possible results in any given set of circumstances. They have very little power of concentration, and though generally amiable, well-meaning and what is sometimes called "harmless," are apt to blunder into difficulties through lack of imagination and consequently of tact. Their memory is sometimes deficient—or possibly only rather slow. Important details are forgotten till it is too late to consider them, and their work is too often attacked in a hesitating and apparently headless kind of way peculiarly exasperating to more capable and practical types. Another accusation frequently brought up against them is that of moral and physical cowardice; and there certainly is a peace-at-any-price tendency about most of them. At the highly evolved stage they may possibly be induced to fight for what they feel to be important truths, or in defence of those weaker than themselves; but anyone skilled in strategy and the methods of warfare can get the better of them, at any rate for the moment, for they are easily betrayed into allowing their attention to wander to abstract questions of right and wrong when they ought to be holding themselves in readiness and concentrating their energies on points of possible attack or defence. Most of them, and especially the women, are apt to feel flurried and bewildered by the onset of the enemy, and when they have blundered into a battle—as primitives often do—they have no resource beyond getting their back up against the rock of some cherished conviction and hitting out clumsily and blindly, goaded to the effort chiefly by the desire to get the trouble over as quickly as possible. In the confusion of the moment, point after point may possibly be yielded to the adversary, but when the noise and tumult of the battle have died away and the atmosphere is clear again, the chances are that our Aquarian will be found just exactly where he or she was before; for if the outlook is really a wide one, it cannot well be narrowed to please those who do not share it. This fact taken in conjunction with the typical truth seeker's attitude of mind towards tradition, results in all sorts of disconcerting departures from precedent; and makes the sons and daughters of this sign anything but favourites with Mrs. Grundy in consequence. They develop in harmony with law just as every other type does, but the laws they hold in honour are not necessarily those most revered by the particular communities in which their lot is cast, and Aquarians are apt to go their own way, ignoring convention and authority, and so meet with a good deal of hostility and criticism, especially if they are women.

Many students have been puzzled by the fact that this inclination to defy public opinion is much stronger in people born with Uranus rising than in those born with Aquarius rising; and find it difficult to accept Uranus as the ruler of Aquarius in consequence. Developed Aquarians, generally speaking, are too tranquil in temperament, too gentle and kindly in disposition, to outrage the feelings of their families and friends by startling eccentricities of conduct; but the planet Uranus rising in any of the more energetic and enterprising signs, and especially in any of the Cardinal signs, with their tendency to come before the public in one capacity or another, may easily lead to what seems to others amazing and unaccountable decisions and extremely peculiar behaviour, especially if associated with an undeveloped and ill-disciplined nature. In the case of those who have sufficient balance and self-control to avoid foolish extremes, Uranus rising is often associated with a dash of genius; but to have it rising where the nature is ill-balanced and the judgment faulty, suggests a stormy career indeed, especially if it is in Aries or Gemini.

Love and Friendship This eleventh sign of the Zodiac is naturally associated with the eleventh house in the horoscope, which, according to tradition, tells us something of the special relationship of any man to humanity as a whole. It speaks of his friends and of the experiences that come to him through friendship, and also suggests the favour or disfavour of the general public. The Water-bearer is represented as pouring forth liberally the Water—the emotion—which he carries; and the affections of the true-born Aquarian are certainly far-reaching and widespread. His attitude to the whole world is kindly and humane, and he extends his friendships to nations of alien race and unknown tongue, besides cherishing an almost sentimental tenderness for his younger brethren of the animal kingdom. People of this type will take any amount of trouble to increase the comfort and well-being of those around them, and find great satisfaction in devising simple and healthful pleasures for others. Charities such as the country-holiday fund, and societies for the amelioration of social conditions among the poor, often find in them willing contributors; but sometimes the sorrows and sufferings of humanity weigh upon them to an almost paralysing extent, and if the views held are more or less those of the doubter or agnostic, any practical work that they undertake loses part of its value through being carried on in a rather dejected spirit. They lack the abounding faith necessary to carry people hopefully through times of difficulty and darkness; and though they share a certain breadth of view and largeness of mind with their Leonian brethren, they have a way of looking at life's problems from the outside rather than from the centre, which makes it harder to tackle them effectively. The same kind of difference is seen in the dealings of the two types with their fellowmen. The Leonian takes them on trust, instinctively realising that in moral evolution the majority of mankind are really ahead of their outward actions, though they may be tied by evil habits to a tendency to fall below their own level; and very often the faith he shows in them helps them to break these fetters, and rise to the highest of which they are capable. The Aquarian, instead of trusting others, studies them, scrutinising their words and actions and if possible even their thoughts, earnestly, patiently and carefully; and as humanity, conscious of its own shortcomings, is not particularly keen on being vivisected, it is apt to grow restive during the process. It also craves for personal and particular appreciation and attention, and the acquaintances of the Aquarian often find it somewhat of a shock to realise that the very same kindliness and interest, which tickled their vanity and delighted their egotism when they first met him, are equally at the disposal of later comers. If they are of a jealous and exacting disposition, friendship with him will prove impossible; but in rejecting it they show little judgment, for the friendship of the Aquarian is founded on an understanding and personal esteem which go right down to the foundations of character, and his tranquil affection is crystalline in its purity and sincerity, and very well worth having, in spite of the fact that its somewhat general tendency makes it appear less of a personal compliment than the concentrated devotion of the blinder and narrower types.

It will be readily understood that the above characteristics sometimes result in a certain isolation and soul loneliness so far as intimate affections are concerned, and that at the primitive stage the trouble is accentuated by a real incapacity for settling down to anything like a steady-going friendship, or definitely and distinctly entering upon terms of affection and intimacy for more than a very brief space of time. Where memory is not a strong point, loyalty to individuals cannot be expected to flourish, and if imagination is lacking and the thirst for knowledge great, the chances are that the individual will spend a good deal of time in putting his foot in it with his fellow-men, however amiable and well-meaning he may be. As a matter of fact we find primitive Aquarians constantly getting into hot water through asking tactless and point-blank questions about the feelings and actions and opinions of others. They seem to lack the intuition that penetrates behind the veil, and yet cannot rest content so long as they realise that the veil is there; and when they have pulled it away and got at the heart of the mystery they often seem puzzled and a little disappointed to find that the hidden treasure didn't really amount to much after all—and are apt to add insult to injury by naïvely expressing their opinion to that effect; with results that are again a matter for bewildered speculation and astonishment.

The sons and daughters of Aquarius—and especially the sons—are slow to wed, although they generally do so in the end. They frequently make friendship the foundation of love, and choose a partner who is not merely a mate but a "chum" as well, and consequently capable of sharing in some at least of the many interests which go to make up the Aquarian's mental life. They are naturally well equipped for matrimony, possessing the priceless treasure of a wide and unprejudiced outlook, which can make allowances for difference of heredity, environment, training and education. The kindliness and humanity of the sign also favour marriage; for the typical Aquarian is inclined by nature to exact little and to give much, is incapable of petty tyranny and puerile jealousy, and carries a certain tender consideration into all the more intimate relations of the conjugal state—a consideration born of innate reverence for universal law, and associated with the highest possible aspirations for the welfare of the coming race. This being the case, the dilatoriness of the sons of this sign is the more to be regretted; but it springs quite naturally from the characteristics of the type. Both men and maidens find it extraordinarily difficult to let themselves go, and cling to the delusion of a safe and pleasant friendship long after that has become an impossibility for the prospective partner. Even after the goal of matrimony is actually in sight, they shrink from any approach to definite love-making, hesitating and vacillating and evading to an extent that is really unfair and unkind. In favourable circumstances the first ardour of youth may possibly carry an occasional Aquarian into an early engagement, but, if so, it will probably be years before any further step is taken. There are always lions in the way for anyone who takes a dispassionate all-round view of marriage; and as this type does not take to money-making pursuits, poverty is very frequently one of the most ferocious of them. The very kindliness and consideration of this sign prevent an Aquarian wooer from urging his betrothed to face circumstances that he deems too hard for her, and makes his astrological sister shrink from becoming a burden to the man she loves; and consequently in the case of both sexes, courage and faith and hope are shoved into the background while fear and doubt and delay win the victory all along the line. The Gordian knot may be cut for the maiden by the impetuosity of a lover who refuses to wait, and, in the case of her brother, an irate father-in-law elect may feel called upon to speak out in plain terms, bidding him make way for some more manly suitor; so that the chances are that some rival with a little more fire about him will cut our poor Aquarian out; in which case, after heaving a few sentimental sighs, he will probably relapse into friendliness again, repeating the experience from time to time as the years go on, without even beginning to understand just how and where he blunders. "Faint heart never won fair lady," and the maiden who is called upon to choose between a man who, whatever his faults may be, can and does play the convincing lover with energy, and one who is apparently not very sure whether he wants to marry at all, is not very likely to place her happiness in the hands of the doubter; and nothing is more absolutely fatal to romance than the discovery that the supposed admirer is a cold-blooded examiner in disguise, who is testing and trying, weighing and deliberating—as he has probably done in the case of innumerable other "possibilities" already. So the years slip by till middle age is past, and then the fortieth birthday or the happy wedding of the last available bachelor friend suddenly awakens our sentimentalist to the fact that he is preparing for himself a childless and lonely old age; and having long ere this done his part as dutiful son and generous brother, he sets about his wooing in earnest, and enters gravely and earnestly on the heavy responsibilities incident to the state of holy matrimony.

At the primitive stage the tendency to hesitate and vacillate is naturally much more accentuated, and a great many very prosaic details go to make up the *pros* and *cons* that are so frequently turned over and over and examined inside and out. At the same time the kindly good-nature of this type, together with its sentimentality and its interest in character study, strongly favour a series of foolish flirtations, which prefer to describe themselves as platonic friendships, and rarely reach the stage of a respectable heartache even when they come to an abrupt conclusion—at least so far as the Aquarian himself is concerned.

In spite of his own exemplary conduct as husband and father, the Aquarian type is rarely rigidly orthodox on the subject of the marriage law. Faithful and loyal to his promises himself—at any rate *after* the tie has been definitely formed—he is ultra-tolerant in his estimation of those who are not, and his tendency to legislate for minorities often makes him a conscientious supporter of those who would fain see some drastic alteration in the said law in England, especially where it presses heavily on the weaker sex. The ignorant, the undeveloped and those of uncontrolled and uncontrollable passions also come in for a share of his careful consideration, and the conclusions at which he arrives are distinctly disturbing to the consciences of those who prefer to shut their eyes to the conditions that exist around them to-day. Caring nothing for any theoretical presentation of life, this seeker after truth will dive straight into the facts, and face them fearlessly, however appalling they may be. He will reckon up as accurately as possible, just how many men and women are bound for life to drunkards, criminals and lunatics; how many more are struggling along hopelessly handicapped by husbands or wives who are actually deficient in mental capacity or utterly unbearable through lack of self-control; and he will ask himself how far it is desirable, for the race and for the state, that these people should be allowed—much less compelled—to remain bound. Lunatics* and imbeciles are not permitted to marry, but their lunacy or imbecility do not annul a marriage which has already taken place; and he will find that their bereaved partners—among the working men at any rate—are in many cases impelled by circumstances to replace them, and driven by the pressure of the law to replace them by those who cannot but be undesirable mothers for their children. Continuing his investigations, our Aquarian will come up against the results of a system which dooms people of utterly incompatible tempers and dispositions to struggle along together—possibly in very restricted space. He finds that the nagging wife sends her man to the public-house, and that the brutal and tyrannical husband wrecks the nerves and constitution of the woman whose duty it is to bear and to rear strong and healthy citizens. Not sensuality, but common sense, and an earnest desire for the true welfare of his fellow men and women, will make the son of Uranus upset tradition and shock convention by suggesting that divorce should be granted much more freely and easily than it is at present; but in all probability he will neither agitate for such a change nor fight for it; contenting himself with a

* Lunacy, if considered incurable, is now legally admitted as grounds for divorce.

mere statistical demonstration of its desirability, and when more warlike types have carried out the reform, he will still continue to follow the pleasant path of conjugal virtue, shewing by practical example what a beautiful and mutually helpful thing a harmonious marriage can be.

Students of Astrology are frequently puzzled how to reconcile these personally exemplary characteristics with the fact that Uranus is found by all astrologers to be the planet of divorce; that is to say that when a marriage ends disastrously in separation and the law courts, the possibility of such an event is almost invariably indicated by some baleful aspect of Uranus. The clue to the puzzle will be found in the fact so strongly insisted on in this chapter, that Uranus represents the outlook on life, and that a sympathetic point of view is the only thing absolutely and fundamentally necessary to the making of a happy marriage. Characters which clash to begin with, may be modified by experiences in which both partners share. Discordant dispositions may be attuned; mere differences in taste often add piquancy to the union, and diverse types of mind and intellect may still be full of interest for one another; but to change one's whole point of view, to learn to look at life through the eyes of another; to understand and sympathise even when these eyes may give but a limited or distorted reflection of things that are clear and comprehensible to one's own inner vision!—that is what is impossible for all but the very highly evolved, and even they can scarcely hope to compass it excepting through the discipline of sorrow. Hence uncomfortable positions with regard to Uranus are associated with sharp and sudden and disconcerting experiences, which widen a man's outlook and sometimes rob him of cherished illusions. The planet is consequently classed as a malefic, and his evil aspects are dreaded accordingly, but to his own children—to those who feel that "There is no religion higher than Truth" and that "There is nothing worthy to be given in exchange for Truth"—he looks with a favourable eye; and those who know by a careful study of aspects that his hand is stretched out towards them should go fearlessly to clasp it, for although it may lead them through lonely ways and over rough and stony ground, it is ever drawing them upwards to the heights upon which true breadth of vision may be attained.

Literary Style

Students who wish to understand the chief characteristics of

Aquarian style, cannot do better than take up the poems of Wordsworth and read first his most famous passages and then some of his more prosaic and less popular poems. His theories as to how verse ought to be written are typical; for he puts Truth first and foremost and always protested against the practice of keeping up a poetic diction, because it inferred that there was no poetry to be found in the simple language of our daily life. We can see in such an attitude of mind something of that reverence for natural law which is the hall-mark of all great souls belonging to this type, and the wide sweep of subjects, ranging from the tattered cloak of the poverty-stricken orphan, to the history of man's soul, and the wonders of the starry firmament, all suggest the son of Uranus. The language in which this poet speaks of the great mysteries of life is as direct and straightforward as that of the Leonian, but there is far more descriptive power. In fact the accuracy of detail given in certain passages is positively overdone. Many of Wordsworth's most popular poems come perilously near to being commonplace; while the great bulk of his work is unread by the majority, precisely because it is prosy.

Wordsworth's birth-hour is unknown, but the writer was helped to the recognition of his type by comparing his poems with the early verses of John Ruskin, whose hour has been recorded and shows the Sun rising in Aquarius, and Uranus close to the Zenith. That Ruskin abandoned verse as he grew older is probably no loss to literature, especially as he gave us in its place some of the most exquisitely beautiful passages of descriptive English prose that have ever yet been penned. The opening chapters of *The Stones of Venice* may be cited as examples of his style at its finest, but to the end of his literary career he shows all the most striking of the Aquarian characteristics—simplicity, sincerity, the attitude of the truth seeker and the habits of the student; and last but not least an intense interest in sociology and the real welfare of humanity as a whole.*

Religion The religious tendency of the Aquarian is to a thoughtful and reverent agnosticism, founded on the recognition of the fact that the finite human mind cannot hope to grasp the Infinite. If he takes any

* Among other writers who have the Sun in this sign and who answer strongly to the influence of Uranus, are Francis Bacon and Charles Darwin, both renowned as having altered and enlarged the outlook of their brother scientists to a remarkable extent. Both had the Sun—indicating the success—in Aquarius and probably Darwin had it at the Zenith, for his life suggests Cancer as ascendant

interest in forms and ceremonies it is to examine and compare them, and he treats the scriptures of the world and the traditional teachings of the great founders of religion in the same way, accepting no other man's verdict, be he priest or layman, but probing, searching aud inquiring into the matter for himself. If he attempts to give us the foundations of his belief he will draw up a statement with accuracy and care, taking pains to make it a thoroughly straightforward and conscientious document; but it will probably be so hedged about with modifications and saving clauses as to be somewhat dull reading. His notes for such a work are often better reading than the work itself, and some of the finest that have been left to us have never been worked up into elaborate book form at all. The jottings and journals of Marcus Aurelius, the great philosopher, Emperor of Rome, suggest the Aquarian mind at its noblest and best. This grand old pagan viewed life steadily and viewed it whole, and in spite of his moods of agnosticism, in which he realised that the greatest of all facts—those that seemed to him most essential—were not, and could not be, logically proved, and that there was possibly much human error mixed with the dearest and most sacred of his own convictions, he could ring out his creed more bravely and sincerely than many a so-called Christian of modern days. "Whatever the gods ordain is full of wise forethought. . . . Gods there are, and assuredly they regard human affairs, and they have put it wholly in man's power that he should not fall into what is truly evil." Such phrasing may strike strangely upon our ears; but, in reading, we must be careful not to misinterpret it. Many great and reverent souls prefer to speak of the Heavens or the divine Powers, rather than utter the name of God. Jewish prophets and teachers frequently make use of plural forms—*the Elohim* or *the Orions*—in the Old Testament, although our translators sometimes conceal the fact. It is the Powers that say, "Let US make man in Our own image"—a sentence full of meaning for the astrological student of the different types of humanity. The Protestant Church pays little heed to old traditional teaching concerning the ministry of the angels, and even in early times much was kept back from the people, probably because the ignorant all tend to worship isolated aspects of deity and to forget their essential oneness; but certain learned Fathers of the Church, notably Dionysius, made a very special study of the Heavenly Hierarchies and there is much curious and interesting lore in all great religions about these mighty forces, which are invariably associated with the heavenly bodies. This is a branch of comparative religion which will probably appeal very strongly to the thoughtful and earnest son of Aquarius as worthy of examination. If he carries his studies further on the same cautiously comparative lines, he will gradually realise that the teaching of Astrology, taken at its highest and best, really places religious dogma before him in a more acceptable form than any creed or catechism however carefully compiled, can possibly do. Even the study of Astronomy will move any man strong enough to bear its revelations of his own insignificance, to wonder and awe; but the observation of the outer form alone will never satisfy the whole man, and it is not until the physical Universe appeals to him as merely the Garment of God, Who is as omnipresent in the world of thought and of spiritual emotion as in the world apparent to the senses, that he is in a position to realise what it means to be in body, soul and spirit an integral part of such a wondrous Whole. In what concerns practical religion, the question "Am I my brother's keeper?" stands ever before the Aquarian's mind; and he answers it emphatically in the affirmative by giving his hearty sympathy and practical or monetary aid to active and well-organised philanthropic work; but outward forms of worship mean little or nothing to him, and there is seldom any tendency to regard one place or object as more worthy of reverence than another; so that in spite of his tender heart and upright life and disinterested conduct, the Aquarian is apt to be swept aside by the narrow-minded and the "unco guid" as a God-forsaken and utterly irreligious man. In connection with this curious tendency of modern Christianity to shut the truth seeker out of religious life, we may take the persistent discouragement by the Church of the scientific spirit of inquiry and research. The Christ may find room for the doubting Thomas among the chosen twelve, but His nominal adherents cannot follow Him so far, and the typically agnostic book of the Bible, that strange drama that tells of the doubts and sorrows of Job—a book full from end to end of characteristic Aquarian questionings—is an altogether forbidden book in the Church of Rome, so far as the laity is concerned, while not even priests are permitted to translate it. The fact that it is drama, and the style in which it is written, suggest that it was penned by a Cancerian hand, but the spirit and conclusion of the book show the unmistakable influence of Uranus over the mind of the writer, and the problems presented are such as have occupied the student from the beginning of the race.

Where wast thou when I laid the foundations of the earth?
Whereupon were the foundations thereof fastened?
By what way is the light parted?
Or the east wind scattered upon the earth?
Hath the rain a father?
Or who hath begotten the drops of dew?
Who hath put wisdom in the inward parts?
Or who hath given understanding to the mind?

And the result of all this searching is the conviction that man can know nothing, but that in the fear of the Lord—and in reverence for the wonders of the created Universe—is the beginning of wisdom.

The extreme width and tolerance of the Aquarian view make it difficult to assign to him any marked partiality for one form of observance over another. The advanced will probably show the same grave and courteous tolerance for all—and show it by preference through absenting himself impartially from everything in the way of special ritual and ceremonial. But if the inner meaning and wide universality of sacred symbols—and especially of mathematical symbols such as the circle, the cross, the triangle, the cube, the spiral, etc.—be demonstrated to him, he will certainly regard them with peculiar reverence, and among the homelier and more material objects used in the presentation of religious truth there is one which makes a particular appeal to this type. The essential sacredness of bread—the symbol of the Body of the Lord—has an inner significance that only the man of clear vision and world-wide sympathies can grasp. From time immemorial the staff of life has been associated with the thought of the Giver of all good, and His relation to the children of men; and whatever form the recognition may take, whether it be the laying of rice or maize* or simple cake of barley-meal on the altar or the presentation and dedication of the Shew-bread and of the Sacred

* *Cf* the maize mentioned as being given to Hiawatha, in Longfellow's poem—Hiawatha representing the Saviour in these Indian legends. These are other strange old tales and assertions about the bringing down of wheat from Heaven, possibly echoed in the Manna story of the Old Testament.

Wafer—he who gives earnest consideration to the subject will find his heart and his imagination caught and held by the thought underlying the act. It may be that he will prefer the silent thanksgiving of the Quaker to the elaborate celebration of the Mass—that will depend on his race and environment—but the idea that bread is the symbol of something beautiful and holy—that besides being the Gift of God it actually represents the toil and endurance of striving humanity—will appeal to him very strongly, and he will dislike intensely to see it wasted or neglected, allowed to go mouldy or hard, or thrown aside to be trampled underfoot in the dust—a sight too frequent in the prosperous England of to-day. In Italy and other Catholic countries, the maid-servant who drops a piece of broken bread by mistake, raises it devoutly to her lips and kisses it in apology; and the tourist who smiles in a superior manner over such "rank superstition" would do well to carry home with him some thought of the ancient teaching from which such custom has arisen; and, duly pondering it, learn to impart to both the employers and the employed in his own land, some Aquarian enthusiasm for the value and the dignity of human labour, and some reverence for its most appropriate symbol.

Physical Characteristics

The influence of this sign often shows physically in remarkable nobility of feature, and especially of profile. It is emphatically the sign of the man, and even in the undeveloped specimens there is never any suggestion in form or feature of any of our brethren of the lower brute creation. The dispassionate and platonic tendency of the type in its emotional life finds a curious echo in the physical vehicle, for the men not infrequently show some feminine trait, and the women some characteristic that is censured in them as masculine. Sometimes a man otherwise well proportioned will have a breadth of hip almost as great as his breadth of shoulder, suggesting that his manly form has somehow been built upon a feminine skeleton*; and narrow hips and a masculine habit of movement and posture have been noted in exceptionally fine and essentially womanly specimens of this type. As a rule these people are tall and fair, with blue or grey eyes, deep-set and wide apart; and many of them have the student's trick of the

* Astrologers observe with interest that doctors are now describing people who in structure or measurement show characteristics of both sexes, as "Uranians." The type is increasingly common, as humanity is at present responding freely to the influence of Aquarius.

slightly drooping head, suggesting that the thoughts revolving in the busy brain have actual weight. Their voices are gentle, and somewhat monotonous, and they seldom laugh; but many of them have a peculiarly winning and delightful smile which has a special charm from its unexpectedness. At times when some enthusiastic or energetic friend is attempting to goad them into making a prompt decision about something that seems to him important, their habitually grave expression changes to one of serious anxiety, and transverse wrinkles of worry appear on the broad forehead. Their movements are generally as leisurely as their thoughts, but in spite of their serene and tranquil ways they can be exceedingly out-spoken and even severe at times—especially if what has roused them is some manifestation of the vices they detest most heartily—slyness, hypocrisy and double-dealing. Nothing will shake their conviction that the truth ought to be trusted, and those who tell it so ingeniously as to give a false impression to their hearers without actually uttering a falsehood themselves, arouse Aquarian indignation as strongly as those who pervert it or keep it back.

Health Aquarius is said by the older astrologers to "rule the blood" and the only characteristic symptom of Aquarian ill-health is a sluggish circulation, manifesting in cold hands and feet and sometimes in chilblains. Friendship and fresh air are the best remedies, and a walking tour amid beautiful scenery with congenial companionship is an ideal prescription which will work wonders. The thoughts should be turned frequently in the direction of the advantages of good health and the duty to others of keeping one's own body in order through obedience to nature's laws; for the type is somewhat phlegmatic, and apt in consequence to be a little lazy, especially at the primitive stage.

Poesy alone can tell her dreams ;—
With the fine spell of words alone can save
Imagination from the sable chain
And dumb enchantment. Who alive can say
" Thou art no poet—may'st not tell thy dreams " ?
Since every man whose soul is not a clod
Hath visions ; and would speak, if he had loved,
And been well nurtured in his mother tongue.

KEATS.

Sorrow is hard to bear, and doubt is slow to clear,
Each sufferer says his say, his scheme of the weal and the woe ;
But God has a few of us whom he whispers in the ear ;
The rest may reason and welcome ; 'tis we musicians know.

BROWNING.

♓ PISCES ♓

THE FISH.

The Sign of the

POET OR INTERPRETER

A mutable watery sign.

Keynote—Love.

Watchword—Unity.

Ruler—Neptune.

♆

Mystical Gems—Chrysolite, Moonstone.

Colour—Pale Heliotrope? *Metal*—Aluminium?

Physical Manifestation—Solution.

Mental Manifestation—Insight.

Our revels now are ended, these our actors,
As I foretold you, were all spirits, and
Are melted into air, into thin air:
And like the baseless fabric of this vision,
The cloud-capt towers, the gorgeous palaces,
The solemn temples, the great globe itself,
Yea, all which it inherit, shall dissolve;
And, like this insubstantial pageant faded,
Leave not a rack behind. We are such stuff
As dreams are made on, and our little life
Is rounded with a sleep.

THE TEMPEST.

From the unmanifested all the manifested stream forth at the coming of day; at the coming of night they dissolve, even in That called unmanifested. This multitude of beings, going forth repeatedly, is dissolved at the coming of night; by ordination, O Pârtha, it streams forth at the coming of day. Therefore, verily there existeth, higher than that Unmanifested, ANOTHER UNMANIFESTED, *eternal, which, in the destroying of all beings, is not destroyed. . . He, the highest Spirit, O Pârtha, may be reached by unswerving devotion to Him alone, in whom all beings abide, by whom all this is pervaded.*

THE SONG OF THE LORD, OR BHAGAVAD GÎTÂ.

CHAPTER XII.

THE PISCARIAN TYPE

THE ruling deity associated with this sign is Neptune, the God of the *Sea*—that wonderful world of waters which is the most fitting physical symbol of the astral, emotional, or psychic plane. The ocean, even when apparently at rest, is never absolutely still, but always stirred by natural ebb and flow and mysterious undercurrent. Steel cannot grave it, nor hot iron brand, but it answers by a quiver to every passing breeze; and as a pebble cast into its depths sends vibrations travelling far and wide in every direction, so some message of joy, of danger or of anger, thrown into the midst of a multitude of men and women, awakens and unites their emotional natures, sending ripples of mirth, great waves of shuddering panic, or stormy billows of malice and hate through the entire crowd. The sea mirrors the sky above it; its waters rest upon the solid earth beneath. So does emotion bind thought to action and carry the fruits of action back again to the realms of thought; and it is through the gradual evolution of the emotional or psychic body that a man learns to choose aright his pleasures and his pains, and to look behind and beyond them for something that will outlast either. Further, it is through this process of emotional development that salvation,—the true *health* of the whole man in body, soul and spirit—is attained. For the heart of man once aroused from indifference and lethargy by realising its relation to the heart of the universe—in other words, by the process of conversion—yearns upwards for right thought or heavenly wisdom, and downwards for liberation through right action, and thus, gradually, the whole triple nature is unified, perfected and healed of all its follies and flaws. Consequently we find that Neptune, the ruler of this psychic plane, was hailed by his ancient worshippers as the "Saviour" —the Power that stirs and awakens the emotions and guides them aright; and that the symbol given into his hand is the Trident—a Ruler three-fold emblem, used by him to still the tumult of the waves, and calm the troubled waters into repose. Like the element over which he reigns, he is represented as sometimes asleep, and sometimes in a state of violent agitation; and his form is not unlike that of Jupiter, kingly and dignified, with flowing beard, and noble brow, but attended by *fish*—the symbols of this sign, instead of by the eagle. He is the brother of Jupiter and Pluto, and stands for the second person in the Greek Trinity when that Trinity is personified.

The deity corresponding to this aspect of Divine energy in Indian mythology is Vishnu,* whose title, "The Preserver," very strongly suggests "The Saviour" of the classic writers, and shows us a very striking resemblance between both systems of teaching and our own familiar Christian mode of expression. The analogy is further accentuated by the fact that it is Vishnu who is said to come to the rescue of mankind by incarnating periodically on earth in some practically helpful form, thus acting as teacher and guide to the developing race. Love is the greatest and deepest and most enduring of the emotions —the emotion which gives the strongest impulse to self-sacrifice—,so such divine incarnation—the taking on of physical limitations for the benefit of others—is naturally ascribed to the presiding deity of the psychic or emotional plane; and it is therefore peculiarly fitting that the members of the early Christian Church should have chosen Pisces, the fish, as the †emblem of their religion—the sign by which they recognised each other in the days of danger and persecution. It is also interesting to note the constant recurrence of the watery element in the Gospel story. Our Lord is described as walking on the waves and stilling their tumult, an assertion which can be interpreted both psychically and physically. He chose His disciples among fishermen and their friends, gave them fish to eat, and taught them so to cast their nets that they might bring great multitudes of fish to land *with*

---

* The Hindoo teaching really acknowledges seven planes, but four cannot be symbolised effectually. They are suggested by the *four heads* of Brahma, the first Person. The second Person of the Trinity is described in Assyrian, Celtic and many other religions as the *Saviour* or *Mediator*

† The cross is a pre-Christian symbol found all over the world, and was adopted by the Church as its special symbol at a comparatively late date It is interesting to note the prominence once more given to the fish in Christian art and architecture of the present day.

the net still unbroken. Would that their successors in authority had always striven for the same end!

Regarded simply as a form of energy, Neptune represents the dissolving or unifying principle as opposed to the differentiating and separative tendencies typified astrologically by Vulcan and Mars. Mars especially drives man's energies downwards towards the physical plane, giving him an eager desire for action and teaching him primarily to fight for his own hand—making of him, in fact, an ego, and sometimes also an egoist. The Power represented by Neptune and Pisces withdraws a man from the warfare of the physical plane and sets him longing and yearning first for emotional experiences, then for a wider knowledge and a deeper consciousness, and ultimately for full and perfect union with the Divine.

Evolved Type

In seeking to understand the children of Neptune the above definition of its power will be our safest guide. The strength of the typical Piscarian lies in his ideals and aspirations rather than in his actions. He has little or no worldly ambition, cares nothing for rank or place or power; seldom succeeds in making money, and rarely accumulates it. He is indifferent about restrictions and limitations in this earthly life, so long as the inner self is left free to feel and to dream and to grow according to the laws of its own nature. Thus, many people born under this sign are attracted to the cloister, or imprison themselves voluntarily within the limits of house or studio, garden or library, shrinking from the society of their fellow men, and from anything like competition, rivalry and strife. Many others go to sea, or spend all available recreation time within the narrow confines of yacht or fishing smack, preferring the silent world of waters to the most beautiful scenery on the face of this earth. With the vast ocean below and the star-spangled sky above, with only a few frail boards between them and the abyss, they rest content and calm and fearless; for solitude and solitary musing are very frequently the luxuries most prized by people of this type, especially if their lives are passed in uncongenial and unsuitable surroundings.

And yet it is difficult to say that any particular profession is impossible or unsuitable for a Piscarian. On the whole, individual commercial enterprise is least likely to be a success, and the son of Neptune will do wisely to consult some clear-headed man of business before choosing his investments; but if the business signs—Taurus and Virgo—are well accentuated in his horoscope, and aspects are favourable, it is possible that the quick intuition and plastic mind given by Pisces may favour daring undertakings in this or other lines of ambition rather than hamper them. But as a rule the Sun, the Moon, the ruler or any striking group of planets in Pisces must be taken as inimical to worldly prosperity, because these positions indicate that the native will never make it his first consideration, but rather tend to sacrifice it to his ideals and aspirations, and to the imperious need he feels for harmony and inward peace. Curiously enough, it is this yearning for unity and for the sense of completion which carries many of the children of Neptune on to the stage, which, in some ways, seems to be the last place one would expect to find them. It may to a certain extent prove trying and uncongenial, but the actual work of interpretation will always give these people intense delight, and they are almost invariably capable of undertaking some form of it. Receptivity of mind makes them accept the thought of the poet or playwright as naturally as if it were their own, and once possessed or inspired by that, they positively revel in calling up the necessary emotions. These, in their turn, dominate the action, and so transform, for the time being, the whole personality. Further, the psychic sensitiveness peculiar to the type, gives Piscarians a very special pleasure in the feeling that they are in touch with their audience; for that is to them a kind of foretaste of the enlarged consciousness for which they yearn. In proportion to their delight in such achievements, however, is the measure of their despondency after failure; and, in some cases, fits of unreasoning apprehension beforehand, and all the horrors of actual stage fright, are among their recurrent woes. Analysis of the horoscopes of successful actors and actresses will show an amazing preponderance of this particular influence; and there are few, if any, of the first rank without at least one planet in the sign. To name only a small selection of widely differing types, Garrick, William Terriss, Mrs. Kendal, Mr. F. R. Benson, Henry Irving*, and J. L. Toole all have it emphasised in one

* Henry Irving is the least Piscarian of those named, and his success was really due to the power and personal magnetism given by his ascendant, Scorpio Still, he had the mystic outlook from Uranus, and love of interpretive art from Venus, both placed in Pisces; but he was handicapped by a lack of plasticity in the physical vehicle:—the true cause of the mannerisms so easily imitated by lesser men. Mr Forbes Robertson is another Scorpio actor. He has Neptune in Pisces, well aspected; which adds inspiration to his magnetic power.

way or another, and Miss Ellen Terry has actually a quadruple accentuation, consisting of Neptune, the Sun, Saturn and Mercury! Apart from theatrical life altogether, the true-born Piscarian generally learns sooner or later that "all the world *is* a stage," and whether he plays lead or simply walks on as a humble super, he realises more fully than it is possible for other men to do that his little life is only part of a stupendous whole, and that the setting of the scene is transitory and elusive, and of very little importance compared with the rendering of the piece. This is why many Piscarians are peculiarly fitted to enter the church, the army, and the navy, or to take employment in large institutions such as hospitals, universities, colleges, and theatres. Any kind of service which emphasises the fact that the whole is greater than any of its parts, or teaches a man to regard himself as a mere unit, whose duty it is to put self and self-seeking absolutely aside, gives opportunity for the rapid assimilation of the special lessons assigned to the sons and daughters of this sign. Government service is peculiarly suited to this very improvident type; because government salaries, though small, are steady and regular, and a suitable provision is generally made for old age. Life is often simplified for highly-developed Piscarians by the fact that they accept celibacy easily, and many, especially among the women, lead cheerful and busy lives as maiden aunts or other unimportant members of the household, unselfishly content to sink their own individuality and to fill up the odd corners of family life.

Primitive Type

Manifesting in humanity in the early stages, the power of Neptune seems to our blind eyes merely negative, if not wholly malevolent, for the primitive Piscarian is almost invariably a burden and anxiety to his friends. Lacking the spur of worldly ambition, and even, sometimes, the rudimentary desire to be self-supporting and independent, he drifts aimlessly through life, always waiting vaguely for the prompter and incapable of using his discrimination when the prompt comes. He will accept any suggestion that chimes in with the emotional condition of the moment, and, as a variety of emotional experiences is the true path of his evolution, that condition is constantly changing. Like a rudderless boat he drifts on a sea of sensations, caught by every passing current, driven by every wind that blows. The wistful yearnings for completion which make the real compelling force of the sign and which will ultimately take the form of a devout desire to become One with the Father, are mistranslated into cravings for creature comforts, for emotional excitement and, too often, for stimulants, opiates, and narcotics; and over-indulgence in these naturally leads to physical break-down, to hallucinations, delusions, delirium and many sorrowful forms of insanity. Even the fitness for celibacy and the monastic life which shows later on as a favourable influence, has its dark side in the earlier stages, merely manifesting as a peculiar inability to understand the sanctity of the marriage contract or to appreciate the qualities of faithfulness and loyalty; and even, in certain cases, leading to unwholesome and morbid perversions of the natural instincts. When highly developed these people are pure and passionless and yet at the same time very loving; but in the earlier stages they are prone to strange and unaccountable adorations and antipathies which they do not attempt to control—revelling in the emotional exercise of a devotion that is positively abject, or shrinking with shuddering repulsion from some apparently harmless and innocent fellow creature. As they are always more or less psychic and intuitional even when not actually mediumistic, these vagaries may be the result of telepathic communication or possibly of the latent memories of former lives, and so actually have some sort of comprehensible basis; but as obsession and hallucination are among the dangers of this sign, it is never wise to accept such an explanation too readily; and in every case the duty of self-control in such matters ought to be strongly insisted on. In fact the whole training and education of this type ought to be such as to lead them steadily in the direction of greater balance and self-restraint in every kind of way. Otherwise nervous irritability, varied by sudden explosions of temper of a type suggesting positive "possession" by the demon of anger, will become habitual, and in the case of women, the tyranny of tears will make the lives of those who have to live with them a burden. At the lowest depths, the cloistered seclusion appropriate to the type is often replaced by the prison cell; for though incapable of daring crime on their own account, Piscarians easily drift into the position of cat's-paw or scape-goat, and are extremely helpless in the matter of self-defence. They also lack the sense of proprietorship, and consequently cannot see why they should not be allowed to help themselves from the superfluity of others. Commercial integrity and conscientious discharge of debts are in fact altogether beyond them; and though, if they have money they are always quite willing to part with it, they can never understand why someone else—who has the cash at hand—should not meet their obligations for them without demur.

Physical Characteristics

Manifesting physically, the influence of Neptune and of Pisces shows a characteristic indifference to the possibilities of the physical plane. The stature is generally insignificant, the muscles weak, the limbs short, especially from the knee downwards. The skin is very soft and easily wrinkled, the hair fine and silky, of a nondescript colour; the eyes light, and the complexion pallid. The best-looking specimens have better proportions, clear complexions, dimples instead of wrinkles, and a golden gleam as of sunshine in their hair: but actual beauty among the sons and daughters of Neptune is very rare. Even the comelier specimens are apt to have their plain moments, and the type at its worst is very plain. Its disadvantages are, however, generally atoned for by the plasticity of feature, mobility of expression and extraordinary grace of movement and gesture associated with the sign. Even the somewhat deficient colouring of those born under it seems to change and brighten as they forget themselves and their shyness in really congenial society; but their psychic sensitiveness to surroundings often makes them fail to do themselves justice, and it is only at inspired moments that they are seen at their very best. A touch of the Neptune influence often adds great charm to childhood, and even in old age a certain child-like grace is sometimes retained, making the personality extremely lovable. The step-sons of Neptune, as the primitive specimens are called, are to be sought among the most shiftless and incapable and unfortunate of mankind; and they usually look the part—weak in health, consumptive, morbidly shy, depressed and depressing. They are generally extremely sensitive to the influence of alcohol or other deleterious drugs, so that very little self-indulgence disgraces them in the eyes of their fellowmen, and brings on deplorable reaction, which in its turn drives them again to excess. Luckily such types rarely survive to old age, so that their state of abject misery is seldom so prolonged as the severer discipline meted out to sinners of a more robust type.

In Drama and Fiction

Piscarians are common in literature, but rarely play leading parts. An exception is found in Hamlet, Prince of Denmark, the precise interpretation of whose character has been the subject of so much debate. He is psychic, emotional, and impressionable; prone to moods of loneliness and despondency, liable to sudden outbursts of severity which contrast strangely with his habitual gentleness; deeply religious, yet unrestrained, in his flights of daring speculation, by mere formalities of orthodox belief; so utterly devoid of ambition that he declares he could be bounded in a nut shell, and yet count himself king of infinite space; always on guard against his own sensitiveness to suggestion, and insistent in demanding proof that his ghostly visitant is no goblin damned, luring him to destruction; keenly interested in acting, and exquisitely true to the best principles of the actor's art in his discourse thereon. Students of Astrology who wish to have a clear conception of the tendencies of this type cannot do better than read and re-read his utterances, remembering, as they strive to realise the character, that, if recent authorities on Shakespeare are correct, we have in it, inextricably mixed up, a youth of twenty and a man of thirty. For it is looked upon by many as practically certain that, in the original draft of the play, Shakespeare gave poignancy and pathos to the plot by making the unfortunate Prince really a student at College, as certain of the lines seem to show· and that his age was afterwards advanced ten years, and some of the more philosophic speeches added, because Burbage was too fat and heavily built an actor to play so youthful a part effectively. The play, by judicious omission, can still be taken either way, but at whatever age the character is read, the influence of Neptune sways it, from beginning to end. Richard II. suggests the Piscarian type at a less highly-developed stage, and at the very other end of the scale we have Jenny Wren's unfortunate Father, "Mr. Dolls" in *Our Mutual Friend*—too pitiful and degraded a specimen of humanity to be described as a "burlesque," in spite of the humour with which Dickens has drawn it.

Health As Neptune is a planet which calls a man to consciousness on the higher planes, its summons is naturally sometimes to be interpreted literally in a horoscope as the demand for the entire cessation of physical life; and it will be found that those who are strongly dominated by its vibrations have rarely any fear of death and are even apt to long for it at times of despondency or ill-health. They are frequently somewhat frail in physique, delicately formed and deficient in muscular power; but if the nature is finely balanced and the various activities, mental, emotional and physical, are wisely guided into suitable channels, it is probable that they will enjoy excellent bodily health and fair length of days. Very careful attention to hygienic laws and scrupulous cleanliness of person, habitation and clothing, with plenty of fresh air and sunshine, are their best protectors on the physical plane, and these will also react favourably on the emotional and mental planes. A good vigorous tubbing followed by friction, does wonders in the way of dispelling the gloom and despondency due to contact with a psychic atmosphere that is uncongenial or unclean. If at the same time mental affirmations of a wholesome and robust type are made and held, strength, both moral and physical, will quickly return, and the sunshiny sweetness of temper which ought to be characteristic will re-assert itself. These fits of despondency and depression due to infection are naturally more appalling in the primitive specimen, who has neither moral back-bone nor mental ability to help him in the fight against them, and whose psychic and clairvoyant faculties—so easily stimulated in Piscarians—may produce all kinds of hallucinations and delusions due to ignorance of astral conditions or misinterpretation of astral vision. There is also danger of obsession—of domination by the will of another, whether incarnate or discarnate—and as such experiences are always very exhausting and sometimes induce sleeplessness, there may be a recurrent temptation to have recourse to alcohol and drugs. Total abstinence is the only really safe rule for Piscarians if they desire to live at their highest level and maintain their self-control; and a simple vegetarian diet is often advisable; some of the finest specimens finding it necessary to confine themselves to cereals and fruit, and avoiding even such mild stimulants as tea and coffee.

Literary Style

The literary style of the Piscarian is particularly hard to define and practically impossible to parody, for it is so plastic that it tends to vary with the mood of the moment, and not only adapts itself very easily to the subject in hand, but takes on tone and colour and form according to the circumstances of production and the audience addressed. It abounds in delicate shades of expression and is characterised by peculiarly appropriate and therefore illuminating turns of phrase. It is subtly suggestive without innuendo, graceful and facile without weakness, absolutely natural and yet never commonplace. Even if the passing years have made the diction of those who used it old-fashioned, their works retain their hold upon the reading public, because they deal with underlying realities, even while apparently discussing the ordinary events of everyday life. Such a gift of expression, or rather of interpretation, belongs pre-eminently to the poet, and all who feel the divine afflatus, and whose works have in them a touch of what is called *inspiration*, are really responding to the influence of Neptune at its highest and best. Of course every human being possesses this power of response at least potentially, but even among those who have eyes to see and ears to hear, the power of bringing the message through to the physical plane for the benefit of others is not always at command, and the majority are prone to relapse into a form of utterance that is trivial or dull. The true son of Neptune never does. When inspiration fails him he sinks dumb, and consequently although his output of work—his actual achievement—may be small in bulk, he usually attains a very high level in the work he produces. He gives everything—or nothing!—is far too fastidious to publish rubbish, and, even when he has done his best, he is often oppressed and disheartened by a sense of failure, because what he felt and saw and *knew* with absolute certainty during the glorious moments of inspiration is so inadequately represented by the fragment of composition which remains after the vision has faded.

At his supreme moments, the Piscarian's realisation of the essential unity of all things is so overwhelming, that sense-impressions are transcended, and their record blended or fused together in some measure, so that colour and sound and emotion become one and indivisible: a state of consciousness which finds utterance in marvellously pregnant phrases, full of vitality and essentially true, but which are nevertheless condemned by the colder critics because the metaphor is mixed or the adjectives misapplied. Thus when Keats—whose life and personality strongly suggest the Piscarian type—used the expressions "purple riot" and "argent revelry" they aroused the unmitigated scorn and contempt of those who clung to conventional usage; but they captured the ear of the true lover of literature all the same, because they actually presented living pictures to the inner eye that lengthy paragraphs would have failed to suggest: and they have consequently passed into current use among the minor poets.

Those who wish to study this blending of colour and emotion in another form should turn to the works of Fra Angelico, the saintly Dominican of Fiesole, and should note especially the wondrous rainbow hues of the draperies that clothe the happy souls and radiant angels in his lovely presentations of Paradise. His clairvoyance is attested by the fact that his colour symbolism is precisely that of modern visionaries, who in this more scientific age define and analyse and describe the impressions made upon the inner eye by psychic visions of thought-forms and auras, and who may recognise the clear yellow of intellect and the orange of pride, the scarlet of anger and the blue of devotion, the rose-colour of love and the violet of spirituality, in the colour schemes of this mediæval monk. Among other painters the works of a modern pre-Raphaelite—Edward Burne-Jones—make a somewhat similar impression on the astrological lover of art, an impression considerably deepened by perusal of the very charmingly written biography by his wife. Like the Beato Angelico, Burne-Jones painted the very souls of things—the inner realities veiled by the outer form. Both men were upright and pure in heart, gentle in speech and manner, and intensely devout. The Italian painter was a recluse, and the Englishman, despite his Protestant up-bringing and his happy marriage, was ever harping on the charms and sweetness of the celibate religious life. Perhaps he was a reincarnation of his great predecessor, and such utterances were only the half-awakened memories of his years of labour in the quiet cloisters of St. Mark, or on the sunny slopes of Fiesole; or possibly he had merely been a favourite pupil or friend. In any case he had the same idealism and the same insight, and both in his life and in his work showed forth the strivings of the poet soul to find expression. The fact that there is no planetary accentuation on Pisces in Burne-Jones' horoscope impels one to the conclusion that it must have been strong by position, otherwise it would have been obscured by Virgo, which is accentuated very heavily, by the Sun, Mercury, Mars and Saturn. Pisces rising would throw this accent very suitably on the house of marriage and of partnership; for much of Burne-Jones' best work was actually done in partnership with William Morris, and harmony in the home-life was an important factor in his success.

A more pathetic picture is brought before us when we turn to the field of musical expression, and seek for our typical Piscarian there. The horoscope of Frédéric Chopin—the hour of whose birth was duly registered by his parents—shows the sign of Pisces *descending with the Sun in it;* which points out an astrological truth of which students should make a mental note. Part of the contrariness and incomprehensibility of this sign seems to be expressed by the fact that it is often much more powerful descending than ascending—*and especially is this to be observed in the case of highly developed souls who live chiefly on the mental plane.* The quality it gives is receptivity. Rising, it makes the body receptive, plastic and easily influenced; at the Zenith it does the same for the soul, or emotional nature—a position which it probably held in the case of Dante—and descending it opens the portals of the mind. It will easily be seen that of these three gifts, that of the receptive mind is of the highest importance, and the one which would most directly result in inspirational work, whether in poetry, music or art. Jupiter, the planet of the mind, placed in Pisces, has a somewhat similar effect as this angular position of descendant; and when the sign descends with Jupiter in it, *or with Neptune in any powerful position,* then we may, with favourable aspects, look for very high achievement indeed. Most astrologers are agreed —for various reasons—in thinking that Pisces was in this descendant position when Shakespeare was born, in which case his horoscope works out with Neptune in Gemini at the very Zenith, thus making the Piscarian influence a dominant one, and accounting for his marvellous intuition and inspiration, as well as for the perfect ease and naturalness of his expression. It would also account for the type of part allotted to him as a player. The Virginian actor does not, as a rule, play the hero, but often excels in character parts and can, even in extreme youth, give a very faithful and discriminating rendering of age and infirmity. It is recorded on the authority of Shakespeare's own brother, who was a member of his company, that the poet's interpretation of the beautifully drawn character of Adam, the aged retainer in "As You Like It," was exquisitely pathetic and affecting. This Virginian trait and tendency *plus* the inspirational influence of Neptune and Pisces would fully account for the verdict of another contemporary critic who pronounces him "excellent in the quality he professes"; a phrase which is always understood as referring directly to his work as an actor, although the passage from which it is quoted is more concerned with singing his praises as a poet and a man.

One of the tests of good composition is an exceedingly simple one. —*try to learn a passage from the author by heart.* If his verse—or his prose—absolutely refuses to be memorised, and if there is an irresistible inclination on the part of the learner to reverse or alter the position of words or phrases, there is some flaw in the style—some misfit or miscarriage in the process of translating the thought into utterance. Nobody misquotes the line—so often taken as an example of perfect expression:—"After life's fitful fever he sleeps well"; and the prose of Shakespeare is almost as easy to learn as his verse, because whatever his subject may be—however lofty and great—he can almost invariably place it before us in the simplest and most natural and at the same time most illuminating form. Something of this natural simplicity, together with a certain delightful quaintness of expression, is to be found in the prose of two lesser men, Charles Lamb and Izaak Walton, who call for mention as showing Piscarian traits both biographically and in their writings; but as usual, if we want to see the characteristic literary qualities given by the sign in full perfection, we must turn to sacred literature, and pass on to the consideration of the religious tendencies of its children.

Religion

Ask any group of people who have been fairly well grounded in Bible study, which of the writers in the New Testament they can quote most easily, and the majority will assuredly answer "St. John," and the quotations which rise to their lips will probably be taken from the most mystic—and consequently the most Piscarian—of his chapters. "I am the vine, ye are the branches," is as clear and concise and illuminating a statement of the essential unity of the human and the divine as has ever been penned; and the passage beginning "Let not your hearts be troubled," is so exquisitely perfect from the literary point of view that it can be easily learnt by a child of five, and once committed to memory is a precious possession for life. Sometimes the writer of these and similar passages falls into a series of quiet meditations which begin or conclude with the vivid realisation of some tremendous truth; and in the Book of Revelation we find lyrical outbursts characterised by the blending or mixture of metaphor and by that rapid substitution of one image for another which is so frequent in the writings of the seers that come under the influence of Neptune. Among the saints and mystics of the early Christian

Church many suggest the domination of that planet and especially is this the case with St. Francis of Assisi, whose most famous hymn proclaims his love for his brother the Sun and his sister the Moon and shows his glorious certainty of the essential unity of all consciousness. Biographical details are also instructive and worth study. The life of St. Francis is one long record of ceaseless devotion and self-sacrifice, and the descriptions of his physical characteristics and constitution also point to the influence of the mystic sign of the Fish. His stature was insignificant, his health fragile, and he had what his devoted disciples envied as "the gift of tears." He was utterly indifferent to the ties of home and kindred, regarding all men equally as his brethren. He chose "The Lady Poverty" for his bride, and preached the excellence and beauty of the celibate life. He was gentle, quiet and unassuming—as humble-minded as a little child; but when actually face to face with a crowd of people he could hold them so absolutely entranced by the power of his preaching that his listeners declared it to be "inspired." Lastly, he was extremely psychic—a visionary from his youth up.

This mystic sign of love and self-sacrifice rules Judæa and has been always associated with the dawn and development of Christianity; but the Piscarian influence can be found in the sacred lyrics of all nations, and each ancient religion has in it some kind of ritual which suggests the typical outward form that the devotion connected with Pisces and with Neptune would find congenial as symbolising in some way the influx of Divine Grace and its uplifting effect upon the worshipper. All the wonderful sacred symbolism connected with the Cup and with wine should be studied carefully in connection with this sign. The simple libation of the Eastern devotee, the stately Mass in St. Peter's at Rome, and the Highland Communion on the heathery hillside are all akin to far older forms of religious observance—Jewish, Mithraic, Cymric, and others older yet—and are all connected with the idea of a great out-pouring which is to increase spiritual vitality and so lead to the true health or salvation of the whole man. The fact that such ceremonial has sometimes become degraded to a terribly low level—as was the case with the rites of Bacchus—should not blind us to the inward beauty of the ideal celebration.

The physical vehicle of the vitalising principle that pervades the whole vine is the sap, which, circulating through every leaf and twig and tender bud, carries with it health and energy and endless possibilities of future development. In the animal kingdom "The blood is the life," and plays the part of vivifier throughout the whole frame, and, as is often the case, a scientific examination of the mystical statements that have been made by great teachers in times past, only makes them show forth more meaning. Thus we are told in the first epistle of St. John that *the blood of Jesus Christ . . cleanseth us from all sin;* but we now know that there is only one way in which blood can cleanse, and that is from within. If there are impurities or poisonous secretions lurking about our bodies, it is the blood that carries them away and gets rid of them through the natural processes connected with the nutrition and renewal of the tissues. If the circulation is unsatisfactory, impeded or inefficient, we must get rid of all obstacles to its freedom of movement,* increase the supply and improve the quality of the blood. Again, if a wound has been made by some unclean instrument, the physician encourages bleeding so that all impurities may be washed away, even at the expenditure of a certain amount of vital force. But we also know that nothing can be more dangerous and deadly than blood that is stagnant and apart from the living body; and any attempt to wash anything whatever in *that* would be madness.

Mystically interpreted then, the blood is the life-principle, the sap of the great tree whose branches we are, and so represents the source of that Divine Energy which wills to manifest in and through us. If by binding ourselves with chains of guilt and attempting to grow in wrong and unnatural directions, we hinder the full flow of that wonderful sap, we wither away, and the only way back to true health or salvation is by removing all barriers and restrictions between us and the divine Source of all. The best method of doing so is to come into close personal relation with the Master who points out the path. For the Christian disciple Jesus Christ is the Way and the Truth and the Life; and the true Mystics of all religions who can rise to the heights of perfect comprehension and know the essential unity of all spiritual life, can understand this declaration and accept it.

So also, in the light of such an interpretation, the assertion that

* This increase is sometimes obtained by transferring a quantity of healthy blood from the veins of some self-sacrificing friend, physician or relative, to the veins of the sufferer—also a suggestive illustration.

Jesus Christ is always willing and ready to give His life-blood as a ransom—a means of liberation—for the many still in the bondage of sin, takes a fuller and deeper meaning. All characteristically Christian teaching is founded on this conception, and its beauty has never been entirely lost sight of by the Church, although the symbolism of the early founders has often been misconstrued or crudely set forth. There are so-called Christian hymns that revel in a gory imagery that is gross and sensual and entirely misapplied; and the more ignorant among our street preachers and missionaries fall into the same kind of error as the writers of such verses. "The blood of slaughtered beasts" may be used as a propitiatory sacrifice in the ceremonial of older and more primitive faiths; but the ritual that was chosen by Christians as a reminder of that gift of grace which came through the incarnation of the Christ, was the simple act of drinking from the wine cup, which was passed from hand to hand when the family gathered together after the toil of the week, for the benediction of the evening meal with which the Sabbath Day began. The degradation of this custom of the first converts, into the riotous "love-feasts" of a later generation, necessitated some change that should recall the dignity and importance of the rite; and the scene of the communion was transferred from the peaceful home circle to the basilica or church, when the Mithraic* ceremony, which is still carried out in the ritual of the Mass, was substituted for the Jewish ceremony of the Passover. But whatever the surroundings of the symbolic action may be, the religious significance remains the same. The worshipper is drinking in, on the higher planes, the vitalising energy or symbolic life-blood of his Lord, and so partaking of His spiritual essence; and by that act he is acknowledging his own need of healing and of help, and accepting the salvation offered to him. Is it any wonder that no legend has ever drawn the poet heart more strongly to its study or lifted it to greater heights than the legend of the Holy Grail?

There is an ancient Egyptian and astrological tradition which

* The attempt of Presbyterians and others to restore the simplicity of the older ceremonial to the Church is unsatisfactory because the Passover Supper was a family gathering and was never intended to be carried out as a temple service An interesting reversal to Druid custom has resulted, the highlanders preferring to celebrate their communion—their most sacred ceremonial—on the open hillside. Ritual is racial, and imported rites usually die or degenerate

declares that when the Sun enters a new sign at the vernal equinox a change comes over the spirit of religion, and a new aspect of the truth is revealed through the coming into incarnation of One who possesses the Divine wisdom and has the power to reveal it. "Once in every 2155 years . . . the Prince of Peace was to be reborn. He had been born as a calf in the sign of the Bull; as one of the twins in the sign of Gemini, as a beetle in Cancer, as the Lion in Leo, as the red shoot of the Vine in Virgo, as the Lord of the Balance in the Scales. . . . He was to be reborn as the lamb in the sign of the Ram, as Ichthus the Fish in the sign of Pisces." . . . "The rebirth of Atum Horus as the fish of Iusaas and the bread of Nephthys was astronomically dated to occur, and appointed to take place, in Bethlehem of the Zodiac about the year 255 B.C. at the time when the Easter Equinox entered the sign Pisces, the house of corn and bread." There is, for the ordinary reader, always a good deal of mistiness about these ancient utterances,—which are quoted from Mr. Gerald Massey's curious book *Ancient Egypt, the Light of the World*, Vol. ii., p. 734,—but the main idea underneath the elaborate symbolism is clear. Students of the doctrine of reincarnation will however note how easily the uninitiated may misunderstand the form of expression. To say that one born under Pisces or Leo is born as a fish or a lion naturally suggests metempsychosis into animal forms, a retrogression contrary to our ideas concerning the building up and evolution of mind and character; but the idea that each great teacher who comes forth to save and inspire and raise humanity has a fresh aspect of deity to show us is very beautiful. It is also, from the historical point of view, very suggestive, for while the Sun entered Taurus at the Vernal Equinox, that sign of steadfastness and of material prosperity was worshipped in Egypt as the Golden Calf. During the next great period, while the Sun gave us his Easter greeting from Aries, Moses led his people out of Egypt into the strenuous life of warfare and of wandering in the wilderness, and gave them a new teaching, associating it with the symbol of the sacrificial lamb—or young *Ram*—of the sacred Passover. Then came the turn of Pisces and, with the advent of that Power, the preaching of self-abnegation and self-sacrifice by the Buddha and the Christ. The gradual breaking down of ignorance and prejudice in the West, has shown students how very much the two great faiths of Buddhism and Christianity have in common; and as time goes on, and the study of comparative religion is given its right and proper place in the schools and colleges of this great Empire, the differences that do exist will be understood, and so reduced to their true proportions. In view of the fact that the great change from Pisces to Aquarius has been calculated by various astronomers to take place in recent years—dates varying from 1881 to 1901 having been assigned to it—it is worth while to pause for a little and ask to what point these three latest revelations have brought us. For ancient Egypt the Earth was the Lord's and the fulness thereof; and everything upon it might be considered as a symbol of something sacred and worthy of care and reverence—even to the carcase of a cat or the clay image of a creeping thing. Moses taught his people that through Right Action alone, through the practical acceptance of and obedience to the Law, could man hope to find favour with God. The next revelation appealed to the very centre of man's being, to the heart and soul of him, cheapening action and minimising the value of this earthly life, which was described as a weary pilgrimage and a vale of sorrows, a place of unceasing disappointment and tribulation, a school for the destruction of egotism and consequent growth of the spiritual nature. The Buddha viewed life on earth as an oft-recurrent calamity, and preached self-sacrifice, self-denial and devotion to duty, as the only means of liberation from the necessity of constant reincarnation on earth. Our doctrine of salvation from hell is a closely parallel teaching; for salvation is liberation, and hell is described as a state or *condition* of continual suffering. To those who attain this salvation or liberation, is promised by the Christian teacher the joy of absolute oneness with God,—and by the Buddhist, the bliss of Nirvana, which, properly understood, is precisely the same thing, namely the utter destruction of that sense of separation which is due to egotism.

In the matter of rites and ceremonies also, Buddhist and Christian might, in the early days of their respective faiths, very easily have joined hands. Both Founders swept aside ritual and observances as of little importance, thus undermining and wrecking the authority of the priesthood; and the Piscarian influence has always the same tendency to simplify the outward form, and to realise mystically the inner side of religion. Difficulty arises for the followers of these two faiths when they come into touch with people who are incapable of understanding mysticism, and who consequently require the crutch of ritual to support their steps on the upward path; for without its help they may degenerate into indifference and irreverence, as has happened among the materialistic nations of Western Europe. So far have we lost sight of the ancient altruistic ideals so beautifully set before us in the New Testament that our commercial and social procedure is actually lower than that obtaining in many nations whose standards of conduct are supposed to be far beneath our own. When the great Aquarian revelation comes, may it awaken in us those ideals of truth and honest dealing, of gentleness and consideration for the ignorant, the weak and the erring, that will carry us forward to the realisation of all that is summed up in the one great word of Brotherhood.

After Pisces, Aquarius, and after Aquarius Capricorn, and after Capricorn Sagittarius, and so the great wheel revolves, turning ever slowly backwards, while the lesser wheels bring up the signs in what seems to us their normal order.

> "The mills of God grind slowly
> But they grind exceeding small,"

and of the fine flour that they are producing, who knows the destiny or the end? What food for angels, what heavenly manna for those yet in the wilderness may not one of those minor revolutions produce! Each influence in its turn brings its own lesson. Warrior, Builder, Artist, Prophet, King; Servant, Statesman, Governor, and Counsellor; Priest or Ambassador, seeker after Hidden Wisdom, Mystic or Poet or Saint; Man is each in turn and all of them potentially always. For though the Powers are twelve they are also seven; and the seven are three, and the three are One, Infinite, Indivisible and Eternal.

To those who ask, " Where hast thou seen the Gods ? or How dost thou comprehend that they exist, and so worshippest them ? " I answer, " In the first place they may be seen even with the eyes ! In the second place, neither have I seen even my own soul, yet I honour it. Thus then, with respect to the Gods, from what I constantly experience of their power, from this I comprehend that they exist, and I venerate them."

MARCUS AURELIUS.

Part II.

ANALYTICAL

It is the stars,
The stars above us, govern our conditions.

King Lear.

Man is his own star, and the soul that can
Render an honest and a perfect man
Commands all light, all wisdom and all fate—
Nothing to him falls early, or too late,
Our acts our angels are, or good or ill,
Our fatal shadows that walk by us still.

EMERSON.

What a glorious power is given to man, never to do any action of which God will not approve, and to welcome whatever God appoints for him.—MARCUS AURELIUS.

CHAPTER I.

The Horoscope and its Message

The horoscope map is a symbolic presentation of the life and opportunities of the individual coming into incarnation at the hour and place for which it is drawn. The Circle which forms the boundary line suggests the limitations of physical existence; the Cross which cuts it symbolises the discipline of his earthly life and experience; and the Signs of the Zodiac placed around the circle represent the various influences which are ever with him, pressing forward his evolution.

Those signs indicated by the four arms of the cross—*i.e.*, the signs at the Zenith and Nadir, Ascendant and Descendant—are always important. The sign at the Zenith influences the emotions and aspirations, and consequently the choice of a profession; the sign at the Nadir generally suggests the basis of character; the sign ascending affects the outward man, his expression and action, and is therefore the most easily recognised; the sign descending indicates the elements most wanting in the native, and, consequently, the qualities desirable in his partners and redoubtable in his adversaries. Planets placed in appropriate or congenial signs, intensify and accentuate such signs; but planets in diverse or uncongenial signs modify them very considerably. For example, Mars in Aries doubles the warrior influence in a horoscope; but in Pisces he loses half his energy in awaking the poetic and mystical Pisces element to some realisation of the importance of the physical plane.

It is probable that there are ten planets in our system, *possible* that there are twelve, a planet for every sign; and many students believe that each sign has thus its own planetary representative, or "ruler," as it is termed, in our solar system. In the following list, the planets whose existence is merely surmised, are named according to the affinity of their signs with the character and powers of the

Latin deities. Taurus is associated with "the Earth-mother," under the name of Vesta, because that steadfast and kindly goddess of the hearth and home best expresses the stability of the sign. Pluto suggests what is called the "negative" side of Mars, and Vulcan the "negative" side of Mercury. Each planet is further associated with the particular element in human nature with which its influence comes most readily into touch.

The Signs and their Ruling Planets

♈	ARIES — THE WARRIOR.	*Ruler:* Mars, ♂.	The Energy; physical action, courage and passion.
♉	TAURUS — THE BUILDER.	*Ruler:* Vesta (the Earth), ♁.	The Disposition; persistence and stability.
♊	GEMINI — THE ARTIST.	*Ruler:* Mercury, ☿.	The Intellect; versatility and variety.
♋	CANCER — THE PROPHET.	*Ruler:* Diana (the Moon), ☽.	The Memory; imagination and sympathy.
♌	LEO — THE KING.	*Ruler:* Apollo (the Sun), ☉.	The Glory; radiance and renown.
♍	VIRGO — THE BUSINESS MAN.	*Ruler:* Vulcan. ☿.	The Nature; practical utility, purity and health.
♎	LIBRA — THE STATESMAN.	*Ruler:* Venus, ♀.	The Appreciation; affection, and desire for *balance* or completion.
♏	SCORPIO — THE GOVERNOR.	*Ruler:* Pluto, ♇.	The Power; progress, regeneration and liberation.
♐	SAGITTARIUS — THE COUNSELLOR.	*Ruler:* Jupiter, ♃.	The Mind; liberty of thought; wisdom.
♑	CAPRICORN — THE PRIEST.	*Ruler:* Saturn, ♄.	The Character; the sum of past experience.
♒	AQUARIUS — THE SCIENTIST.	*Ruler:* Uranus, ♅.	The Outlook, or point of view.
♓	PISCES — THE POET.	*Ruler:* Neptune, ♆.	The Emotions; dissatisfied cravings and yearnings.

The symbols here shown for Vesta, Vulcan and Pluto are quite arbitrary, being merely those of Venus, Mercury and Mars inverted.

Each of these signs is associated theoretically, or rather analogically, with one of the twelve divisions or houses of the horoscope; and each house represents a particular field of activity in which experience may be gathered. It is gathered more easily and effectually with the help of its most appropriate sign, especially if that sign is emphasised by the presence therein of its own ruler, but though modifications introduced by inappropriate signs and rulers may hinder specialisation, they are good for all-round development, and prevent any tendency to lopsidedness. The list of houses is as follows, each having a dual aspect or presentation which may be described as the higher and the lower, or the advanced and the elementary.

I.—House of the Personality: The Field of Action and Enterprise; *or*, of Strife and Warfare. *Appropriate Sign and Ruler:* Aries ♈ and Mars ♂.

This house is chiefly concerned with the battle of life or struggle for existence, and the qualifications or disqualifications for the same.

II.—House of Possessions and Repose: The Field of Peace, Prosperity and Gratitude; *or*, of Self-indulgence, Greed and Idolatry. *Appropriate Sign and Ruler:* Taurus ♉ and Vesta ⚶.

This house is chiefly concerned with the power of acquisition and (in its lower influences) the worship of the golden calf or almighty dollar.

III.—House of Brethren and Contemporaries: Field of Expression, Intellect and Art; *or*, of Exaggeration, Craftiness and Artifice. *Appropriate Sign and Ruler:* Gemini ♊ and Mercury ☿.

This house is chiefly concerned with intellectual development and all that forwards its growth and power of expression, including frequent change of environment and intercourse with equals.

IV.—House of Parents and Guardians: Field of Heredity, Home and Fatherland; *or*, of Handicaps, Racial and Local Prejudices. *Appropriate Sign and Ruler:* Cancer ♋ and Diana (the Moon) ☽.

This house is chiefly concerned with the native's early home and environment, his relations to his family or clan, and sometimes also to his teachers, especially those that have inspired and influenced him in such directions as patriotism and the duties of citizenship.

V.—House of Children, Subjects and Dependents: Field of Love, Happiness and Glory; *or*, of Lust, Excitement and Notoriety. *Appropriate Sign and Ruler:* Leo ♌ and Apollo (the Sun) ☉.

This house is chiefly concerned with the power of radiation and giving forth, and consequently speaks of the native's *standing* among his fellow men, and especially among those who are in a position to look up to him. The Sun is sometimes said to sum up the planets, and the glory of this house may be won in any of the fields of activity, commercial, scientific, artistic, etc. Indications of the *kind* of glory —or notoriety—must be sought elsewhere in the horoscope.

VI.—House of Employers and Employed: Field of Health and Active Service; *or*, of Sickness and Incompetence. *Appropriate Sign and Ruler:* Virgo ♍ and Vulcan ⚴.

This house is chiefly concerned with the service of humanity on the physical plane—feeding it, clothing it, tending it in sickness. It is often a very important house in the horoscopes of doctors and nurses.

VII.—House of Partners and Adversaries: Field of Balance and Harmony; *or*, of Opposition and Discord. *Appropriate Sign and Ruler:* Libra ♎ and Venus ♀.

This house is chiefly concerned with "duets and duels" of all kinds, thus including both partnership and quarrels, both marriage and divorce. Well aspected and favourable this house brings the happiness due to the sense of completion and harmony.

VIII.—House of Progress through Discipline and Loss. Legacies are shown here: also psychic influence of dead relatives or friends. *Appropriate Sign and Ruler:* Scorpio ♏ and Pluto ♇.

This is the true "House of Education," for it is concerned with progress of *every* kind—moral, mental and spiritual. It is always important in the horoscopes of those strongly interested in movements of progress and reform, and its older and more gloomy title of the "House of Death" is only appropriate because death is the greatest step forward known to us at our present stage of evolution. Badly aspected, malefics in this house may suggest the danger of the native's choosing the downward path of degeneration instead of the upward path of regeneration. If the house is accentuated at all he will certainly not stand still, but progress rapidly in one direction or the other, learning—possibly by bitter experience—as he goes.

IX.—House of Paternal Influence: Field of Religion, Philosophy and Law; *or*, of False Doctrine, Scepticism and Lawsuits. *Appropriate Sign and Ruler:* Sagittarius ♐ and Jupiter ♃.

This house is chiefly concerned with the mental plane and the awakening and development of the power of thought by such influences as travel in distant lands, and contact with other minds. Its influence is described as *paternal*, because the example and teaching of the father usually determine the direction of mental development; and for this reason Jupiter frequently represents the father in the horoscope, but may equally well stand for any strong stimulus to activity on the mental plane.

X.—House of Maternal Influence: Field of Ambition, Aspiration and Attainment; *or*, of Covetousness, Superstition and Failure. *Appropriate Sign and Ruler:* Capricorn ♑ and Saturn ♄.

This house is chiefly concerned with the awakening of the aspirations and ambitions and the choice of a profession or career. Hence it is associated with the maternal and feminine influence, and Saturn* often denotes the mother in the horoscope.

XI.—House of Friends and Patrons: Field of Science, Philanthropy and Humanity; *or*, of Scepticism, Sentimentalism and Cowardice. *Appropriate Sign and Ruler:* Aquarius ♒ and Uranus ♅.

This house is chiefly concerned with the attitude of the native to the rest of mankind; his power of establishing friendly and fraternal relations and of coming into touch with the mass of men represented by the public. In order to do so he must lay aside all bias and prejudice, and face facts. Hence this is the house of the truth-seeker, or scientist, and is sometimes associated with much doubt and difficulty connected with the outlook or point of view. Among the friends suggested by this house are those of the four-footed order—intelligent quadrupeds; and in many cases the sympathies of this house extend beyond mankind, to the whole animal kingdom.

XII.—The House of Large Institutions: Field of Spiritual Development; of Unification, Purification and Obedience; *or*, of Suffering, Sorrow and Bondage. *Appropriate Sign and Ruler:* Pisces ♓ and Neptune ♆.

* Astrologers disagree on this point and often reverse the signification of Saturn and Jupiter, possibly because parents often reverse *rôles*, so that the mother aids the mental development, and the father stimulates ambition and aspiration. Hence possible error in interpretation.

This house is chiefly concerned with the breaking up of egotism, and the abolition of all separative tendencies. When it is emphasised in a horoscope the native goes through experiences that make him realise himself as a mere unit—as part of the great whole. At its highest, this training leads to cosmic consciousness, and "One-ness with the Father"; but to the undeveloped and primitive man, rebelling against fate, the lesson is a weary grind, and sometimes literally, as well as figuratively, the treadmill. Slavery and imprisonment, and chains, moral, mental and physical, are associated with this house. Its dark side may even threaten the bitterness of bondage to alcoholism or other slavish habit; but only, of course, when the planets in the house are badly afflicted; and on the other hand well aspected planets in this house may indicate attainment of the highest positions in connection with Government work, with large associations, public bodies, schools, almshouses, hospitals and theatres; in short with every sort of organisation that exacts rigid regularity, punctuality, conformity and dependence on the co-operation of numbers of other people. The importance of this field of activity at its best may be seen in the horoscope of the late Queen Victoria, who had a brilliant group of planets, including the Sun, the Moon, and her own ruler, Mercury, in this mystic and difficult house of self-sacrifice and obedience. Perhaps its best title is the briefest: the House of Duty.

The foregoing definitions might easily be further elaborated, but the reader who takes the subject up seriously can think out such matters for himself. The symbols must be committed to memory before any progress can be made in reading the horoscope, but that is easily done, and it is astonishing how soon the little charts begin to assume significance even at a casual glance, and how much more living their wonderful symbolism can be, than the most speaking likeness of the professional photographer.

The first glance given to a map by an experienced astrologer always goes straight to the first house, and marks the sign and planets ascending at the moment of birth. These at once suggest the kind of personality or outer man, his methods of tackling—or evading—the practical work he is called upon to do, his manner of speech, mode of expression and general bearing towards his fellow-men. If many planets are ascending this outer man will be complex and difficult to understand, and the two most unaccountable planets in this position are Neptune and Uranus—because they have been more recently discovered than the rest, and the astrologer has no great body of tradition to guide him. The eye of the student then takes in the sign at the Zenith and its planetary modifications, which together give the clue to the emotional or psychic nature, to the likes and dislikes, the ambitions and desires, and also, to some extent, the point of view. The examination of some hundreds of horoscopes has convinced the writer that many astrologers underrate the importance of the sign at the Zenith, and in some books the assertion is made that the sign in which the Moon is placed gives the key to the emotional nature. This is quite a mistake. The Moon, as far as the writer can make out, suggests and reflects the past, thus giving a clue to habits of thought, emotion and action acquired in previous lives. These acquired habits are not always a boon and a blessing, and when the Moon is unfavourably placed in a horoscope it often represents those inherent tendencies that are apt to lead us astray against our better judgment—those faults and failings that continue to handicap and bind us even after they are recognised as such, and are described in theological parlance as our *Original Sin.*

The student having noted the position of the Moon and realised that its influence will gradually wane as fresh habits are formed during the present incarnation, passes on to the consideration of the Sun, and at once gets behind the personality to the individuality, or larger man, who is called upon to assert himself and to attain, by means of the graces and virtues and opportunities he has acquired and earned, and in spite of the handicaps and limitations imposed upon him by his own past. Roughly speaking he will probably be middle-aged—thirty-five or forty—before the sign that the Sun is in, begins to assert itself; but the further a man is advanced in evolution, the earlier will it begin to shine through and overcome all the obstacles that prevent his success. And here it must be emphatically laid down that astrological success is never to be measured by worldly standards.

"It seems otherwise to the gods," and our guardian angels are far more concerned with the way in which we carry out our appointed task, than with the amount of money or of praise that its accomplishment may bring; for the real reward for duty done is always an increase of power and responsibility. Having accomplished the task indicated by the two talents in one incarnation, the worker starts with a double share of faculty next time. If he uses it well, it will be doubled again; if he lets it atrophy it will be taken from him. That is the law of Action or *Karma*, and it is absolutely relentless as well as absolutely just. There is no finer and pithier exposition of the working out of the law of reincarnation to be found anywhere, than is to be found in this parable of the talents; and our attention is called to the fact that it has an inner meaning not obvious at first sight, by the Master's use of the significant phrase, "He that hath ears to hear, let him hear."

CHAPTER II.

Planetary Aspects

When the Sun has yielded up his information as to the kind of radiance or glory possible for the subject of our study, the other planets have their turn, and actual *conjunctions* or other close groupings which infer a gathering together and concentration of energy in special directions must be examined; after which we pass to the consideration of other aspects. This is a very elaborate subject and is quite outside the sphere of this volume, but a few general ideas about the matter may be given as a basis for further inquiry; and most earnestly I would exhort all students of Astrology to cease from frightening both themselves and other people by talking so much and so gloomily about bad or malefic aspects, and still more earnestly to leave materialistic views entirely behind when diagnosing a horoscope. The call of the angels or gods to man is always there, and always wholly good. If in our ignorance and blindness we mistake the call, and use the opportunities they give us amiss, trouble comes to us, but it comes from our own action or response. This is proved by the fact that the same aspect which will crush an ignorant and undisciplined man will call out heroic virtues in one more evolved, and it is almost impossible to predict what a great soul will do, because he has arrived at the point of ruling his stars and using the forces placed at his disposal in ways that the average man would never dream of. Roughly speaking, mediæval astrologers class everything that favours personal success of a worldly kind, and especially money-making, as *good*, and everything that favours spiritual and moral development as *bad*. The astrologer who looks at the science from a religious point of view must stand on another platform altogether. He sees through the symbol of the horoscope the man himself, the ego or thinker, brought into relation with the powers at work all around him. If that man can put himself into tune with their vibrations and respond to their stimulus harmoniously and strongly, he will take his own part as a harmonic in the music of the spheres. If he is not yet in tune, the very same play of forces will only produce a jangle and a discord in his life. What are called good aspects are those which suggest only so much stimulus as may be easily and happily answered by average humanity; whereas bad aspects suggest over-stimulus, such an out-pouring of energy as is overwhelming or bewildering to those who cannot understand and use it. Good aspects are associated with the idea of the triangle and sections thereof; bad aspects with the more powerful form of the cross and with subdivisions thereof. There are 360° in the circle of the Zodiac—30° to each sign. Planets placed at a distance of 120° from each other are in the best possible aspect, 60° coming next best, and 30° after that. Planets placed in what is called square aspect—at right angles to one another—are in the worst possible position with regard to each other because they suggest *cross*-currents; and planets at an angle of 45° or in opposition are also considered to send out an influence that is trying and undesirable. Those who have learned to take up their cross and live a life that is pure and noble and full of self-sacrifice will not find that their oppositions or even their squares disturb the current of their existence in any serious way; for "On the renunciation of the fruits of labour followeth peace;" and with that peace comes power.

In the interpretation of aspects, special heed should be paid to the *Ruler*; that is to say, to the planet sympathetically associated with the rising sign, for it is looked upon as in a peculiar sense expressing the personality of the native; and the sign it is in, and the aspects which smile or frown upon it, are given particular weight. The essential significance of all the planets should be committed to memory, and may be summarised thus:

⊙ THE SUN indicates the radiance, glory or renown; the *standing* likely to be achieved by the individual in the eyes of his fellow-men. It is therefore neither benefic nor malefic, but takes colour from the rest of the horoscope. In a good horoscope, showing excellent aspects to the Sun, the native will win honour and fair fame; in a very bad one, showing the Sun afflicted in several ways, he may only achieve notoriety or be a theme for ill-natured gossip. Note that conjunctions with the Sun, the Moon or the Ruler are not necessarily afflictions, even if the planets in conjunction are usually classed as malefics. If the evolution of the individual is so far advanced that he can respond to the higher vibrations of Uranus, Neptune, Saturn and Mars, they will do him good and not evil, all the days of his life.

☽ The Moon, suggesting habits and inherent tendencies that have been acquired in a past life and are likely to be modified in this present one, is usually classed as neither malefic nor benefic—or rather as sometimes one and sometimes the other; and naturally, for a man's habits may help or hinder him according to the problem to be faced. The Moon in Pisces, indicating the unbusinesslike habits of the poet or mystic, often prevents worldly success, but would assist artistic efforts in any direction; whereas in Taurus, a methodical and business-like sign, it is so helpful as regards finance, that there it is described as "exalted." If it is in bad aspect to the Sun or to any planet, the habitual and mechanical actions should be examined and probably reformed in some way.

♅ Uranus suggests the outlook or point of view; and also a tendency to investigate the higher branches of mathematical science or to study astronomy or astrology and occult science. If it is in bad aspect to any planet, it is probably the point of view that requires revision, and that is often a slow process and a painful one. Uranus interfering with friendship or love always means much suffering. If people cannot understand each other's point of view, reconciliation is practically impossible, and only the highly evolved can conquer such crosses as are indicated by Uranus.

♄ Saturn suggests the character, a word which sums up and summarises the amount of reserve force, mental, emotional and spiritual, accumulated by the individual during the experiences of many lives. If he has had many incarnations and used his opportunities and learnt his lessons well, his character will be of the utmost value to him in helping him to overcome obstacles and make favourable progress on the upward path; and Saturn, in spite of its evil name among students of Astrology, will puzzle them by playing the part of a benefic in unmistakable ways. If on the contrary the individual is backward in evolution—ignorant and weak—or unbalanced through lop-sided development, he will be born when Saturn is badly aspected and that planet in his horoscope will represent hardships and disappointments, obstacles, limitations and hindrances, in a word the *discipline* he has earned and which he requires for his fuller development.

♃ JUPITER is the planet of the mind, and is chiefly active in the realm of thought; but as right and wrong thinking work out respectively in health and efficiency or their opposites, and as what we *think* is really at the back of everything we *do*, his influence in the horoscope is of enormous importance, and if he is badly aspected, a very strong effort should be made to lead the thoughts into pure and healthy channels of activity. The older books declare that, even in evil aspect, Jupiter never does much harm to anyone; but lack of wisdom is the root of almost every kind of trouble and wrong-doing, and all great teachers emphasise the necessity of guarding and guiding the thought of the individual and the race. The most immediately visible result of Jupiter in unfavourable direction, is ill-health; but that reacts in turn upon the emotions, and a whole chain of causes is set up, each with its undesirable effect. To break such a chain the thinker must first wish to do so. In the words of the old theologians he must attain to *conviction of sin*, and get back to the root of it, which is spiritual darkness. Hence it is of enormous importance that Jupiter should work hand in hand with Neptune, the planet of spiritual enlightenment, and Jupiter is consequently given great value by astrologers when found in Neptune's sign of Pisces;—as great a value, in fact, as when it is in Cancer, where it is *exalted* by the characteristic gifts of that sign, Memory and Imagination, and is of immense practical use.

♂ MARS stands for the amount of physical energy and enthusiasm possessed by any individual, so that its position in the horoscope gives a clue to the particular direction in which that energy and enthusiasm will most easily find an outlet. It also stands for the amount of hope and courage available in times of difficulty and danger; or, badly aspected, for the amount of vitality squandered through ineffective, ill-considered or recklessly imprudent speech or action. It also gives a clue to the attitude habitually assumed towards the opposite sex.

♀ VENUS is generally taken as indicating the affections or powers of appreciation and sympathetic emotional response. When this planet is adverse in a horoscope, the affections are in want of control or culture—are either undeveloped or undisciplined; whereas, when it is in benefic aspect, they act as a stimulus to good work and steady progress, and add immensely to the happiness of the life.

☿ MERCURY represents the intellect, the servant of the mind, the instrument through which thought finds expression. It is particularly active and efficient in Virgo, Gemini and Aquarius, sluggish in Taurus, restless in Aries, listless in Pisces, and ordinarily serviceable in the rest. In bad aspect this planet denotes intellectual worry and the possibility of nervous break-down.

and ♇ What is said here of the value of the planets called VULCAN and PLUTO is of course only tentative, and although the orbit of the former is by some accepted as near the Sun, and there are rumours of the approaching discovery of a planet beyond Neptune, the positions are not yet ascertained, and their aspects cannot therefore be profitably discussed. The word chosen to express the Vulcanian element in man may be described as his *nature*, the stuff of which he is made, something in him which eludes analysis and cannot be accounted for. Theosophical readers will understand the suggestion that the position of Vulcan may indicate those characteristics due to the essential quality of the particular ray of manifestation to which the *ego* belongs; for the Smith among the Gods puts everyone into the furnace, and by burning away the dross, gets down to the essence of our being, thus completing and assisting the work of the unknown ruler of Scorpio, the planet that represents the *power* of the individual, which, of course, being essentially Divine Power, is only limited in its action by the limitations of a man's own personality; and these limitations gradually disappear as he evolves to his great goal—perfect union with God.

♆ NEPTUNE is left to the last, as his aspects are not yet understood, and there is practically nothing in the way of tradition to guide the student, owing to the fact that the discovery of this planet was comparatively recent. Astrologers were at first inclined to regard him as a powerful malefic, and certainly in bad aspect his discipline is apt to be severe. Loss of money, of position, of friends and of those nearest and dearest—all those experiences that make a man feel that this life on earth is not worth living—have been associated with Neptune in adverse relation to the native; and it is only when the inner ear is opened that we can hear his gentle voice whispering to us the great secret that all the changing physical conditions that seem to us so important are merely illusive and temporary, and that there is a state of consciousness in which sorrow and separation and loss are absolutely unknown—that consciousness or condition which we describe as Heaven. Consequently, bad aspects from Neptune crush and dishearten undeveloped natures; and they misunderstand his call to the higher planes to such an extent that some drown their sorrows in alcohol or seek oblivion or temporary exaltation through the use of opiates. In extreme cases, where the nervous system has been shattered and the reason thrown out of gear by habitual lack of self-control and proper discipline, the call of this great ruler to the higher planes may even be misconstrued into an inward impulse to get rid of the physical body by suicide; in which case the method adopted will probably be by drugs or drowning, for it is the martial suicide who takes to fire-arms or steel. Even if a death in which Neptune is concerned is due to natural causes, one of these causes will probably be the cessation of all desire to live. Such tragic misreadings of the stimulus of Neptunian vibrations do not, of course, affect ordinary normal humanity, and it cannot be too strongly insisted upon that this influence or aspect of the Deity is never really evil; it is only our blindness and ignorance that make it appear so. The sight of the gleaming wave or the tranquil pool lifts up the poet's heart and inspires his pen, and even the average man is helped and spiritually strengthened by communion with the beautiful world of waters. The very same sights and sounds only suggest to the wretched prostitute and the miserable drunkard that here is a chance to throw off the useless and degraded physical body and its chains "for ever"; and until the teaching of reincarnation with its companion teaching of the inevitable nature of Karma is more widely spread, suicides of that type will continue to abound, and souls will consequently continue to be reborn to a drunken and dissolute and suicidal heredity; for no man can shirk reaping what he has sown.

In good aspect the influence of Neptune gives a call to some form of unselfishness, renunciation, devotion or self-sacrifice which can be easily and even happily undertaken, and which will bring an exceeding great reward. In any strong aspect, but especially in cross aspect to Uranus, there is indicated a recurrent tendency to have gleams of clairvoyance or other psychic experiences; but this will depend upon the stage of evolution, both the very primitive and the highly evolved individuals being more likely than the half-developed, to sense such impressions; the first because he has not sufficient mentality to absorb his activity, and the second because he has transcended the realm of thought and acquired the higher intuition.

Reviewing the horoscope more generally, and balancing one aspect against another, it may be said that a striking preponderance of bad aspects—especially squares—denotes that the incarnating *ego* has been out of harmony with its past conditions and that the fruits of labour are unlikely to be reaped in the present life, although much excellent work may be done, which will pave the way for future triumphs. A marked preponderance of good aspects, on the other hand, promises success and happiness in the present life, and suggests the gathering in of a goodly harvest before it closes. Where we find good and evil aspects evenly balanced, the possibility of a fresh start in any direction preferred by the native is indicated. In other words Free Will is likely to be stronger than Destiny in that particular incarnation.

CHAPTER III.

Conclusion

Readers who have been sufficiently interested in the foregoing chapters to desire further knowledge on the subject are advised to learn the simple process of casting the horoscope for themselves, either by the study of manuals on the subject or, preferably, through taking a few lessons from a practical astrologer. No abstruse reasoning or difficult calculations are required, for the necessary figures are supplied by the mathematicians who compile the almanac and ephemeris; and with the aid of a little simple arithmetic the rising sign can be ascertained and the little wheel of life described. If a man is born exactly at noon the necessary arithmetic is reduced to a minimum. Reference to the almanack or ephemeris for the year of his birth will show the *Sidereal Time* at noon on his birthday, and the sign rising at that hour will be easily found in the lists given in any astrological manual which includes a "Table of Houses." *Raphael's Manual*, which gives the tables for a variety of latitudes, including England and Ireland, only costs a shilling—which is also the price of an ephemeris. If many horoscopes are to be drawn, however, it is an economy to purchase Mr. Alan Leo's second volume of *Astrology for All*, which summarises the ephemeris for every year from 1850 to 1905. In the case of those born some hours earlier than noon, the number of these earlier hours—or minutes—must be subtracted from sidereal time at noon; and in the case of those born some time after noon, these later hours or minutes must be *added* to sidereal time at noon. Sometimes this subtraction of morning hours brings out a minus quantity, in which case add twenty-four; and sometimes the addition of afternoon or evening hours brings out a sum greater than twenty-four, in which case subtract twenty-four. Needless to say this is a very unintelligent and rule-of-thumb way of beginning and will never satisfy anyone with a scientific bent; but, such as it is, it will serve its immediate purpose.

Accurate reading of a horoscope takes time and care, and of course the date, hour and place of birth must be known if the chart is to be drawn aright. Further, if the hour has been hastened or delayed by accident, surgery or drugs, some rectification will be needed. Doctors are resourceful in methods of saving life or lessening suffering, and even slight interference with the hour of birth may change the zenith or the rising sign, disconcerting the astrologer. No seven months baby ever fits its horoscope; though the premature map shows a sort of adjustment, for the sign the Sun ought to have been is generally shown as rising. If the expected date is ascertainable, the sign the Moon was in *ten lunar months before that*, will probably be rising—or setting—in the true horoscope.

The hour of birth is registered in many European countries now Scotland began to do that in 1855, France some years earlier, and England about sixty years later. The custom is a great help to students collecting statistics; and it is hardly necessary to add that the hour used must be actual time. Greenwich time is minutes ahead of places further West. Paris time is an hour wrong for Chamounix, and so on.

In the pages that follow, a short summary of the values of the signs in various positions, and an analysis of each of the twelve types, will be found. These tables are drawn up from the careful analysis of the horoscopes of friends, relatives and acquaintances, and are illustrated by the names of famous persons whose horoscopes are known or surmised—the latter being marked by a note of interrogation. These "specimens" have been gleaned from the pages of *Modern Astrology*—the magazine edited by Mr. Alan Leo—and the works of Mr. George Wyld, or taken from a collection of some two hundred horoscopes very kindly lent to me by a fellow student, and drawn by himself and by a learned astrologer who writes under the name of "Kymry," and to whom I am also much indebted for various items of information. Others have been drawn by two of my sisters from data furnished by biographical notices or the records of Register House. It is difficult to acknowledge all my debts or to give anything like a full list of the books into which I have dipped during the writing of the foregoing chapters. Comparatively few of them were astrological and I have to own that I have never yet read an astrological work through from beginning to end, and know hardly anything at all about the higher mathematics. In fact, even my arithmetic is shaky at times, and I never draw out a horoscope if I can get anyone to do it for me.* I am not a professional astrologer, I never dabble in prediction, have never studied progressions and cannot give directions to anyone—not even to myself. As a dramatist—by predilection if not by achievement!—I have been attracted to this study by interest in character analysis, and by that alone. If I have, by anything I have said in these pages, succeeded in giving any of my readers some little help towards the understanding of their fellow creatures, the primary aim of this book has been attained. Its secondary aim, which as I wrote gradually eclipsed the first, has been to interest those who had the patience to bear with my digressions, in the marvellous teachings of the ancient mythologies, and in the relations of those teachings to our own current beliefs. I fancied when I first took up my pen that what I meant to do could easily be accomplished in a few weeks. It has taken over four years; and although many and many a time the subject has seemed so vast, so illimitable, that I have been tempted to give it up in despair, Cancerian tenacity has carried me through. I mention this fact because among the various friends and acquaintances I have made during the publication of these pages in magazine form, the majority have begged me to tell them my rising sign, and no one has ever guessed it correctly without meeting me face to face. I was born with the Moon and Uranus rising in conjunction in Cancer, square to Neptune in Aries and in direct opposition to Venus; but trine to Jupiter, which is at the Zenith in Pisces. The Sun is in Sagittarius in conjunction with Mars, and semi-sextile to Saturn in Scorpio in conjunction with Mercury. The bad aspects have worked out chiefly in accidents, illness and loss of money; so, in spite of the serious number of my *squares*, students are warned not to waste their pity on one who has all her heart's desire and knows how to be grateful

* This statement is self-protective. I have already received letters from various quarters of the globe, asking for advice as to the buying or selling of stocks and shares, or begging me to assume the *rôle* of a private detective, or to do other uncongenial and impossible tasks No notice will be taken of such requests.

for it. Some of my readers may be interested to know that this attitude of mind is due to the study of Theosophy and acceptance of its teaching, and that, but for the constant kindness, encouragement and help of the members and ex-members of the Theosophical Society, with whom I have come into personal contact, this book would have never been written. And how it has come to be written at all is something of a puzzle—unless it is true, as certain clairvoyants have asserted, that in a previous incarnation in ancient Egypt, as a student and teacher of Chaldean Astrology, I prepared myself for the task. Certainly, as far as actual astrological study goes, I have had no preparation this time. After a cursory glance at one or two manuals and a little talk with a sister who took it up as a summer hobby, I went straight into the detailed examination of horoscopes, and within a very few weeks had made up my mind to try to classify the types clearly without delay. At first I worked literally day and night; sometimes awaking two or three times from sleep to write down another pair of precious analytical adjectives, or make a correction on the paper that lay beside me. Yet, certain astrologers who had worked at the subject for years, assured me, even in those first weeks, that my conclusions were correct. Gradually, as the subject unfolded itself before me, the delight and interest grew, threatening to crowd out all other interests until it arrived at the point when, instead of excluding, it embraced them all. There are astrological theories and teachings and explanations not even hinted at in this volume; the history of the subject has never been written, the works of some of its greatest students lie in forgotten corners of library shelves unappreciated and unread. There are three manuscript volumes on this subject by the great Kepler still lying untranslated and unpublished at the British Museum; and those who reverence Astrology as he did, are hampered in their studies by lack of statistics as well as by the false deductions of the charlatan, whose absurd pretensions have too often brought the study into disrepute. Beginning as an absolutely sceptical inquirer I have learnt during these four years of labour that there is far more in this subject than I can hope to understand, even if I follow it up for several successive lives. How much its symbolism means to me even now, I cannot possibly express, and only those whose tastes lie in the same direction are likely to understand. Of course, too, like all Cancerians, I am hampered by personal prejudices and predilections. Other types would have found a different form of presentation and possibly, to many, a more acceptable one. The mathematical mystic—and he exists—would rejoice in classifying and re-classifying, subdividing and again unifying the types according to their numerical relation, and he would have found plenty to interest and possibly also to puzzle him. The signs were not always reckoned as twelve but appear in earlier tradition as ten;* and other systems of analysis give the number of the Gods as neither twelve nor ten but as seven.† A study of sacred numbers is found helpful by some students, who point out that $3 \times 4 = 12$ and that $3 + 4 = 7$; but to many readers such assertions are meaningless, and a musical analogy will probably prove more suggestive to the majority. The notes of the diatonic scale—major or minor—are seven. The notes of the chromatic scale, in which the musician uses all the half tones, are twelve. The three notes of the common chord sum up the scale, and when preceded by the four notes of the chord of the dominant seventh, form the cadence which expresses the AMEN, one of the most ancient and impressive names for the Supreme. It is significant that even in that noble and beautiful expression of Deity, however reverently and richly chanted and in whatever key it may be sung, there is still one note of the scale awanting. Even in the three-fold repetition, with its changes of harmony, the expression is still incomplete, and only the full choral rendering of the sevenfold AMEN with its glorious succession of stately chords sweeping on from key to key, can represent to the listening worshipper something of the depth and breadth and height of the Glory and the Love and the Wisdom and the Power and the Peace of God, which whether manifest or unmanifest, pass all human understanding.

* *Cf.* Apollo and the nine muses; a symbolic presentation much used in the school of Pythagoras.

† *Cf* the seven great spirits which are before the throne, the seven Rishis of India

Part III.

SUMMARY

ANALYTICAL SCHEME

The Ascendant Sign gives the:	Watchword	*which is modified by the Sign the Moon is in*	☽
	Type	*which is modified by the sign the Sun is in*	☉
	Method	*which is modified by the sign the Moon is in*	☽
	Style	*which is modified by the sign the Moon is in*	☽
	Intellect	*which is modified by the sign Mercury is in*	☿
	Speech	*which is modified by the sign Mercury is in*	☿
	Manner	*which is modified by the sign Saturn is in*	♄
	Bearing	*which is modified by the sign Mars is in*	♂
	Temperament	*which is modified by the sign the Ruler is in*	
The Sign at the Zenith gives the:	Function	*which is modified by the sign the Sun is in*	☉
	Outlook	*which is modified by the sign Uranus is in*	♅
	Nature	*which is modified by the sign Vulcan is in*	[illegible]
	Affections	*which are modified by the sign Venus is in*	♀
	Attitude	*which is modified by the sign Mars is in*	♂
	Sex-attitude	*which is modified by the sign Mars is in*	♂
	Disposition	*which is modified by the sign Jupiter is in*	♃
The Descendant Sign gives the:	Mind	*which is modified by the sign Jupiter is in*	♃
The Sign at the Nadir gives the:	Character	*which is modified by the sign Saturn is in*	♄
	Keynote	*which is modified by the sign the Sun is in*	☉

The position of Neptune shows where the call to self-sacrifice will come: easily obeyed if aspects are good; with difficulty if adverse. The position of Pluto shows the direction in which the Will is set. Good aspects show aspirations and ambitions working out harmoniously and well. Adverse aspects show obstacles.

SUMMARY

Sun ☉.—The Sun gives forth radiance and glows as Central Fire. Hence its position in the zodiac suggests the sphere of activity in which the native is most likely to meet with success, and also the essential impulse or driving force which will urge him to seek it. This solar influence increases steadily with advancing years.

Moon ☽.—The position of the Moon in the zodiac gives a clue to the inherent tendencies of the native; tendencies which possibly represent habits of thought, emotion and action acquired during the previous incarnation. This lunar influence is strongest in early childhood, and wanes with advancing years.

Ascendant.—The Sign rising on the horizon at the moment of birth gives a clue to the outer personality or medium through which the ego will have to work during its present incarnation; and also suggests the type of intellect, the method of attacking work, and certain characteristic modes of expression generally described as bearing, style, temperament, speech and manner.

Zenith.—The sign at the Zenith gives a clue to the inner man of feeling or emotion, and suggests his outlook and aspirations as well as his ambitions and desires, thus influencing, to a large extent, his choice of a profession.

Descendant.—The sign descending on the horizon at the moment of birth gives a clue to the type of mental energy.

Nadir.—The sign at the Nadir suggests the basis of character and the keynote to which the activities should be attuned.

♈ ARIES ♈

The Ram

The Sun is in Aries from March 21st to April 20th

☉.—Those born when the Sun is in Aries should find their best success in the field of action and enterprise, and will generally do well in the battle of life, many of them finding themselves in a position to play a leading part among their equals and contemporaries before they have reached middle age. An indication of their type, function and keynote is given on the opposite page.

The driving force that urges them forward will be hope for the future, sometimes perverted into impatience of and rebellion against the environment or conditions of the present.

Born with ☉ in ♈. Bismarck. General Booth.

☽.—The Moon in Aries gives habitual hopefulness and a tendency to take up new ideas and fresh enterprises with enthusiasm; but possibly also to drop them again before they have come to anything.

Aries as Ascendant suggests attainment through personal leadership and active combat; or through the facing and fighting of strong opposition, an opposition which will probably be largely aroused by the speech or action of the native himself, and which will consequently be doubly hard to overcome.

Born with ♈ rising. King George V. General Gordon (Khartoum). Mrs. Annie Besant.

Aries at the Zenith gives spiritual aspirations for complete manifestation, and practical ambitions to be always in the vanguard and to take part in pioneer work of some kind. The outlook is bright and hopeful, expectant and progressive; sometimes rather unsettled.

Aries descending suggests the type of mind which is ready to take in fresh ideas, and inclines to progress in thought, passing quickly from one idea to another and sometimes lacking the power of persistence and application.

Aries at the Nadir suggests, as a basis of character, the courage born of hope; which in some cases only manifests as recklessness and impatience.

♈ ARIES ♈

A The influence of Aries as Ascendant is felt chiefly on the physical plane, and asserts itself strongly in childhood

Watchword. ACTION

		Perfected Stage	Primitive Stage
OUTER PERSONALITY	*Type*	Enterprising	Headstrong
	Method	Militant	Belligerent
	Style	Oratorical	Misleading
	Intellect	Quick	Impatient
	Speech	Daring	Imprudent
	Manner	Lively	Forward
	Bearing	Spirited	Audacious
	Temperament	Enthusiastic	Fanatical

B The influence of Aries at the Zenith is felt chiefly on the emotional plane, and asserts itself strongly in youth

Function. THE WARRIOR *or* PIONEER

		Perfected Stage	Primitive Stage
PSYCHIC PERSONALITY	*Outlook*	Expectant	Unsettled
	Nature	Impetuous	Hasty
	Affections	Impulsive	Short-lived
	Attitude	Courageous	Reckless
	Sex-attitude	Ardent	Inflammable
	Disposition	Generous	Extravagant

C The influence of Aries descending is felt chiefly on the mental plane, and asserts itself strongly during middle age

Mind	Active	Roving

D The influence of Aries at the Nadir is associated chiefly with the building of character and asserts itself strongly in old age

Character	Indomitable	Uncontrollable

Keynote: HOPE *Ruler:* MARS, ♂

♉ TAURUS ♉

The Bull

The Sun is in Taurus from April 21st to May 20th

☉.—Those born when the Sun is in Taurus should find success in the sphere of constructive work of an enduring type; in some achievement of permanent value to the family or race, something on which future generations may safely build. An indication of their type, function and keynote is given on the opposite page.

The driving force of the sign is a desire for peace and stability—for the attainment of a resting-place among the things that cannot be shaken. This force may be perverted into a craving for the sense of security given by great possessions, and so degenerate into mere greed of gain.

Born with ☉ in ♉. Shakespeare, Browning, Fielding, Huxley, Marconi, J. M. Barrie.

☽.—The Moon in Taurus is associated with practical business ability, a determination to meet and discharge all monetary obligations and a tendency to undertake work in an orderly and methodical way, and to persist in it with industry. These habits go so far to ensure success in life, that the Moon is said to be exalted in Taurus.

Taurus as Ascendant suggests attainment through steadfast adherence to plans laid down; through routine and regularity and possibly through drudgery so monotonous that it requires either dogged resolution or constant goading to carry it through. Work associated with the beginnings and foundations of achievement rather than with their completion, is entrusted to this type.

Born with ♉ ascending. Chaucer? Burns? Miss L. Braithwaite?

Taurus at the Zenith awakens aspirations for the peace that passeth understanding and a practical ambition to enjoy in this world a well-earned rest, and enter into the fruits of labour; an ambition which may become altogether material and somewhat deadening. The point of view is settled and determined, and difficult to change.

Taurus descending suggests the type of mind which is steadfast and unshakeable; possibly even exceedingly stubborn and unyielding.

Taurus at the Nadir suggests as the basis of character stability and persistence—sometimes perverted into obstinacy.

♉ TAURUS ♉

A The influence of Taurus as Ascendant is felt chiefly on the physical plane, and asserts itself strongly in childhood.

Watchword: STABILITY

		Perfected Stage	Primitive Stage
OUTER PERSONALITY	*Type*	Steadfast	Stubborn
	Method	Constructive	Obstructive
	Style	Humorous	Grotesque
	Intellect	Persistent	Plodding
	Speech	Appropriate	Colloquial
	Manner	Leisurely	Lazy
	Bearing	Calm	Indifferent
	Temperament	Tranquil	Lethargic

B The influence of Taurus at the Zenith is felt chiefly on the emotional plane, and asserts itself strongly in youth

Function: THE BUILDER *or* PRODUCER

		Perfected Stage	Primitive Stage
PSYCHIC PERSONALITY	*Outlook*	Settled	Limited
	Nature	Restful	Self-centred
	Affections	Enduring	Dogged
	Attitude	Stoical	Stolid
	Sex-attitude	Kindly	Amorous
	Disposition	Just	Exacting

C. The influence of Taurus descending is felt chiefly on the mental plane and asserts itself strongly during middle age

Mind	Contemplative	Slow

D. The influence of Taurus at the Nadir is associated chiefly with the building of character and asserts itself strongly in old age.

Character	Trustworthy	Obstinate

Keynote: PEACE. *Ruler:* VESTA (*The Earth*—Traditionally *the Negative aspect of Venus*).

♊ GEMINI ♊

The Twins

The Sun is in Gemini from May 21st to June 20th

☉.—Those born when the Sun is in Gemini should find success in the sphere of intellectual achievement or artistic expression, possibly in both; for this sign of the twins is dual, and many persons under its influence pursue two callings, either contemporaneously or alternately. An indication of their type, function and keynote is given on the opposite page.

The driving force of this sign is a certain exuberance or overflow of energy which must find expression and prefers to find it in a variety of ways. At its highest it is a divine rapture or joy; and at its lowest a feverish excitability leading to constant change of plans and occupation, and consequent waste of time and energy.

Born with ☉ in ♊. King George V., Queen Mary, Dante, Walt Whitman, Balzac, Sir Oliver Lodge.

☽.—The Moon in Gemini is associated with intellectual eagerness and ingenuity, versatility and readiness of resource, and also with a strong dislike of drudgery and routine work.

Gemini as Ascendant suggests attainment through variety of intellectual experience, leading to frequent alternations between joy and grief, which stimulate the native to constant and insistent efforts to express himself with sufficient energy to arouse sympathy or response in others.

Born with ♊ rising. Dante, Francis Bacon, G. B. Shaw, Rossetti.

Gemini at the Zenith gives spiritual aspirations for perfection of expression and ambitions for some kind of artistic or intellectual achievement that has in it an element of freshness and originality. The outlook is free and untrammelled, and keenly intellectual.

Gemini descending suggests the type of mind which is extremely fertile in ideas, but which does not always follow them up to a logical or practical conclusion, thus giving a certain impression of flightiness and irresponsibility.

Gemini at the Nadir suggests as the basis of character a certain joyous impulsiveness which may possibly carry the native far in several successive directions.

♊ GEMINI ♊

A The influence of Gemini as Ascendant is felt chiefly on the physical plane, and asserts itself strongly in childhood.

Watchword: VARIETY.

		Perfected Stage	Primitive Stage
OUTER PERSONALITY	*Type*	Versatile	Variable
	Method	Experimental	Tricky
	Style	Expressive	Exaggerated
	Intellect	Inventive	Inaccurate
	Speech	Eloquent	Redundant
	Manner	Sympathetic	Effusive
	Bearing	Eager	Insistent
	Temperament	Joyous	Excitable

B. The influence of Gemini at the Zenith is felt chiefly on the emotional plane, and asserts itself strongly in youth.

Function · THE ARTIST or INVENTOR.

		Perfected Stage	Primitive Stage
PSYCHIC PERSONALITY	*Outlook*	Untrammelled	Lawless
	Nature	Sensitive	Huffy
	Affections	Spontaneous	Changing
	Attitude	Resourceful	Shifty
	Sex-attitude	Responsive	Fickle
	Disposition	Lavish	Spendthrift

C. The influence of Gemini descending is felt chiefly on the mental plane and asserts itself strongly during middle age

Mind	Fertile	Flighty

D. The influence of Gemini at the Nadir is associated chiefly with the building of character and asserts itself strongly in old age

Character	Impulsive	Wayward

Keynote JOY. *Ruler* MERCURY, ☿

♋ CANCER ♋

The Crab

The Sun is in Cancer from June 21st to July 21st

☉.—Those born when the Sun is in Cancer should find success in the sphere of teaching or preaching, or in otherwise appealing to the imaginations and sympathies of their fellow creatures and especially those of the rising generation. An indication of their type, function and keynote is given on the opposite page.

The driving force of the sign is the power which manifests in patriotism, and which is associated with the growth and evolution and well-being of the race rather than of the individual.

Born with ☉ in ♋. Prince of Wales, Garibaldi, Parnell, Kitchener, Joseph Chamberlain.

☽.—The Moon in Cancer is associated with facility in teaching, or tenderness in nursing, and sometimes with an inclination to employ effective and even startling methods, calculated to strike the imagination of the onlooker or listener.

Cancer as Ascendant suggests attainment through teaching or preaching or public-speaking; or through motherhood or, its equivalent, the guardianship, nursing or tending of the helpless, the ignorant or the infirm; work which requires endless patience, tenderness, adaptability and tenacity of purpose.

Born with ♋ rising. Carlyle, Mme. Blavatsky, Emperor William II., Bulwer Lytton, J. M. Barrie.

Cancer at the Zenith gives aspirations for perfect comprehension and an ambition to influence one's fellow-creatures by appealing to their imaginations and enlisting their sympathies. The point of view is that of the patriot, national, clannish, and possibly prejudiced.

Cancer descending suggests the type of mind which is imaginative and retentive; and inclined, at times, to fancifulness or brooding.

Cancer at the Nadir suggests as the basis of character a patience which at its highest is a marvellous adaptability to environment plus tenacity of purpose.

♋ CANCER ♋

A. The influence of Cancer as Ascendant is felt chiefly on the physical plane and asserts itself strongly in childhood

Watchword SYMPATHY

		Perfected Stage	Primitive Stage
OUTER PERSONALITY	*Type*	Parental	Brooding
	Method	Effective	Startling
	Style	Metaphorical	Untruthful
	Intellect	Retentive	Reticent
	Speech	Picturesque	Slangy
	Manner	Dignified	Distant
	Bearing	Self-reliant	Proud
	Temperament	Intense	Bitter

B The influence of Cancer at the Zenith is felt chiefly on the emotional plane, and asserts itself strongly in youth

Function THE PROPHET *or* TEACHER

		Perfected Stage	Primitive Stage
PSYCHIC PERSONALITY	*Outlook*	Patriotic	Clannish
	Nature	Sympathetic	Touchy
	Affections	Loyal	Partisan
	Attitude	Prepared	Defensive
	Sex-attitude	Constant	Unadaptable
	Disposition	Economical	Miserly

C. The influence of Cancer descending is felt chiefly on the mental plane, and asserts itself strongly during middle-age

Mind	Imaginative	Fanciful

D. The influence of Cancer at the Nadir is associated chiefly with the building of Character and asserts itself strongly in old age

Character	Tenacious	Grasping

Keynote PATIENCE *Ruler*. DIANA ☽ (*The Moon*)

♌ LEO ♌

The Lion

The Sun is in Leo from July 22nd to August 21st

☉.—Those born when the Sun is in Leo should find success in some sphere of activity which gives them a chance to shine in the eyes of their fellow men and women. They ought in some way to irradiate or brighten or inspire or harmonise the energies of others, either through the exercise of their own faculties, or through the occupation of positions of responsibility which are associated with some sort of kingly or fatherly office. An indication of their type, function and keynote is given on the opposite page.

The driving force of this sign is an abounding faith in God or in Destiny; sometimes perverted into a habit of leaving everything to Providence—or to other people—and of shirking strenuous personal exertion of any kind.

Born with ☉ in ♌. Napoleon Buonaparte, King Haakon of Norway, Sir Walter Scott, Alfred Tennyson, G. B. Shaw and Harry Lauder.

☽.—The Moon in Leo is associated with a certain inner harmony or centralisation of force which is a great help towards practical achievement; and also with a preference for simple, straightforward and direct methods of dealing with matters and with men.

Leo as Ascendant suggests attainment through Kingship or Fatherhood; through responsibility for the welfare of others; a position sometimes attained too early, and very unwisely, through lowering the standards of life and deliberately choosing a position involving constant association with inferiors.

Born with ♌ rising. King Victor Emmanuel III., Bismarck ? and Harry Lauder.

Leo at the Zenith gives aspirations to glorify God by letting one's light shine before men and by thus irradiating the lives of others. The ambitions are for glory and renown; sometimes perverted into a desire for praise and flattery even from those whose verdict is of no value. The point of view is central. In other words the Leonian looks at every side of a question from the heart of it.

Leo descending suggests the type of mind which is large and comprehensive but apt to lack clearness and precision.

Leo at the Nadir suggests as a basis of character that quality of mercy which springs from a radiant and irradiating faith in God and in man, a faith which makes it possible to believe the best even against apparent evidence of injustice or depravity, and which sometimes manifests as a too slack and easy-going tolerance of things as they are.

♌ LEO ♌

A. The influence of Leo as Ascendant is felt chiefly on the physical plane, and asserts itself strongly in childhood

Watchword. FAITH.

		Perfected Stage	*Primitive Stage*
OUTER PERSONALITY	*Type*	Regal	Lordly
	Method	Deputing	Shirking
	Style	Straightforward	Bald
	Intellect	Comprehensive	Wandering
	Speech	Deliberate	Slow
	Manner	Stately	Pompous
	Bearing	Magnanimous	Condescending
	Temperament	Energetic	Fussy

B. The influence of Leo at the Zenith is felt chiefly on the emotional plane, and asserts itself strongly in youth.

Function. THE KING *or* PRESIDENT

		Perfected Stage	*Primitive Stage*
PSYCHIC PERSONALITY	*Outlook*	Tolerant	Lax
	Nature	Hospitable	Convivial
	Affections	Generous	Ill-bestowed
	Attitude	Benevolent	Easy-going
	Sex-attitude	(*m*) Chivalrous (*f*) Confiding	Quixotic Undiscerning
	Disposition	Trustful	Gullible

C. The influence of Leo descending is felt chiefly on the mental plane, and asserts itself strongly during middle-age

Mind	Large	Hazy

D. The influence of Leo at the Nadir is chiefly associated with the building of character and asserts itself strongly in old age.

Character	Merciful	Slack

Keynote GLORY *Ruler*: APOLLO ☉ (*The Sun*).

♍ VIRGO ♍

The Virgin

The Sun is in Virgo from August 22nd to September 21st

☉.—Those born when the Sun is in Virgo should find success in some sphere of activity which gives constant opportunity for the exercise of keen discrimination and critical acumen, and through minute attention to apparently unimportant details. It will probably be their duty to test and to try—to sift, to select and to reject materials or men—and so to aid in the work of purification necessary to the healthy growth of the individual or of the state, or possibly of some great public enterprise. From their verdict there is no appeal, and if their efforts are unavailing it is probably because of this element of rigidity in their decisions, which make no allowance for growth and expansion; their critical faculty may in fact paralyse activity instead of crystallising it into beautiful forms. An indication of their type, function and keynote is given on the opposite page.

The driving force of the sign is the desire for holiness, otherwise perfect purity or health, an impulse which makes a man constantly seek for perfection. It is however sometimes perverted into a captious habit of noticing nothing but flaws, and rejecting or condemning all available methods and materials.

Born with ☉ in ♍. Goethe, Samuel Johnson, Burne-Jones, Queen Wilhelmina of Holland.

☽.—The Moon in Virgo gives practical and business-like methods of attacking work, habits of industry, irritability, and a critical rather than an appreciative turn of mind and style of expression.

Virgo as Ascendant suggests attainment through disinterested and faithful service; through painstaking and possibly highly skilled labour done on behalf of others with little or no thought of recognition or reward; through work of some kind which requires discrimination and critical acumen and an industry that never flags.

Born with ♍ ascending. Jane Austen, Sir Joshua Reynolds, the King of Spain.

Virgo at the Zenith gives aspirations for perfect purity, and ambitions to raise the standard of public morality or public health or both, by enforcing obedience to the universal laws, which affect these matters. The point of view is that of the examiner or critic, who tries and tests everything and everyone, condemning and rejecting the unworthy, the inefficient and the unclean.

Virgo descending suggests the type of mind which is clear and practical but somewhat lacking in imagination and consequently rather unsympathetic with the thoughts and ideas of others.

Virgo at the Nadir suggests as the basis of character that instinct for health and purity which leads to upright dealing and makes a man shrink from all that is morbid, hysterical and unclean.

♍ VIRGO ♍

A The influence of Virgo as Ascendant is felt chiefly on the physical plane, and asserts itself strongly in childhood.

Watchword SERVICE

		Perfected Stage	*Primitive Stage*
OUTER PERSONALITY	*Type*	Practical	Prosaic
	Method	Selective	Rejective
	Style	Concise	Dry
	Intellect	Discriminating	Calculating
	Speech	Pointed	Sharp
	Manner	Serious	Worried
	Bearing	Helpful	Officious
	Temperament	Active	Irritable

B The influence of Virgo at the Zenith is felt chiefly on the emotional plane, and asserts itself strongly in youth

Function · THE CRAFTSMAN *or* CRITIC

		Perfected Stage	*Primitive Stage*
PSYCHIC PERSONALITY	*Outlook*	Critical	Captious
	Nature	Prudent	Selfish
	Affections	Well-regulated	Cold
	Attitude	Alert	Apprehensive
	Sex-attitude	Faithful	Unresponsive
	Disposition	Thrifty	Mean

C The influence of Virgo descending is chiefly felt on the mental plane, and asserts itself strongly during middle age

Mind	Clear	Common-place

D The influence of Virgo at the Nadir is chiefly associated with the building of character, and asserts itself strongly in old age

Character	Upright	Rigid

Keynote · PURITY *Ruler* VULCAN ♁ (Traditionally the *Negative side of Mercury*).

♎ LIBRA ♎

The Balance

The Sun is in Libra from September 22nd to October 22nd

☉.—Those born when the Sun is in Libra should find success in some sphere of activity which requires all-round capacity rather than concentrated specialisation, and which is concerned with the maintenance of the moral and mental equilibrium of the individual or the state rather than with pioneer work. Many of them, indeed, tire of their profession and change it, and if they do specialise, it will probably be in connection with music and the fine arts, or in some line which tends to beautify and to complete human life. An indication of their type, function and keynote is given on the opposite page.

The driving force of this sign is that desire for beauty and for balance which in its sterner form is a strict sense of justice, and which, in weaker manifestations, works out as a tendency to shrink from what is disagreeable, ill-balanced, ugly or unjust, without attempting to set it right.

Born with ☉ in ♎. John Bright, Paul Kruger.

☽.—The Moon in Libra gives a tendency to pass easily and naturally from one kind of work to another, to adapt oneself to changing conditions and environment and make the best of them. This position gives a well-balanced, lovable and loving nature, and ensures a certain amount of popularity.

Libra as Ascendant suggests attainment through statesmanship or arbitration, or through the exercise of the natural affections and the efforts they inspire towards adjusting the environment and beautifying the life by bringing harmony out of discord, possibly through training or practice in one of the fine arts.

Born with ♎ rising.* Emperor Francis Joseph of Austria, Jenny Lind, Mary Anderson.

Libra at the Zenith gives aspirations for beauty of life, and for perfect poise or balance, such as is obtained by free natural growth and all-round development. The ambitions are for personal popularity and public recognition. The point of view is that of the arbitrator who sees both sides of the question, and is consequently tempted to vacillate.

Libra descending is associated with the type of mind that is broad and impartial, but sometimes vague and undecided.

Libra at the Nadir suggests as the basis of character a scrupulous sense of honour and a love of balance or "fair proportions," which involves an appreciation of beauty.

---

* Our King George VI was born with Libra rising and a Leo zenith. Mary, Queen of Scots was also Libran, but with the emotional sign Cancer at the zenith instead of the royal Leo.

♎ LIBRA ♎

A The influence of Libra as Ascendant is felt chiefly on the physical plane, and asserts itself strongly in childhood

Watchword HARMONY

		Perfected Stage	*Primitive Stage*
OUTER PERSONALITY	*Type*	Adaptable	Opportunist
	Method	Weighing	Hesitating
	Style	Persuasive	Cajoling
	Intellect	Judicial	Indecisive
	Speech	Polished	Pedantic
	Manner	Gracious	Smooth
	Bearing	Tactful	Cowardly
	Temperament	Cheerful	Equable

B The influence of Libra at the Zenith is felt chiefly on the emotional plane, and asserts itself strongly in youth

Function THE STATESMAN *or* MANAGER

		Perfected Stage	*Primitive Stage*
PSYCHIC PERSONALITY	*Outlook*	Impartial	Aloof
	Nature	Compassionate	Soft
	Affections	Overflowing	Shallow
	Attitude	Conciliatory	Temporising
	Sex-attitude	Tender	Susceptible
	Disposition	Careful	Niggling

C The influence of Libra descending is felt chiefly on the mental plane, and asserts itself strongly during middle age

Mind	Broad	Vague

D The influence of Libra at the Nadir is associated chiefly with the building of character and asserts itself strongly in old age.

Character	Honourable	Punctilious

Keynote : BEAUTY *Ruler .* VENUS, ♀

♏ SCORPIO ♏

The Scorpion

The Sun is in Scorpio from October 23rd to November 21st

☉.—Those born when the Sun is in Scorpio should find success in some sphere of activity which demands the exercise of concentration and of personal magnetism; or which is associated with the mastery of men or of natural forces; with work that is vitalising or regenerating or dominating in some way; in any case with the use—or misuse—of *power*. An indication of their type, function and keynote is given on the opposite page.

The driving force of this sign is excess of energy which must find an outlet, and prefers to find it either in the generation or creation of new forms and fresh bodies, or in the destruction of those that are old and outworn. At its best it is a vivifying and vitalising force, but when perverted takes delight in hastening the devil's work of destruction, degeneration and death.

Born with ☉ in ♏. King Edward VII., The Mikado of Japan, Martin Luther, Schiller.

☽.—The Moon in Scorpio gives the habit of concentrating thoroughly on the task of the moment, but this position is often associated with narrow and limited views concerning life and work, and is consequently something of a handicap, excepting for the very highly developed.

Scorpio as Ascendant suggests attainment through heroic endurance and self-control, and the determination to conquer disease and weakness and temptation of every kind, mental, moral and physical, both in oneself and in others. The special work will probably be concerned with the domination of natural forces involving some kind of scientific training or the exercise of absolute authority over others.

Born with ♏ rising. Goethe, Milton, Napoleon Buonaparte, Sir Henry Irving.

Scorpio at the Zenith gives aspirations for perfect realisation of divine strength, and practical ambitions for power over the lives of others, through the exercise of the will. The point of view is that of the Governor, concentrated on the immediate future and always on guard; vigilant, forethoughtful, possibly inclined to pessimism.

Scorpio descending is associated with a mind that is deductive in a curiously instinctive or intuitive way that seems to be independent of actual logic, and is very accurate—except where strong feeling is involved.

Scorpio at the Nadir suggests strength as the basis of character, a strength which may prove at times somewhat unmerciful in its manifestation.

♏ SCORPIO ♏

A The influence of Scorpio as Ascendant is felt chiefly on the physical plane, and asserts itself strongly in childhood

Watchword POWER

		Perfected Stage	*Primitive Stage*
OUTER PERSONALITY	*Type*	Commanding	Tyrannical
	Method	Analytical	Destructive
	Style	Trenchant	Cutting
	Intellect	Penetrating	Shrewd
	Speech	Decided	Dogmatic
	Manner	Authoritative	Severe
	Bearing	Heroic	Superior
	Temperament	Reserved	Secretive

B The influence of Scorpio at the Zenith is felt chiefly on the emotional plane and asserts itself strongly in youth

Function THE GOVERNOR *or* INSPECTOR

		Perfected Stage	*Primitive Stage*
PSYCHIC PERSONALITY	*Outlook*	Forethoughtful	Pessimistic
	Nature	Thorough	Vindictive
	Affections	Passionate	Exclusive
	Attitude	Unflinching	Callous
	Sex-attitude	Devoted	Jealous
	Disposition	Investive	Gambling

C The influence of Scorpio descending is felt chiefly on the mental plane and asserts itself strongly during middle age

Mind	Deductive	Suspicious

D The influence of Scorpio at the Nadir is chiefly associated with the building of character and asserts itself strongly in old age

Character	Strong	Hard

Keynote JUSTICE. *Ruler* PLUTO ♇ (Traditionally the *Negative side of Mars*).

♐ SAGITTARIUS ♐

THE ARCHER

The Sun is in Sagittarius from November 22nd to December 20th

☉.—Those born when the Sun is in Sagittarius should find success in some sphere of activity which involves the constant exercise of the reason and the development of the logical faculty. Everything which favours these—travel, exploration, contact with other minds and inquiry into unfamiliar systems of philosophy, theology or law,—will prove helpful and congenial, for wisdom and understanding will be the heart's desire. An indication of their type, function and keynote, is given on the opposite page.

The driving force of the sign is this craving for wisdom and the determination to seek it out through the exercise of the reason, which is sometimes perverted into a tendency to argue or chop-logic, to doubt, to dispute and to deny, till the lamp of Truth is obscured in a fog of casuistry and the enquirer is lost in a mist of his own making.

Born with ☉ *in* ♐. Carlyle, Beethoven, Mark Twain.

☽.—The Moon in Sagittarius gives a fair share of practical common-sense; an inquiring and somewhat sceptical habit of mind, a friendly and general interest in one's fellow creatures, and a strong inclination to argue every point.

Sagittarius as Ascendant suggests attainment through some form of "sport"—mental or physical; that is to say, through the eager pursuit of something which eludes capture. This may either take the form of the search for Truth through the exercise of the reason—unaided by the intuition—or of some sort of exploration or enterprise which stimulates the mind, and involves the use of all the physical faculties.

Born with ♐ *rising*. King Edward VII., King Haakon, Sven Hedin, Cecil Rhodes, Theo. Roosevelt, Sir W. Scott? H. M. Stanley?

Sagittarius at the Zenith gives aspirations for perfect wisdom and understanding, and an ambition to make them of practical use to the world by carrying out the ideals grasped, and living according to conviction; an ambition sometimes perverted into a tendency to make them square comfortably with the life. The point of view is that of the practical philosopher or sage, ever ready to learn.

Sagittarius descending is associated with boundless mental curiosity; a mind that is constantly inquiring or probing into some new matter and is not easily satisfied.

Sagittarius at the Nadir suggests as the basis of character a certain sturdy independence akin to pride, which asks no favour and flatters no man, and may even at times be ungracious.

♐ SAGITTARIUS ♐

A **The influence of Sagittarius as Ascendant is felt chiefly on the physical plane, and asserts itself strongly in childhood**

Watchwords · LAW AND LIBERTY.

		Perfected Stage	*Primitive Stage*
OUTER PERSONALITY	*Type*	Original	Eccentric
	Method	Argumentative	Disputatious
	Style	Vigorous	Rugged
	Intellect	Logical	Casuistical
	Speech	Frank	Blunt
	Manner	Genial	Boisterous
	Bearing	Friendly	Familiar
	Temperament	Buoyant	Irrepressible

B The influence of Sagittarius at the Zenith is felt chiefly on the emotional plane, and asserts itself strongly in youth

Function THE SAGE or COUNSELLOR.

		Perfected Stage	*Primitive Stage*
PSYCHIC PERSONALITY	*Outlook*	Optimistic	Over-confident
	Nature	Transparent	Child-like
	Affections	Honest	Grudging
	Attitude	Uncompromising	Defiant
	Sex-attitude	Sincere	Brusque
	Disposition	Contented	Careless

C **The influence of Sagittarius descending is felt chiefly on the mental plane, and asserts itself strongly during middle age**

Mind	Inquiring	Sceptical

D. **The influence of Sagittarius at the Nadir is associated chiefly with the building of character and asserts itself strongly in old age**

Character	Independent	Proud

***Keynote*.** WISDOM. *Ruler* : JUPITER ♃.

♑ CAPRICORN ♑

The He-Goat

The Sun is in Capricorn from December 21st to January 19th

☉.—Those born when the Sun is in Capricorn should find success in some sphere which gives scope for ambition—either personal or vicarious—and is associated with a recurrent possibility of promotion of some kind, preferably of a kind that is outwardly manifest to the eyes of men. Such ambition may be transmuted into aspiration and carry the energy wholly into the religious life, but even there, the outward and visible forms will absorb much of the attention, and the personal element—the office of mediator or ambassador to others—will be given tremendous weight. An indication of their type, function and keynote is given on the opposite page.

The driving force of this sign is reverence or devotion to the Highest, giving an earnest desire to attain. This may be perverted into a dread of sinking to the lowest, which either acts as a spur to exaggerated and even unscrupulous efforts to climb rapidly and at the expense of others, or takes the form of a melancholy heaviness and discontent.

Born with ☉ in ♑. Gladstone, Matthew Arnold, Rudyard Kipling, Andrew Carnegie.

☽.—The Moon in Capricorn gives a grandfatherly tendency to patronise others, and a certain amount of social ambition, together with an inclination to accept tradition and convention and to follow contentedly the path by which other climbers have reached the goal.

Capricorn as Ascendant suggests attainment through social or political ambition, personal or vicarious, leading either to strong concentration and unceasing hard work, or to the development of diplomatic ability and of the tendency to be all things to all men.

Born with ♑ rising. Gladstone, Macaulay (?) Macchiavelli (?)

Capricorn at the Zenith gives aspirations of a soaring nature—a longing or yearning to scale the heights—and an ambition, personal or vicarious, for elevation above the conditions of early environment, an ambition which may be perverted into mere snobbery, either social or intellectual. The point of view is exceedingly reverent and uncritical towards acknowledged superiors but also somewhat patronising and disdainful of acknowledged inferiors.

Capricorn descending suggests the type of mind which is concentrative and profound, and possibly somewhat given to bigotry or narrowness.

Capricorn at the Nadir suggests, as the basis of character, that desire for progress which is the mainspring of both involution and evolution.

♑ CAPRICORN ♑

A The influence of Capricorn as Ascendant is felt chiefly on the physical plane, and asserts itself strongly in childhood

Watchword: EXCELSIOR

		Perfected Stage	*Primitive Stage*
OUTER PERSONALITY	*Type*	* Patriarchal / Filial	Patronising / Dependent
	Method	Traditional	Conventional
	Style	Ornate	Overloaded
	Intellect	Profound	Narrow
	Speech	Significant / Fluent	Sly / Voluble
	Manner	Authoritative / Deferential	Arrogant / Servile
	Bearing	Adaptable / Charming	Capricious / Insincere
	Temperament	Devout	Superstitious

B The influence of Capricorn at the zenith is felt chiefly on the emotional plane, and asserts itself strongly in youth

Function THE PRIEST *or* AMBASSADOR.

		Perfected Stage	*Primitive Stage*
PSYCHIC PERSONALITY	*Outlook*	Reverent	Uncritical
	Nature	Zealous	Unscrupulous
	Affections	Deep-rooted	Limited
	Attitude	Diplomatic	Time-serving
	Sex-attitude	Protective / Submissive	Contemptuous / Slavish
	Disposition	Magnificent	Showy

C. The influence of Capricorn descending is felt chiefly on the mental plane, and asserts itself strongly during middle age

Mind	Concentrative	Bigoted

D The influence of Capricorn at the Nadir is associated chiefly with the building of character and asserts itself strongly in old age

Character	Ambitious	Discontented

Keynote: REVERENCE. *Ruler.* SATURN ♄

---

* The bracketed adjectives are alternatives

♒ AQUARIUS ♒

The Water-Bearer

The Sun is in Aquarius from January 20th to February 18th

☉.—Those born when the Sun is in Aquarius should find success in the sphere of the observer or recorder of phenomena—the truth-seeker—and will probably engage in work which definitely alters their own outlook on life, and possibly also enlarges the sympathies and the mental horizon of great numbers of their fellow creatures. An indication of their type, function and keynote is given on the opposite page.

The driving force of the sign is the craving for enlightenment, a passion for knowledge and especially for knowledge of the occult or hidden truth which underlies the mystery of manifestation. This is often associated with a tendency to reject all incomplete and approximate statements which veil or distort the truth ;—a tendency which may be perverted into a depressed and depressing agnosticism.

Born with ☉ in ♒. Charles Darwin, Francis Bacon, John Ruskin, Charles Dickens, Robert Burns.

☽.—The Moon in Aquarius is associated with habits of careful observation and an inclination to examine searchingly into the truth of any matter which comes up for discussion ; also sometimes a bent towards the study of natural or physical science.

Aquarius as Ascendant suggests attainment through the constant observation and comparison of phenomena or facts, through close investigation or research—possibly into occult matters—and through the unwearying study of fundamental principles in nature, and analysis of the mainsprings of action in mankind.

Born with ♒ rising. John Ruskin, Wordsworth ? Queen Mary, Queen Elizabeth II?

Aquarius at the Zenith gives aspirations for a clear outlook and breadth of vision ; and an ambition to add to the sum of human knowledge and enlarge the views of others ; an ambition sometimes perverted into a tendency to fatigue other people by forcing one's own opinions upon them with too much insistence and at unsuitable times. The point of view is that of the scientist or truthseeker—unbiassed, open-minded, dispassionate.

Aquarius descending is associated with the type of mind that is absolutely open, unbiassed and free from prejudice, and which consequently often appears to be uncertain in its conclusions.

Aquarius at the Nadir suggests as the basis of character a strong sense of brotherhood, springing from the realisation of the common origin of all mankind, and of all manifestation.

♒ AQUARIUS ♒

A The influence of Aquarius as Ascendant is felt chiefly on the physical plane, and asserts itself strongly in childhood.

Watchword : INVESTIGATION

		Perfected Stage	Primitive Stage
OUTER PERSONALITY	*Type*	Scientific	Unimaginative
	Method	Synthetic	Chaotic
	Style	Descriptive	Diffuse
	Intellect	Searching	Prying
	Speech	Accurate	Prosy
	Manner	Earnest	Anxious
	Bearing	Humane	Sentimental
	Temperament	Serene	Phlegmatic

B The influence of Aquarius at the Zenith is felt chiefly on the emotional plane, and asserts itself strongly in youth

Function THE TRUTHSEEKER *or* SCIENTIST

		Perfected Stage	Primitive Stage
PSYCHIC PERSONALITY	*Outlook*	Unbiassed	Agnostic
	Nature	Sincere	Simple
	Affections	World-wide	Scattered
	Attitude	Forgiving	Weak
	Sex-attitude	Dispassionate	Luke-warm
	Disposition	Disinterested	Unbusiness-like

C. The influence of Aquarius descending is felt chiefly on the mental plane, and asserts itself strongly in middle-age

Mind	Open	Undecided

D The influence of Aquarius at the Nadir is associated chiefly with the building of character and asserts itself strongly in old age

Character	Considerate	Vacillating

Keynote TRUTH *Ruler* URANUS ♅ (formerly called *the Negative side of Saturn*

♓ PISCES ♓

The Fish

The Sun is in Pisces from February 19th till March 20th

☉.—Those born when the Sun is in Pisces will find their best success in the field of self-sacrifice and renunciation; in which achievement they will be largely aided by their intuitive knowledge of the reality of the spiritual world and the comparative unimportance of all outward appearances and shows. This knowledge is often accompanied by a power of interpretation which is to some extent a revelation to others; and also by a marvellous receptivity to impressions from the higher planes. An indication of their type, function and keynote is given on the opposite page.

The driving force of the sign is love of the type which manifests as an intense craving for perfect union with the Beloved, who, rightly recognised, is the Higher Self, or the *Christ*, the divine element, in every man. This craving for a fuller and more extended consciousness is often misread or perverted into a craving for such temporary intoxication or uplifting as is associated with the gratification of the lower passions, or the use of alcohol or drugs.

Born with ☉ in ♓. Garrick, Ellen Terry, Ibsen, Chopin.

☽.—The Moon in Pisces gives a certain plasticity or impressionability to the whole nature, a tendency—seen especially in early youth—to accept a message and pass it on to others, striving to interpret what has been grasped as important, but not *necessarily* finding the best method. The effort to do so conduces to a lovable and somewhat wistful humility.

Pisces as Ascendant suggests attainment through obedience or self-sacrifice, leading to the unification of body, soul and spirit, and possibly resulting in high achievement, either in some kind of service to the state or to the race, or in excellence in some form of artistic interpretation, connected with music, colour or word painting.

Born with ♓ rising. Lord Roberts ? Queen Victoria of Spain, Lord Rosebery, Cyril Maude.

Pisces at the Zenith gives aspirations for true insight or clearness of vision, unclouded by illusion; and an ambition to interpret such vision in some way that will bring humanity nearer to the heart of the universe. The point of view is that of the poet, the mystic, the seer.

Pisces descending is associated with a type of mind peculiarly receptive and impressionable, and very frequently alive and responsive to psychic impressions; in short, mediumistic.

Pisces at the Nadir suggests as the basis of character, self-sacrifice and devotion, sometimes exaggerated into an entire lack of initiative and a tendency to be pushed to the wall, and only act when prompted by others.

♓ PISCES ♓

A The influence of Pisces as Ascendant is felt chiefly on the physical plane, and asserts itself strongly in childhood

Watchword UNITY

		Perfected Stage	Primitive Stage
OUTER PERSONALITY	*Type*	Inspired	Mediumistic
	Method	Meditative	Dreamy
	Style	Illuminating	Quaint
	Intellect	Intuitive	Instinctive
	Speech	Suggestive	Indefinite
	Manner	Gentle	Diffident
	Bearing	Unassuming	Apologetic
	Temperament	Sunshiny	Variable

B. The influence of Pisces at the Zenith is felt chiefly on the emotional plane, and asserts itself strongly in youth

Function THE POET OR INTERPRETER

		Perfected Stage	Primitive Stage
PSYCHIC PERSONALITY	*Outlook*	Romantic	Unpractical
	Nature	Plastic	Submissive
	Affections	Adoring	Abject
	Attitude	Peaceable	Pliant
	Sex-attitude	Reverent	Shy
	Disposition	Unworldly	Improvident

C. The influence of Pisces descending is felt chiefly on the mental plane, and asserts itself strongly during middle age

Mind	Receptive	Impressionable

D The influence of Pisces at the Nadir is associated chiefly with the building of character and asserts itself strongly in old age

Character	Self-sacrificing	Weak

Keynote LOVE *Ruler* NEPTUNE ♆ (formerly called *the Negative side of Jupiter*)

THE USE OF THE TABLES

In using this form of analysis it should be remembered that it only gives a starting point from which the student may set out on his investigations into character, and a much more subtle examination of the planetary aspects, exaltations, etc., is necessary before it is possible to say whether the native is a very primitive soul, an average individual or very highly evolved Some clue to the stage of development is, however, afforded by the extent to which the faults cancel each other, and the student will find it helpful to pencil the *primitive* adjectives lightly under the *perfected* adjectives which correspond to them in the analytical tables, and then to erase those which are manifest contradictions Faults which are cumulative may then be suggested as possible, when the horoscope is handed over to the subject of analysis, but care must be taken to avoid giving an impression that these faults are predestined and inevitable, and in the majority of cases it is better to give only the good qualities, adding the remark that this is a description of the man or woman as he might be and ought to be if he is always living up to his highest possibilities It should also be remembered that contradictory statements cancel each other and should never be written out unmodified, that when an adjective occurs twice in the lists it suggests that the corresponding fault may be found in the native The writer is inclined to think that,—

A During childhood the attention is concentrated chiefly on action, and that the ascendant, which strongly affects the physical personality, or outer man, is dominant then.

B. During youth the attention is called to the emotional activities, and that the sign at the Zenith, which strongly affects the psychical personality, or inner man, will probably become the dominant sign

C As a man reaches his prime and passes on to middle age, the mental activities take a more important place, and the descendant sign often becomes dominant

D. In old age the faculties are engaged in summing up and absorbing past experiences and building them into character, at which period the sign at the Nadir asserts itself more strongly than ever before.

Also, that some people remain children all their days and never seem to get much beyond the limitations and possibilities of their ascendant sign!

Appendix

EXAMPLE HOROSCOPES ANALYSED

Zenith
or Southern Point

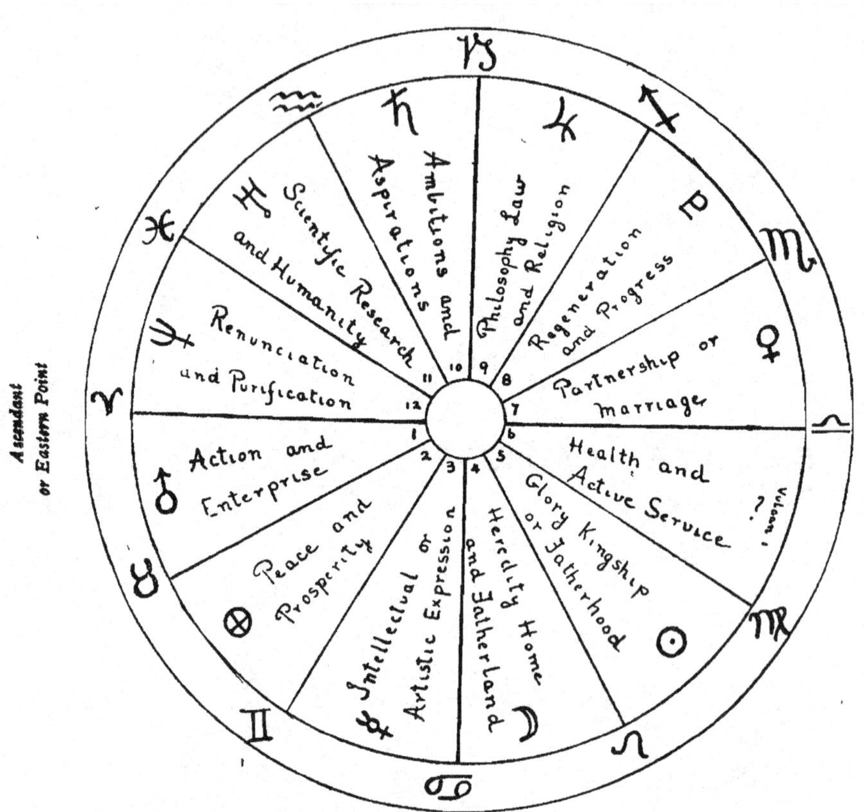

Ascendant
or Eastern Point

or Western Point

Nadir
or Northern Point

Imaginary Horoscope

Showing the order and character of the houses

The figure on the opposite page shows the numbering of the houses in a horoscope The first six are described as being "below the earth," and the activities associated with them are largely physical, necessitating the bodily action of the individual When the planets are all gathered into the upper part of the horoscope, above the earth, the activity will be chiefly mental and emotional, and the native will probably be placed in prominent positions, directing the actions of others The signs are here set round the horoscope in what may be described as their normal position—each governing its own house The first and most energetic sign, Aries, superintending the first house which is associated with enterprise and energy, the tranquil sign of Taurus governing the second house, associated with peace and prosperity, and so on. The four cardinal signs are placed at the four cardinal points, and in every way this position of signs suggests the manifestation of energy through the forces flowing into their appropriate channels Each planet is placed in its own appropriate sign—the sign which it is said to rule; a symmetrical arrangement astronomically impossible The introduction of the Earth, and the two unknown planets as rulers of Taurus, Virgo and Scorpio is peculiar to this writer, and many students will naturally prefer to retain the "negative rulers" of these signs—Venus, Mercury and Mars rather than accept the suggestion given here The planet Vulcan has, however, been tentatively associated with Virgo by some other students of Astrology, and some Theosophical writers assert that it exists, but that the matter of which it is composed is finer than gas, and that consequently it is invisible even at times of transit

Pluto is now generally accepted as the ruler of Scorpio.

EXAMPLE I.

ARIES

Zenith

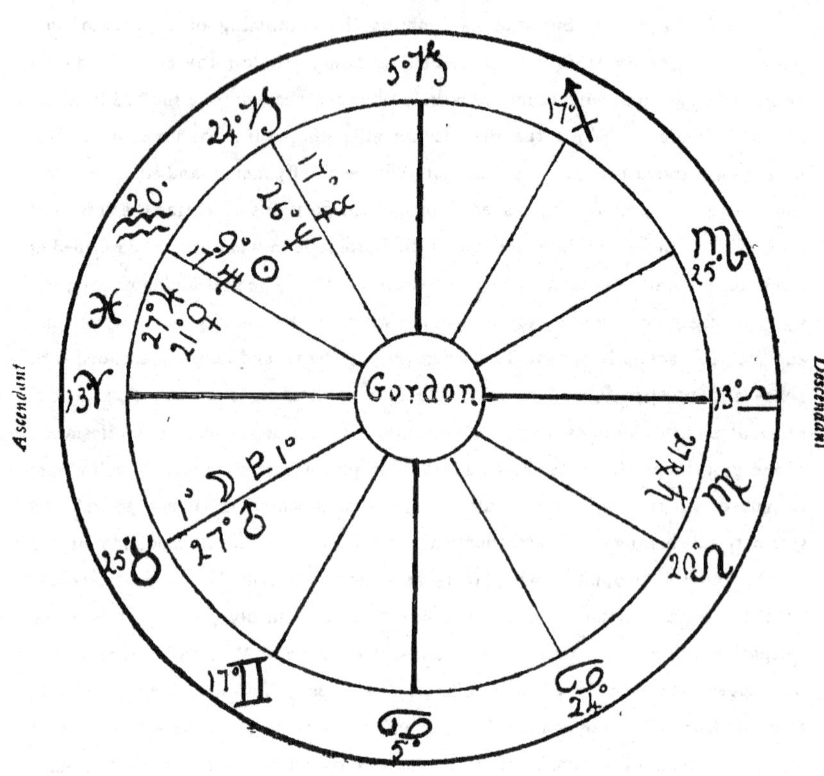

Nadir

GENERAL CHARLES GORDON, THE HERO OF KARTOUM.

Born at Woolwich, January 28th, 1833.

The hour of his birth was entered by his father in the family bible, and the data published by *Sepharial* in his almanac.

GORDON

The aspects in this horoscope are very beautiful when examined from the inner side There is a perfect Trine (120°) between the Ruler (*Mars*), and Saturn, and an all but perfect Trine between both of these and Neptune, all in earthy signs This suggests the physical manifestation, in action, of a perfect harmony between the energetic personality, his aspirations and his character; and this indication is much strengthened by the brilliant conjunction of Jupiter and Venus, the Mind and the Happiness, both in the Twelfth House, which is associated with duty, renunciation and self-sacrifice Saturn in opposition to this conjunction strikes a sterner note, denoting that the duty will often be difficult and that the character will be developed and strengthened through suffering; possibly physical suffering, for this planet of discipline and limitation is in the house of health. As a matter of fact Gordon was wounded early in his career, and hampered by the wound

Pluto is in Taurus a sign already emphasised. It lays good foundations. The work Gordon started for the welfare of boys has grown, and branched out.

ANALYSIS OF THE HOROSCOPE OF GENERAL GORDON

A *Ascendant* —ARIES ♈ *Ruler* —Mars

DESCRIPTION

	According to position of signs		*Modified by position of planets*	
Type	Enterprising	*and*	Scientific	☉ in ♒
Watchwords	Action	*and*	Stability	☽ in ♉
Method	Militant	*and*	Constructive	☽ in ♉
Style	Oratorical	*and*	Humorous	☽ in ♉
Intellect	Quick	*yet*	Profound	☿ in ♑
Speech	Daring	*and*	Fluent (or Significant)	☿ in ♑
Manner	Lively	*yet at times*	Serious	♄ in ♍
Bearing	Spirited	*yet*	Calm	♂ in ♉
Temperament	Enthusiastic	*yet*	Tranquil	Ruler in ♉

B *Zenith* —Capricorn ♑

Functions	Priest or Ambassador	*and*	Truthseeker	☉ in ♒
Outlook	Reverent	*yet*	Unbiassed	♅ in ♒
Nature	Zealous	*and*	Sincere	☉ in ♒
Affections	Deep-rooted	*and*	Adoring	♀ in ♓
Attitude	Diplomatic	*and*	Stoical	♂ in ♉
Sex-attitude	Protective	*and*	Kindly	♂ in ♉
Disposition	Magnificent	*yet*	Unworldly	♃ in ♓

C *Descendant* —Libra ♎.

Mind	Broad	*and*	Receptive	♃ in ♓

D *Nadir* —Cancer ♋

Character	Tenacious	*and*	Upright	♄ in ♍
Keynotes	Patience	*and*	Truth	☉ in ♒

SUMMARY OF GORDON'S HOROSCOPE

Influence of the Sun

☉ *in* ♒. Those born when the Sun is in Aquarius should find success in the sphere of the Truth-seeker—the observer and recorder of phenomena—and will probably engage in work which definitely alters their own outlook on life, and possibly also enlarges the sympathies and the mental horizon of great numbers of their fellow-creatures.

The driving force of the sign is a craving for enlightenment, a passion for knowledge, and especially for knowledge of that occult or hidden truth which underlies the mystery of manifestation This is often associated with a tendency to reject all incomplete and approximate statements which veil or distort the truth. a tendency which may be perverted into a depressed and depressing agnosticism (In the present instance the hopefulness and enthusiasm of the ascendant would cancel that, in all probability)

Influence of the Moon

☽ *in* ♉ The Moon exalted in Taurus is associated with practical business ability, and a tendency to undertake work in an orderly and methodical way, and to persist in it with industry, habits which go far to ensure success in life.

Influence of the Ascendant

♈ Aries as ascendant suggests attainment through personal leadership and active combat, or through the facing and fighting of strong opposition, an opposition which will probably be largely aroused by the speech or action of the native himself, and which will consequently be doubly hard to overcome The kindliness of Taurus and the tolerance of Aquarius would modify this combative tendency in Gordon's case, making him less aggressive than the typical Arietian

Influence of the Zenith

♑. Capricorn at the Zenith gives aspirations of a soaring nature—a longing or yearning to scale the heights—and an ambition, personal or vicarious, for elevation above the conditions of early environment. (This ambition was chiefly vicarious in the case of Gordon, who gave many a fellow-creature a helping hand out of the depths of poverty, misery and degradation) The point of view is exceedingly reverent and uncritical towards acknowledged superiors, but somewhat patronising or even contemptuous towards those considered inferiors (This inclination to despise inferiors would be cancelled by strong feelings of fraternity and humanity in Gordon's case He was large-hearted enough to understand their difficulties and limitations and to make allowances)

Influence of the Descendant

♎ Libra descending is associated with the type of mind that is broad and impartial, but when fatigued, vague and undecided

Influence of the Nadir

♋ Cancer at the Nadir suggests, as a basis of character, a patience which at its highest is a marvellous adaptability to environment plus tenacity of purpose and which, at its lowest, is a mere obstinate determination to have one's own way

Zenith

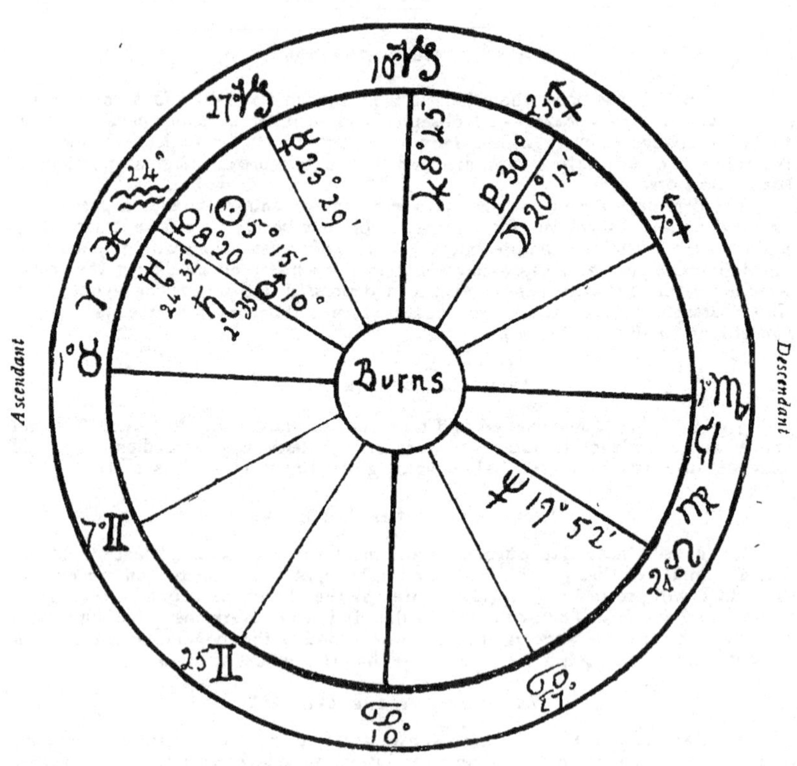

Nadir

ROBERT BURNS

Born at Ayr, January 25th, 1759.

Hour unknown; but the aspects and relations of the planets have been carefully calculated, so that the planetary accentuation of the signs is correct, although their actual position is only guess-work The little wheel may be turned in any way—possibly upside down, but the groupings would remain approximately the same, only the Moon and Mercury moving perceptibly as the hours of the day went on, and this position seems the most likely, considering the career and personality.

Pluto is in Sagittarius, frowning at Uranus in Pisces The action of the Will was impeded by a too sentimental outlook.

BURNS

The most striking note in this horoscope is struck by the brilliant conjunction of Sun, Venus, and Mars, all in Aquarius, a sign associated with the love of nature and of beautiful scenery, and with the power of keen observation and accurate description, and this beautiful group is semi-sextile to Jupiter, thus showing a harmony between the mental activity, the energy, the happiness and the success in life. The Moon, the planet of imagination, is Trine to Neptune, the aspirations, and semi-sextile to Mercury, the intellect—both helpful positions—but *square* to Saturn, the planet of character, which is in one of its weakest signs, Pisces, giving a certain listlessness and want of purpose to the life The horoscope as a whole sadly lacks back-bone and the essentially manly qualities. There is a good deal of gentle sentimentality and a tendency to be easily led, which even Taurus rising would not altogether correct It might, in fact, only add obstinacy instead of those qualities that are really lacking—strength and judgment, and discrimination in practical matters The word "dispassionate" may cause a smile, but it must be remembered that passion does not, as a rule, tend to the production of an infinite variety of tender little love songs all addressed or dedicated to different pretty girls. It runs deeper, and in fewer channels The faults of the peasant poet have been so much discussed, that they are here suggested, in smaller type, as otherwise the list of adjectives might seem inapplicable, but it must be remembered that in this case the hour is only surmised and that consequently the position of the signs is uncertain Therefore it is only the right hand columns of adjectives that can be taken as certainly belonging to him The student will see from these lists what is meant by cumulative indications, noticing the recurrence of the word weak, and coupling it with sentimental, and will also realise how to cancel certain words.—for instance suspicious, which is completely out of tune with the personality as a whole, and especially with the strong Sagittarian and Aquarian elements

ANALYSIS OF THE HOROSCOPE OF ROBERT BURNS

A *Ascendant* —TAURUS ♉. *Ruler* —The Earth

DESCRIPTION

	According to Position of Signs		*Modified by Position of Planets*	
Type	Steadfast or Stubborn	*and*	Scientific or Unimaginative	☉ in ♒
Watchwords	Stability	*and*	Liberty	☽ in ♐
Method	Constructive or Obstructive	*and*	Argumentative or Disputatious	☽ ♐
Style	Humorous or Grotesque	*and*	Vigorous or Rugged	☽ in ♐
Intellect	Persistent or Plodding	*and*	Profound or Narrow	☿ in ♑
Speech	Appropriate or Colloquial	*and*	Significant or Sly	☿ in ♑
Manner	Leisurely or Lazy	*and*	Gentle or Diffident	♄ in ♓
Bearing	Calm or Indifferent	*and*	Humane or Sentimental	♂ in ♒
Temperament	Tranquil or Lethargic	*and*	?	Ruler in ?

B *Zenith* —CAPRICORN ♑

Functions	Ambassador	*and*	Truth seeker	☉ in ♒
Outlook	Reverent or Uncritical	*and*	Romantic or Unpractical	♅ in ♓
Nature	Zealous or Unscrupulous	*and*	Sincere or Simple	♁ in ♒
Affections	Deep-rooted or Limited	*yet*	World-wide or Scattered	♀ in ♒
Attitude	Diplomatic or Time serving	*and*	Forgiving or Weak	♂ in ♒
Sex-attitude	Protective or Contemptuous	*and*	Dispassionate or Lukewarm	♂ in ♒
Disposition	Magnificent or Showy	*and*	Magnificent (*bis*) or Showy	♃ in ♑

C *Descendant* —SCORPIO ♏

Mind	Deductive or Suspicious	*and*	Concentrative or Bigoted	♃ in ♑

D *Nadir* .—CANCER ♋

Character	Tenacious or Grasping	*yet*	Self-sacrificing or Weak	♄ in ♓
Keynotes	Patience	*and*	Truth	☉ in ♒

SUMMARY OF THE HOROSCOPE OF ROBERT BURNS

Influence of the Sun

☉ *in* ♒ Those born when the Sun is in Aquarius should find success in the sphere of the Truth-seeker—the observer or recorder of phenomena—and will probably engage in work which definitely alters their own outlook on life, and possibly also enlarges the sympathies and the mental horizon of great numbers of their fellow-creatures

The driving force of this sign is the craving for enlightenment, a passion for knowledge and especially for knowledge of the occult or hidden truth which underlies the mystery of manifestation This is often associated with a tendency to reject all incomplete and approximate statements which veil or distort the truth, a tendency which may be perverted into a depressed and depressing agnosticism

Influence of the Moon.

☽ *in* ♐ The Moon in Sagittarius gives a fair share of common-sense, an enquiring and somewhat sceptical habit of mind, a friendly and general interest in one's fellow-creatures, and a strong inclination to argue every point

Influence of the Ascendant

♉ Taurus as Ascendant suggests attainment through steadfast adherence to plans laid down, through routine and regularity and possibly through drudgery so monotonous that the native must either possess dogged resolution himself, or be constantly goaded by others, before his work can be successfully carried out

Influence of the Zenith

♑ Capricorn at the Zenith gives aspirations of a soaring nature—a longing or yearning to scale the heights—and an ambition, personal or vicarious, for elevation above the conditions of early environment, an ambition which may be perverted into mere snobbery, social or intellectual The point of view is exceedingly reverent and uncritical towards acknowledged superiors but also somewhat patronising and disdainful of those considered as inferiors

Influence of the Descendant.

♏ Scorpio descending is associated with a mind that is deductive in a curiously instinctive and intuitive way that seems to be independent of actual logic and is very accurate—except where strong feeling is involved

Influence of the Nadir

♋. Cancer at the Nadir suggests, as the basis of character, a patience which at its highest is a marvellous adaptability to environment plus tenacity of purpose, and which at its lowest is a mere obstinate determination to have one's own way

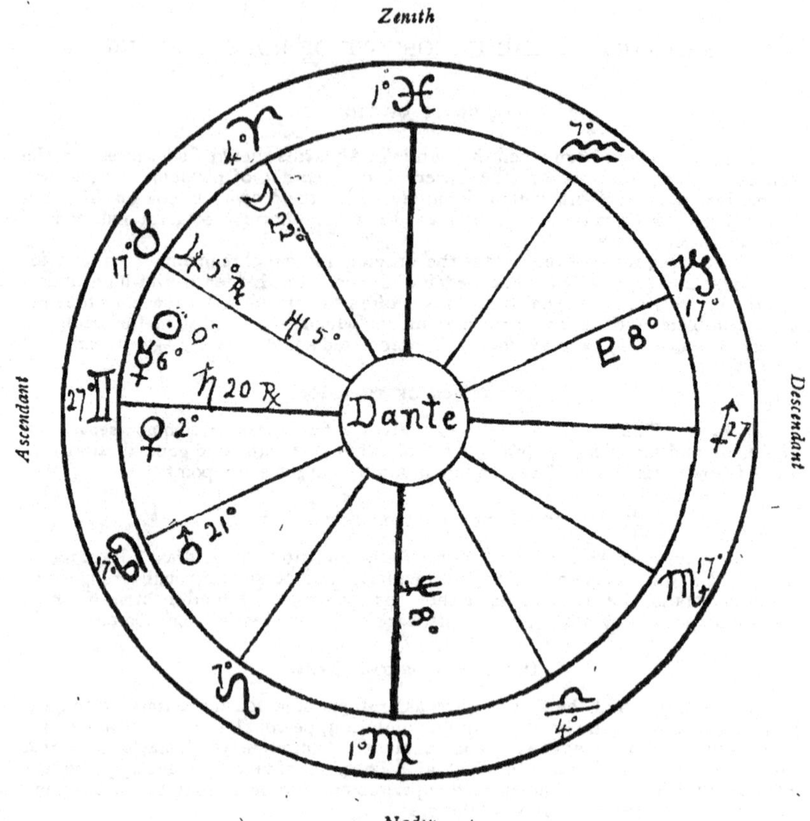

DANTE ALIGHIERI

Born in Florence, May 14th, 1265

The exact day is uncertain, but May 14th has been selected by authorities for the celebration of his birth on great occasions, such as the 500th anniversary. He tells us himself in the *Paradiso* that the Sun was in Gemini, and also that Gemini was rising (see p. 34) The planetary groupings given here have been calculated by three different mathematicians A day later the Moon would have entered its exaltation, Taurus, but Aries is more likely, as the Poet was distinctly polemical in many of his utterances Information through the courtesy of "Kymry"

Pluto is in Capricorn, trine to Jupiter, Uranus, and Neptune. Will well attuned, and operative.

DANTE

This horoscope suggests a much more complex personality than appears in the analysis, for Saturn and Venus are both rising The former gives a sense of rhythm, the latter a love of melody, beauty and harmony, and the power of appreciation Saturn is associated with ambition, and—in *Gemini*—with impulsiveness, which would certainly be intensified by the fact that it is in aspect to both Mars, the energy, and the Moon, the inherent tendencies The fact that these two are frowning at each other, almost exactly square, from Cancer and Aries—the signs associated with combat and patriotism—is very significant, and the sight of Neptune in the house of home and fatherland, square to Mercury, the ruler, suggests worry and trouble connected with the place of birth The inner life of the poet was, however, tranquil and serene and happiness came to him through it. His Mind and Outlook and Spiritual Aspirations were in perfect accord—Jupiter in exact conjunction with Uranus and trine to Neptune. The relationship of these three planets proclaims the seer, and the intuitive and inspirational tendencies would all be much strengthened by the position of Pisces at the Zenith. Looking at this horoscope one realises how all physical experiences must have sunk into insignificance after the glories of the heavenly plane had been revealed. To such a man these spiritual experiences would be infinitely more real and precious than any earthly successes and ambitions could ever be The insight and intuition of the poet can rarely have been equalled

ANALYSIS OF THE HOROSCOPE OF DANTE

A *Ascendant*:—GEMINI ♊ *Ruler*.—MERCURY ☿

DESCRIPTION.

	According to Position of Signs		According to Position of Planets	
Type	Versatile	*and*	Versatile (*bis*)	☉ in ♊
Watchwords	Variety	*and*	Action	☽ in ♈
Method	Experimental	*and*	Militant	☽ in ♈
Style	Expressive	*and*	Oratorical	☽ in ♈
Intellect	Inventive	*and*	Inventive (*bis*)	☿ in ♊
Speech	Eloquent	*and*	Eloquent (*bis*)	☿ in ♊
Manner	Sympathetic	*and*	Sympathetic (*bis*)	♄ in ♊
Bearing	Eager	*and*	Self-reliant	♂ in ♋
Temperament	Joyous	*and*	Joyous (*bis*)	Ruler in ♊

B *Zenith*.—PISCES ♓.

Functions	The Poet	*and*	Artist	☉ in ♊
Outlook	Romantic	*yet*	Settled	♅ in ♉
Nature	Plastic	*and*	Sensitive	☉ in ♊
Affections	Adoring	*and*	Loyal	♀ in ♋
Attitude	Peaceable	*yet*	Prepared	♂ in ♋
Sex-Attitude	Reverent	*and*	Constant	♂ in ♋
Disposition	Unworldly	*yet*	Just	♃ in ♉

C *Descendant*—SAGITTARIUS ♐

Mind	Inquiring	*and*	Contemplative	♃ in ♉

D *Nadir*:—VIRGO ♍

Character	Upright	*yet*	Impulsive	♄ in ♊
Keynotes	Purity	*and*	Joy	☉ in ♊

SUMMARY OF DANTE'S HOROSCOPE

Influence of the Sun

☉ *in* ♊ Those born with the Sun in Gemini should find success in the sphere of intellectual achievement or artistic expression, possibly in both, for this sign of the twins is dual, and many persons under its influence pursue two callings, either contemporaneously or alternately

The driving force of this sign is a certain exuberance or overflow of energy, which must find expression, and prefers to find it in a variety of ways At its highest it is a divine rapture or joy, and at its lowest a feverish excitability leading to constant change of plans and occupation, and consequent waste of time and energy

Influence of the Moon

☽ *in* ♈ The Moon in Aries gives habitual hopefulness and a tendency to take up new ideas and fresh enterprises with enthusiasm and possibly also to drop them before they have come to anything

Influence of the Ascendant

♊ Gemini as Ascendant suggests attainment through variety of intellectual experience, leading to frequent alternations between joy and grief, which stimulate the native to constant and insistent efforts to express himself with sufficient energy to arouse sympathy or response in others

Influence of the Zenith

♓ Pisces at the Zenith gives aspirations for true insight or clearness of vision, unclouded by illusion, and an ambition to interpret such vision in some way that shall bring humanity nearer to the heart of the universe The point of view is that of the poet, the mystic or the seer

Influence of the Descendant

♐ Sagittarius descending is associated with boundless mental curiosity, a mind that is constantly inquiring or probing into some matter, and is not easily satisfied

Influence of the Nadir

♍ Virgo at the Nadir suggests, as the basis of character, that instinct for health and purity which leads to upright dealing, and makes a man shrink from all that is morbid, hysterical and unclean

Zenith

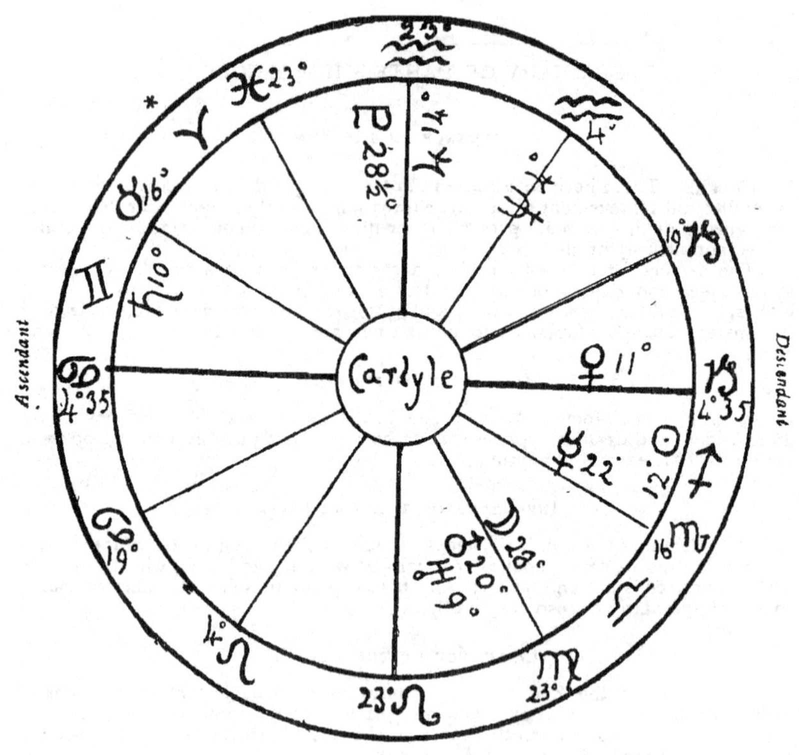

Nadir

THOMAS CARLYLE

Born at Ecclefechan, December 4th, 1795.

The hour is uncertain, but Mr Alexander Carlyle, nephew of the great Thomas, gives the information that almost all the biographical details given in *Sartor Resartus* about Teufelsdrockh were *autobiographical* records on the part of the author, and that the declaration that he was born *towards dusk* is probably one of those Considerable doubt is thrown on the subject by the fact that, in the passage quoted, Carlyle also states that the Sun was in Libra—conceivably a blind, to prevent the entire identification of the character with himself.

---

* Pluto and Jupiter are both at the zenith in Aquarius. The Will is set on stating truths and exposing humbug.

CARLYLE

This horoscope gives us an interesting example of the effect of cross-current in the planetary influences Uranus, Saturn and the Sun, giving the native two squares and a serious opposition to fight The first two represent the outlook and the character, and the third the success in life; so that the fight would be both internal and external, and, if the hour is surmised correctly, the Sun is most appropriately placed—heavily afflicted in the house of health. The outlook was too critical, the character too wayward, and the result was a tendency to worry, producing chronic indigestion, which form of suffering is in itself an argument that Cancer was rising. In spite of this tremendous handicap through lack of harmony, great things were achieved through intellectual and mental energy (Mercury sextile to Mars, and Jupiter sextile to the Sun).

Venus is chiefly beneficial, the affections stimulating the mind, widening the outlook and strongly contributing to the success, for this appreciative planet is sextile to Jupiter, trine to Uranus, and semi-sextile to the Sun. This in itself would be a refutation of the unkind gossip that for a time found a pet theme in his surmised attitude to his wife, and these are suggestions that the marriage meant real gain to him, but Venus opposes the ascendant, an unhappy position If the uncomplimentary adjectives in the tables corresponding to the list given on the following page are written out by the student, he will find that the worst faults—dogmatism, irritability, and over-insistence—were faults of the outer personality, of temperament and manner, and that underneath the rugged exterior beat a very warm and tender heart.

ANALYSIS OF THE HOROSCOPE OF THOMAS CARLYLE

A *Ascendant* :—CANCER ♋ *Ruler* :—DIANA (*The Moon*)

DESCRIPTION

	According to Position of Signs		Modified by Position of Planets	
Type	Parental or Brooding	*and*	Original or Eccentric	☉ in ♐
Watchwords	Sympathy	*and*	Utility	☽ in ♍
Method	Effective or Startling	*and*	Selective	☽ in ♍
Style	Metaphorical	*and*	Concise	☽ in ♍
Intellect	Reflective	*and*	Penetrating	☿ in ♏
Speech	Picturesque	*and*	Decided or Dogmatic	☿ in ♏
Manner	Dignified	*yet*	Sympathetic	♄ in ♊
Bearing	Self-reliant or Proud	*and*	Helpful	♂ in ♍
Temperament	Intense or Bitter	*and*	Active or Irritable	Ruler in ♍

B *Zenith* :—AQUARIUS ♒

Functions	Truth-Seeker	*and*	Sage	☉ in ♐
Outlook	Unbiassed	*yet*	Critical	♅ in ♍
Nature	Sincere	*and*	Transparent	☉ in ♐
Affections	Worldwide	*yet*	Deep-rooted	♀ in ♑
Attitude	Forgiving	*and*	Alert	♂ in ♍
Sex-Attitude	Dispassionate	*and*	Faithful	♂ in ♍
Disposition	Disinterested	*and*	Disinterested (*bis*)	♃ in ♒

C *Descendant* :—CAPRICORN ♑

Mind	Concentrative	*yet*	Open	♃ in ♒

D *Nadir* :—LEO ♌

Character	Merciful	*and*	Impulsive	♄ in ♊
Keynotes	Glory	*and*	Wisdom	☉ in ♐

SUMMARY OF THE HOROSCOPE OF THOMAS CARLYLE

INFLUENCE OF THE SUN.

☉ in ♐. Those born with the Sun in Sagittarius should find success in some sphere of activity which involves the constant exercise of the reason and the development of the logical faculty Wisdom and understanding will be the heart's desire, and everything that favours progress in their direction—travel or exploration, contact with other minds, or inquiry into unfamiliar systems of philosophy, theology or law—may be turned to account by the native

The driving force of the sign is the craving for wisdom and the determination to seek it out through the exercise of the reason, which is sometimes perverted into a tendency to argue or chop-logic, to doubt, to dispute, and to deny, until the lamp of Truth is obscured in a fog of casuistry, and the enquirer is lost in a mist of his own making.

INFLUENCE OF THE MOON

☽ in ♍ The Moon in Virgo gives practical and business-like methods of attacking work, habits of industry, and a critical rather than an appreciative turn of mind and style of expression ; also, as a rule, a tendency to irritability

INFLUENCE OF THE ASCENDANT

♋. Cancer as ascendant suggests attainment through teaching or preaching, or public-speaking, or through motherhood or its equivalent, the guardianship, nursing or tending of the helpless, the ignorant or the infirm, work which requires endless patience, tenderness, adaptability and tenacity of purpose

INFLUENCE OF THE ZENITH

♒ Aquarius at the Zenith gives aspirations for a clear outlook and breadth of vision, and an ambition to add to the sum of human knowledge, and to enlarge the views of others, an ambition sometimes perverted into a tendency to fatigue other people, by forcing one's own opinions upon them with too much insistence and at unsuitable times The point of view is that of the Truth Seeker, unbiassed and open-minded.

INFLUENCE OF THE DESCENDANT

♑ Capricorn descending suggests the type of mind which is concentrative and profound, and possibly somewhat given to bigotry or prejudice

INFLUENCE OF THE NADIR

♌ Leo at the Nadir suggests as the basis of character that quality of mercy which springs from a radiant and irradiating faith in God and in man; a faith which makes it possible to believe the best, even against apparent evidence of injustice or depravity, and which sometimes manifests as a too slack and easy-going tolerance of things as they are

Zenith

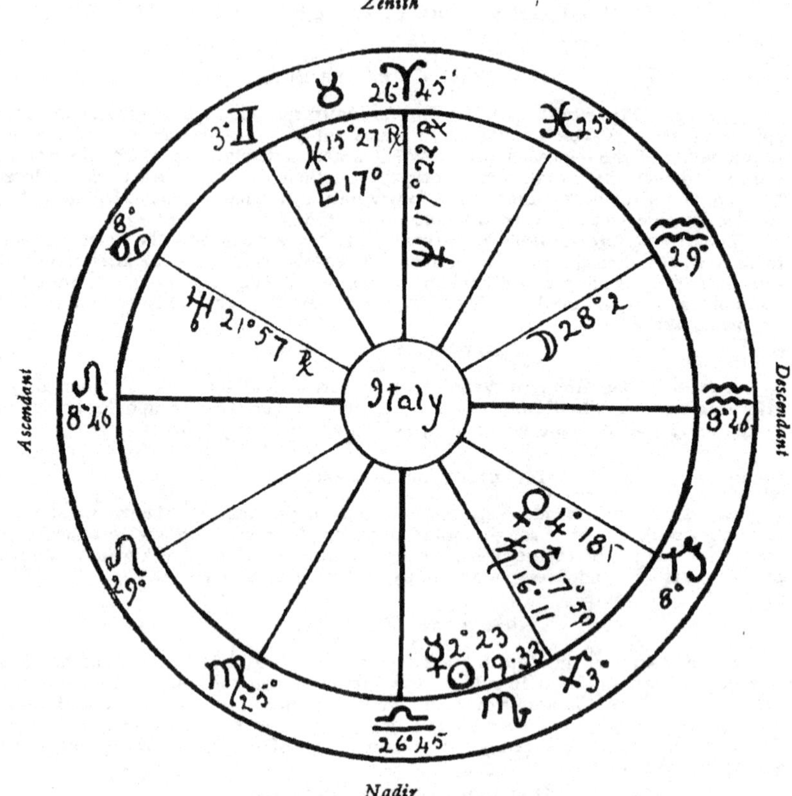

Nadir

KING VICTOR EMMANUEL III OF ITALY.

Born November 11th, 1869, about 10.15 p m., Naples.

Copied, by permission, from "Modern Astrology," July, 1910

The hours of the Royal births are naturally taken from the public announcements in the newspapers of the day.

KING VICTOR EMMANUEL

This horoscope is a thoroughly kingly one, and should be contemplated with lively feelings of satisfaction by all true lovers of Italy, for the Sun, the success, is in the house of His Majesty's Home and Fatherland, a position peculiarly appropriat to a monarch who has set himself steadily from the day of his accession to pull up the level of his country's education, administration and financial integrity, and as a matter of fact Italy has steadily progressed in these directions ever since he came to the throne. This is a peaceful and friendly horoscope, in spite of its martial zenith, and the Pioneer rather than the Warrior is the true description of the man. There are no aggressive tendencies, although there is a certain amount of pride and independence Uranus sextile to Jupiter will give wonderful insight, and Neptune square to Uranus an over-plus of intuition, possibly manifesting occasionally in actual flashes of clairvoyance or clairaudience His success is materially aided by his own personal hard work—Mars, the Energy, in conjunction with Saturn, the Character, and both sextile to the Sun The said conjunction will give trouble when the progressed aspects come up against it by giving more energy than can be well used, but it is normally of enormous benefit Uranus in Cancer gives the patriotic outlook and is trine to the Sun—another excellent point Venus, the affections, and the Moon, which in a man's horoscope often stands for his wife, are very favourable, respectively sextile and trine to Mercury, keeping guard against intellectual worry and waste of power

Italy dethroned this constitutional monarch, and submitted to Mussolini as dictator, with tragic results for herself through wars and invasions. When her patience was exhausted, his murder put an end to his absolute rule. Note in this royal horoscope that the Sun, in the house of heredity and Fatherland, is opposed by Pluto in Taurus.

ANALYSIS OF THE HOROSCOPE OF KING VICTOR EMMANUEL III.

A *Ascendant*.—LEO ♌ *Ruler*:—APOLLO (*The Sun*)

DESCRIPTION

	According to Position of Signs.		Modified by Position of Planets	
Type	Regal	*and*	Commanding	☉ in ♏
Watchwords	Faith	*and*	Tolerance	☽ in ♒
Method	Deputing	*and*	Sympathetic	☽ in ♒
Style	Straightforward	*and*	Descriptive	☽ in ♒
Intellect	Comprehensive	*and*	Penetrating	☿ in ♏
Speech	Deliberate	*and*	Decided	☿ in ♏
Manner	Stately	*yet*	Genial	♄ in ♐
Bearing	Magnanimous	*and*	Friendly	♂ in ♐
Temperament	Energetic	*and*	Reserved	Ruler in ♏

B *Zenith*.—ARIES ♈

Functions	Pioneer	*and*	Governor	☉ in ♏
Outlook	Expectant	*and*	Patriotic	♅ in ♋
Nature	Impetuous	*and*	Thorough	☉ in ♏
Affections	Impulsive	*yet*	Deep-rooted	♀ in ♑
Attitude	Courageous	*and*	Uncompromising	♂ in ♐
Sex-attitude	Ardent	*and*	Sincere	♂ in ♐
Disposition	Generous	*and*	Just	♃ in ♉

C *Descendant*.—AQUARIUS ♒

Mind	Open	*and*	Contemplative	♃ in ♉

D *Nadir*.—LIBRA ♎.

Character	Honourable	*and*	Independent	♄ in ♐
Keynotes	Beauty	*and*	Power	☉ in ♏

SUMMARY OF THE HOROSCOPE OF KING VICTOR EMMANUEL III

Influence of the Sun

☉ *in* ♏ Those born when the Sun is in Scorpio should find success in some sphere of activity which demands the exercise of concentration and of personal magnetism; or which is associated with the mastery of men or of natural forces; with work that is vitalising or regenerating or dominating in some degree, and is in some way associated with the use—or mis-use—of power.

The driving force of the sign is excess of energy, which must find an outlet, and prefers to find it, either in the generation or creation of new forms and fresh bodies, or the destruction of those that are old and outworn At its best it is a vivifying and vitalising force, but when perverted it takes delight in hastening the work of destruction, degeneration and death

Influence of the Moon.

☽ *in* ♒ The Moon in Aquarius is associated with habits of careful observation and an inclination to examine searchingly into the truth of any matter which comes up for discussion, also, sometimes, a bent towards the study of natural or physical science

Influence of the Ascendant

♌ Leo as ascendant suggests attainment through Kingship or Fatherhood; through responsibility for the welfare of others

Influence of the Zenith

♈ Aries at the Zenith gives spiritual aspirations for complete manifestation, and practical ambitions to be always in the van-guard and to take part in pioneer work of some kind. The outlook is bright and hopeful, expectant and progressive, sometimes, rather unsettled

Influence of the Descendant

♒ Aquarius descending is associated with the type of mind that is absolutely open, unbiassed and free from prejudice, and which consequently often appears to be uncertain in its conclusions

Influence of the Nadir

♎. Libra at the Nadir suggests, as the basis of character, a scrupulous sense of honour, and a love of balance, or "fair proportions," which involves a sense of justice and also a keen appreciation of beauty

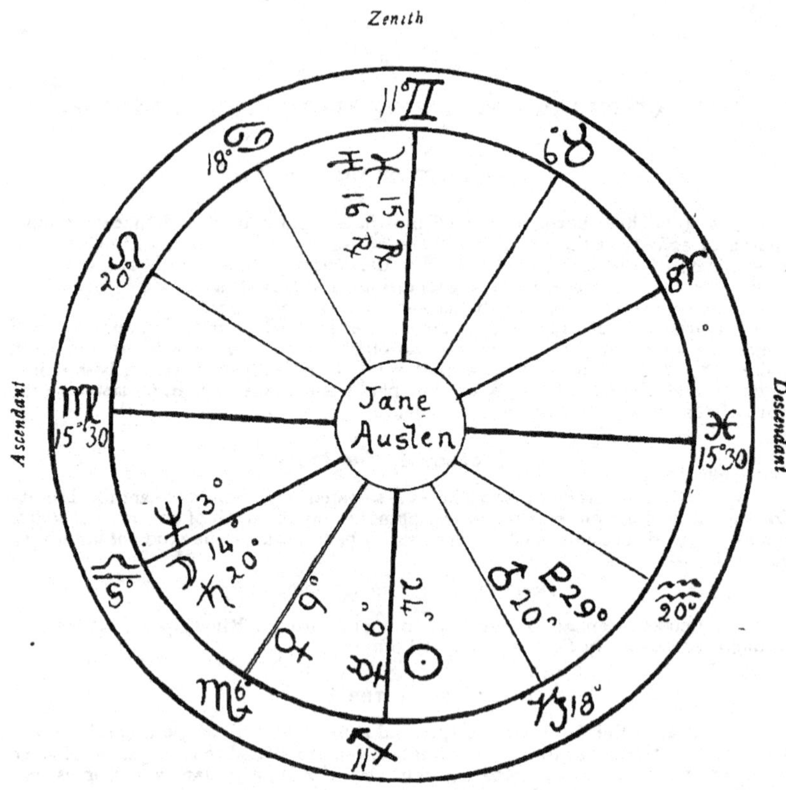

HOROSCOPE OF JANE AUSTEN

Born on the night of December 16th, 1775, before midnight, at Steventon, Hampshire.

Information kindly furnished by William Austen Leigh, Esq., who looked up a letter announcing her birth, written by her father, and still extant. Virgo was rising during the two hours preceding midnight, and her personality, as described by her biographers, makes Leo, the preceding sign, very unlikely.

Pluto in Capricorn gave her a complete understanding of the snobbery rampant in the class she depicted, and which her Sagittarian gifts helped her to castigate.

JANE AUSTEN

In a preceding chapter (page 94) this gifted authoress was claimed as a Libran, because of certain characteristics in her style. Readers will notice that the Moon, Saturn, and Neptune are grouped in Libra, influencing the Style, Method, Character, Manner and Aspirations; so that the mistake was a pardonable one A more experienced astrological student than the writer wrote a criticism of this claim, soon after it was published, pointing out the Virgo traits, shown in the description of her personality, remarking on the Virginian skill of the fingers that succeeded "in everything they tried to do," and adding that the date of her death suggested to him that the twenty-first degree of Virgo was rising, when she was born.

This combination of Virginian and Libran influences works out as an exceedingly lovable type—bright, lively, witty and charming, and the strong Sagittarian accentuation would add buoyancy, vigour and originality. The Sun in the house of *Home and Heredity* is well placed for one who was even more successful as a dutiful, loving and beloved daughter, sister and aunt, than as a novelist.

The high place she has taken in English literature may be associated with the quick insight given by the brilliant conjunction of Jupiter and Uranus at the Zenith, both trine to the Moon Neptune, sextile to Mercury, quickens an already active intellect by adding intuition to it Any aspect between these two makes the intuitive faculties work so easily that it is often difficult for the native to distinguish what he knows intuitively from what he knows by the exercise of the reason. The only bad aspect here is that of Mars to Saturn—which worked out in poor health

ANALYSIS OF THE HOROSCOPE OF JANE AUSTEN

A *Ascendant* :—VIRGO ♍ *Ruler* :—VULCAN.

DESCRIPTION.

	According to Position of Signs		*Modified by Position of Planets*	
Type	Practical	*and*	Original	☉ in ♐
Watchwords	Utility	*and*	Harmony	☽ in ♎
Method	Selective	*and*	Weighing	☽ in ♎
Style	Concise	*and*	Persuasive	☽ in ♎
Intellect	Discriminating	*and*	Logical	☿ in ♐
Speech	Pointed	*and*	Frank	☿ in ♐
Manner	Serious	*yet*	Gracious	♄ in ♎
Bearing	Helpful	*and*	Charming	♂ in ♑
Temperament	Active	*and*	Buoyant	Ruler in ♐

B *Zenith* :—GEMINI ♊

Functions	Artist	*and*	Critic	☉ in ♐
Outlook	Untrammelled	*and*	Untrammelled (*bis*)	♅ in ♊
Nature	Sensitive	*and*	Transparent	☉ in ♐
Affections	Spontaneous	*and*	Passionate	♀ in ♏
Attitude	Resourceful	*and*	Diplomatic	♂ in ♑
Sex-attitude	Responsive	*and*	Submissive	♂ in ♑
Disposition	Lavish	*and*	Lavish (*bis*)	♃ in ♊

C *Descendant* :—PISCES ♓

Mind	Receptive	*and*	Fertile	♃ in ♊

D *Nadir* :—SAGITTARIUS ♐.

Character	Independent	*and*	Honourable	♄ in ♎
Keynotes	Wisdom	*and*	Wisdom (*bis*)	☉ in ♐

SUMMARY OF THE HOROSCOPE OF JANE AUSTEN

Influence of the Sun

☉ *in* ♐ Those born with the Sun in Sagittarius should find success in some sphere of activity which involves the constant exercise of the reason, and the development of the logical faculty Wisdom and understanding will be the heart's desire, and everything that favours progress in their direction—travel or exploration, contact with other minds and inquiry into unfamiliar systems of philosophy, theology or law—may be turned to account by the native

The driving force of the sign is the craving for wisdom and the determination to seek it out through the exercise of the reason which is sometimes perverted into a tendency to argue or chop-logic, to doubt, to dispute and to deny, till the lamp of Truth is obscured in a fog of casuistry, and the inquirer is lost in a mist of his own making The Libran accentuation in this horoscope would cancel any belligerent inclination

Influence of the Moon

☽ *in* ♎. The Moon in Libra gives a tendency to pass easily and naturally from one kind of work to another, and to adapt oneself to changing conditions and environment and to make the best of them This position gives a well balanced, loving and lovable nature, and ensures a certain amount of popularity

Influence of the Ascendant

♍ Virgo as ascendant suggests attainment through disinterested and faithful service, through painstaking and possibly highly skilled labour, done on behalf of others, with little or no thought of recognition or reward, through work of some kind which requires discrimination and critical acumen, and an industry that never flags

Influence of the Zenith

♊ Gemini at the Zenith gives spiritual aspirations for perfection of expression, and ambitions for some kind of artistic or intellectual achievement that has in it an element of freshness and originality The outlook is free and untrammeled, even, in some cases, unconventional

Influence of the Descendant

♓ Pisces descending is associated with a type of mind peculiarly receptive and impressionable, and very frequently alive and responsive to psychic impressions, in short, mediumistic

Influence of the Nadir

♐ Sagittarius at the Nadir suggests, as the basis of character, a certain sturdy independence, akin to pride, which asks no favour and flatters no man

Zenith

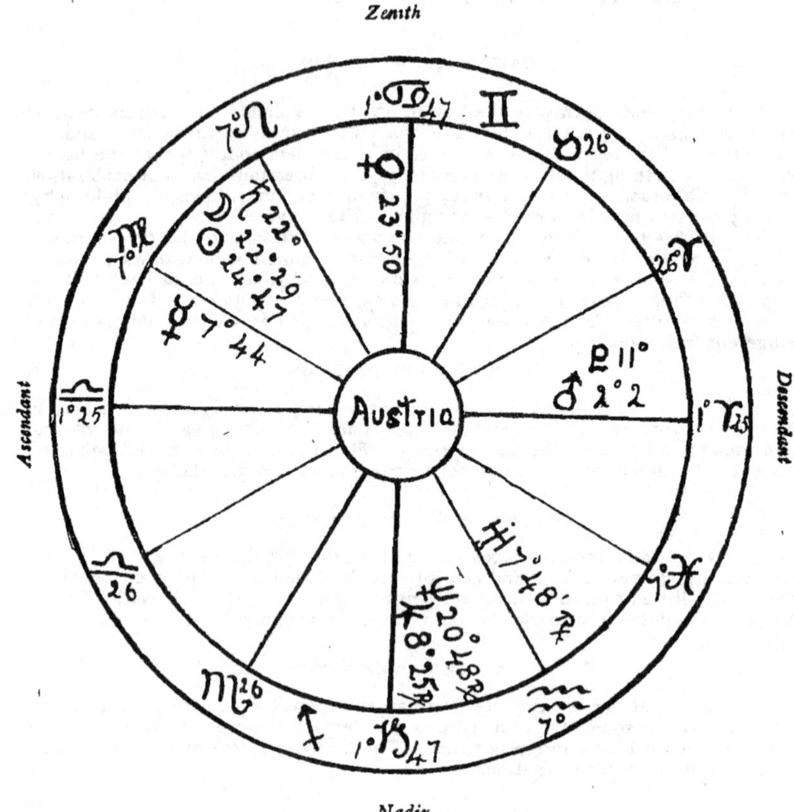

Nadir

HOROSCOPE OF THE EMPEROR FRANCIS JOSEPH OF AUSTRIA.

Born August 18th, 1830, 8 23 a m., Vienna.

Copied, by permission, from "Modern Astrology," July, 1910

Pluto is in conjuction with Mars in Aries in the Marriage house. His Empress was assassinated.

THE EMPEROR FRANCIS JOSEPH

The most striking accentuation in this horoscope is the brilliant conjunction of Sun, Moon and Saturn, all in Leo—a tremendous gathering together and centralising of force in this fixed and kingly sign The Success lies in Kingship of the type which reigns over the hearts of his people, for this group is in the house of the public, and semi-sextile to Venus, the ruler, which smiles benignantly from the Zenith: Jupiter is trine to Neptune, suggesting that the intellect and mind work well in harmony Neptune in opposition to Venus calls for the renunciation of happiness from the house of home and heredity, hinting at the sorrow which has touched this aged monarch so nearly, in his domestic life Uranus, a malefic, in the house of offspring, indicates the possibility of some kind of shock that will widen the outlook in that connection Jupiter, semi-sextile to Uranus, should give keen insight There is much tolerance and considerable understanding of human nature, as well as a strong appreciation of beauty in music, in art, and in life The inner craving is for perfection, and the ambitions go in the directions of organisation and order Mars in the house of partnership reminds us of the fearlessness and energy of his beautiful consort, and there are also suggestions of suffering of some kind connected with her to be found in the conjunction of Saturn with the Moon The Moon, in a man's horoscope, is often taken as signifying the wife, while the Sun in a woman's horoscope signifies the husband

ANALYSIS OF THE HOROSCOPE OF THE EMPEROR FRANCIS JOSEPH

A *Ascendant* —LIBRA ♎ *Ruler* —VENUS

DESCRIPTION.

	According to Position of Signs		*Modified by Position of Planets*	
Type	Adaptable	*yet*	Regal	☉ in ♌
Watchword	Harmony	*and*	Faith	☽ in ♌
Method	Weighing	*and*	Deputing	☽ in ♌
Style	Persuasive	*yet*	Straightforward	☽ in ♌
Intellect	Judicial	*and*	Discriminating	☿ in ♍
Speech	Polished	*and*	Pointed	☿ in ♍
Manner	Gracious	*and*	Stately	♄ in ♌
Bearing	Kindly	*yet*	Spirited	♂ in ♈
Temperament	Cheerful	*but*	Intense	Ruler in ♋

B *Zenith* —CANCER ♋

Functions	Prophet or Teacher	*and*	King	☉ in ♌
Outlook	Patriotic	*yet*	Unbiassed	♅ in ♒
Nature	Sympathetic	*and*	Hospitable	☉ in ♌
Affections	Loyal	*and*	Loyal (*bis*)	♀ in ♋
Attitude	Prepared	*and*	Courageous	♂ in ♈
Sex-attitude	Constant	*and*	Ardent	♂ in ♈
Disposition	Economical	*but*	Magnificent	♃ in ♑

C *Descendant* —ARIES ♈

Mind	Active	*yet*	Concentrative	♃ in ♑

D *Nadir*.—CAPRICORN ♑

Character	Ambitious	*and*	Merciful	♄ in ♌
Keynote	Reverence	*and*	Glory	☉ in ♌

SUMMARY OF THE HOROSCOPE OF THE EMPEROR FRANCIS JOSEPH OF AUSTRIA

Influence of the Sun

☉ *in* ♌ Those born when the Sun is in Leo should find success in some sphere of activity which gives them a chance to shine in the eyes of their fellow men and women They ought in some way to irradiate or brighten or inspire or harmonise the energies of others, either through the exercise of their own faculties or through the occupation of positions of responsibility which are associated with some sort of kingly or fatherly office.

The driving force of this sign is an abounding faith in God or in Destiny, sometimes perverted into a habit of leaving everything to Providence—or to other people—and shirking strenuous personal exertion of any kind

Influence of the Moon

☽ *in* ♌ The Moon in Leo is associated with a certain inner harmony or centralisation of force, which is a great help towards practical achievement, and also with a preference for simple, straightforward and direct methods of dealing with matters and with men.

Influence of the Ascendant

♎ Libra as ascendant suggests attainment through statesmanship or arbitration, or through the exercise of the natural affections and the efforts they inspire towards adjusting the environment and beautifying the life, by bringing harmony out of discord, or possibly through training or practice in one or other of the fine arts

Influence of the Zenith

♋ Cancer at the Zenith gives aspirations for perfect comprehension, and an ambition to influence one's fellow creatures by appealing to their imaginations and enlisting their sympathies The point of view is that of the patriot, national, clannish, and possibly prejudiced

Influence of the Descendant

♈ Aries descending suggests the type of mind which is ready to take in fresh ideas and inclines to progress in thought, passing quickly from one idea to another and which may possibly be lacking in the power of application.

Influence of the Nadir

♑ Capricorn at the Nadir suggests, as the basis of character, that desire for progress which is the mainspring of both involution and evolution.

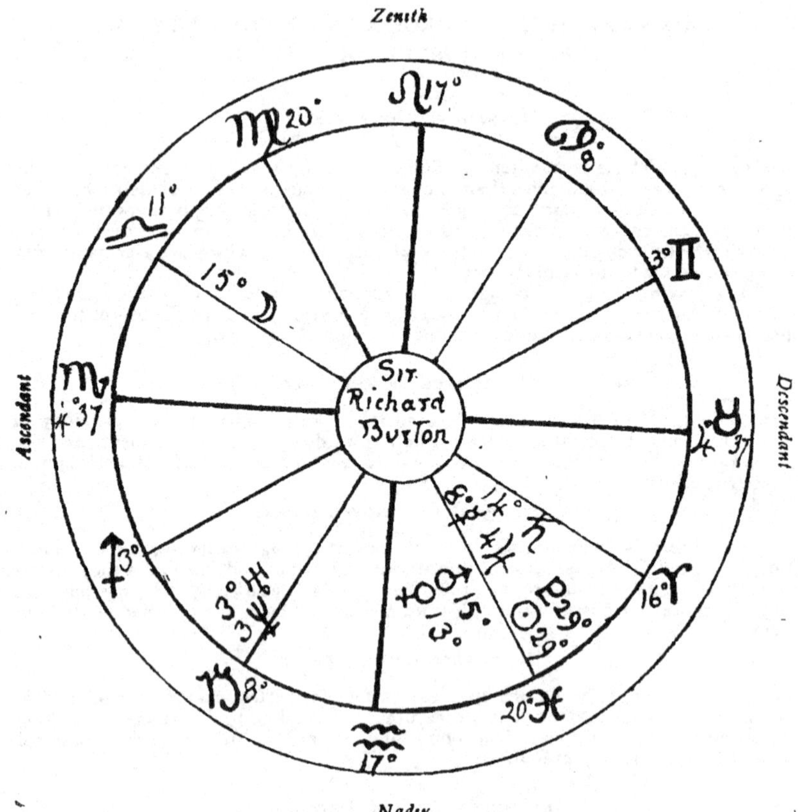

HOROSCOPE OF SIR RICHARD BURTON

Born March 19th, 1821, at Barham House, Hertfordshire, 9 30 p m

Time given by Burton himself in the autobiographical sketch included in the well known biography by his wife

SIR RICHARD BURTON

The conjunctions in this horoscope are positively uncanny Uranus and Neptune close together, and sextile to Jupiter and the Sun, suggest a brilliance and audacity rarely equalled—insight and intuition in absolute harmony with the workings of an exceptionally active mind, all contributing to the success, which is accentuated by the Sun's position in the house of glory. Stress and strain are represented by the opposition of Saturn—the character—to the Moon, which represents the inherent tendencies, and also indicates success or failure in money matters Further, the two conjoined malefics, Uranus and Neptune, are square to the Moon, and as the aspect is from the eleventh house to the third, disturbing and inharmonious conditions of some sort must have lost Burton many friends as well as a good deal of money. A very strange and exceptional personality, how great in achievement no one will ever know, for the scientific book to which he devoted the best years of his life was committed to the flames by his wife after his death, from a conscientious conviction that the subject he treated—the sex instinct—was better left alone In a man's horoscope the Moon is generally taken as representing the wife; that is to say, when the planets are being interpreted as *persons*, and the positions here are very interesting Lady Burton interfered with her husband's intellectual achievement and posthumous fame; not with his happiness She was a devoted and very loving wife, and though possibly her judgment was at fault in this matter of the book, she acted on principle, and not from impulse, fully realising the monetary sacrifice entailed.

Sir Richard Burton was one of the most gifted actors the world has ever seen, and in addition to that, was brilliant enough to improvise his own part and adventurous enough to play it coolly and intrepidly in the face of all manner of risks, in every quarter of the globe—and in every kind of setting—except the limited one of the actual theatre. The Sun, Mars and Venus, all in the Interpreter's sign of Pisces easily account for this power. As a linguist he was so brilliant that he could assume almost any nationality—including that of various oriental nations and tribes He was learned in astrology and in ancient traditions, knew enough of the great religions of the world to take part in their most solemn ceremonial on occasion, and was only once detected as a man of alien race or faith; and he wrote, besides other works, the only complete English translation of the *Arabian Nights* in existence

Piscarians are often good translators, and Pluto in Pisces emphasises his wonderful gifts as actor and interpreter.

ANALYSIS OF THE HOROSCOPE OF SIR RICHARD BURTON

A *Ascendant* —Scorpio ♏. *Ruler*:—Pluto ♇ (*an unknown planet*) *

Description

	According to Position of Signs		*Modified by Position of Planets*	
Type	Commanding	*and*	Inspired	☉ in ♓
Watchword	Justice	*and*	Beauty	☽ in ♎
Method	Analytical	*and*	Weighing	☽ in ♎
Style	Trenchant	*yet*	Persuasive	☽ in ♎
Intellect	Penetrating	*and*	Quick	☿ in ♈
Speech	Decided	*and*	Daring	☿ in ♈
Manner	Authoritative	*and*	Lively	♄ in ♈
Bearing	Heroic	*yet*	Unassuming	♂ in ♓
Temperament	Reserved	*and*	?	Ruler in ?

B *Zenith*:—Leo ♌

Function	King	*and*	Poet	☉ in ♓
Outlook	Tolerant	*yet*	Reverent	♅ in ♑
Nature	Hospitable	*and*	Plastic	☉ in ♓
Affections	Generous	*and*	Adoring	♀ in ♓
Attitude	Benevolent	*and*	Peaceable	♂ in ♓
Sex-attitude	Chivalrous	*and*	Reverent	♂ in ♓
Disposition	Trustful	*and*	Generous	♃ in ♈

C *Descendant*:—Taurus ♉

Mind	Contemplative	*and*	Receptive	♃ in ♓

D. *Nadir*:—Aquarius ♒

Character	Considerate	*but*	Indomitable	♄ in ♈
Keynotes	Truth	*and*	Love	☉ in ♓

* Traditionally the Negative side of Mars. In all the children of Scorpio the position of Mars should be carefully noted, for as *Power* is their chief characteristic, the direction of their *Energy* is of enormous importance.

SUMMARY OF THE HOROSCOPE OF SIR RICHARD BURTON

Influence of the Sun.

☉ *in* ♓. Those born with the Sun in Pisces will find their best success in the field of renunciation and self-sacrifice, in which achievement they will be largely aided by their intuitive knowledge of the reality of the spiritual world, and the comparative unimportance of all outward appearances and shows This knowledge is often accompanied by a power of interpretation which is to some extent a revelation to others, and also by a marvellous receptivity to impressions from the higher planes

The driving force of the sign is Love, of the type which manifests as an intense craving for union with the Beloved, who, rightly recognised, is the higher self or *the mystic Christ*, the divine element in every man. This craving for a fuller and more extended consciousness is sometimes misread or perverted into a craving for such temporary intoxication or uplifting as is associated with the gratification of the lower passions or the misuse of alcohol or drugs.

Influence of the Moon.

♎. The Moon in Libra gives a tendency to pass easily and naturally from one kind of work to another, and to adapt oneself to changing conditions and environment, making the best of them. This position generally gives a well-balanced, loving and lovable nature, and ensures a certain amount of popularity.

Influence of the Ascendant.

♏ Scorpio as ascendant suggests attainment through heroic endurance and self control, and the determination to conquer disease and weakness and temptation of every kind, mental, moral and physical, both in oneself and in others. The special work will probably be concerned with the domination of natural forces, involving some kind of scientific training in investigation, or the exercise of absolute authority over others

Influence of the Zenith.

♌. Leo at the Zenith gives aspirations to glorify God by letting one's light shine before men, and by thus irradiating the lives of others. The ambitions are for glory and renown, sometimes perverted into a desire for praise and flattery even from those whose verdict is of no value. The point of view is central. In other words, the Leonian looks at every side of the question from the heart of it.

Influence of the Nadir.

♒. Aquarius at the Nadir suggests, as the basis of character, a strong sense of brotherhood, springing from the realisation of the common origin of all mankind and of all manifestation.

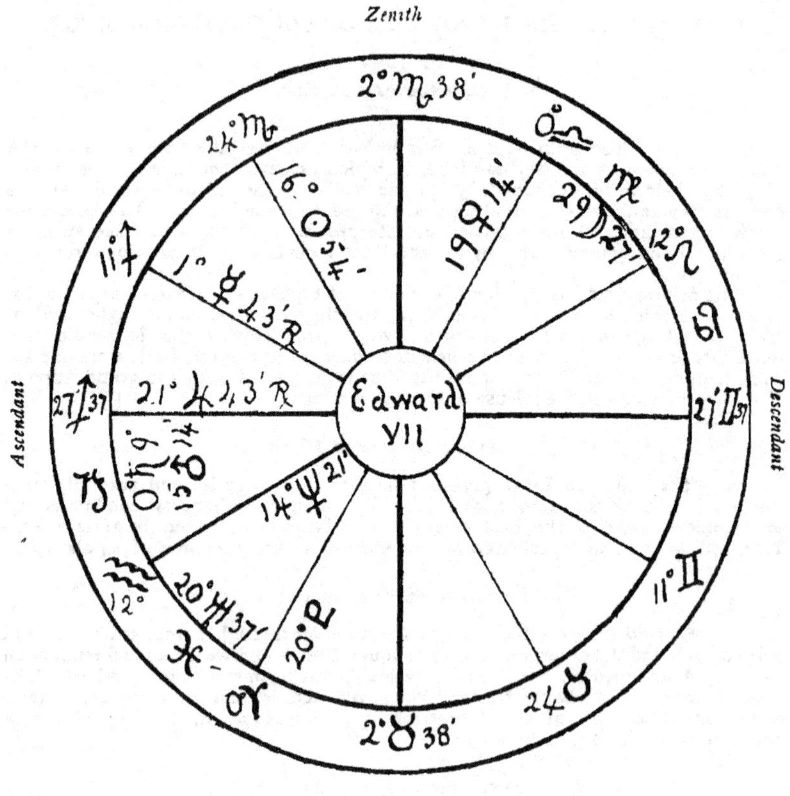

HOROSCOPE OF KING EDWARD VII

Born November 9th, 1841, 10 48 a m , London

Copied, by kind permission of Mr. Alan Leo, from "*Modern Astrology*" for July, 1910.

Information from public announcements of the event

KING EDWARD VII.

This is a horoscope in which the rising sign is emphatically the strongest. Not only has it Jupiter—its own ruler—in it, but Mercury also, so that the outer man, as indicated by speech and manner, as well as the thinker behind, was typically Sagittarian in form and expression. Saturn rising is generally associated with the stern discipline of poverty or hardships in early youth In this case a spartan simplicity of life and a very strict training were meted out by loving parents to their firstborn as the best preparation for the position of great responsibility to which he was born, and the *régime* must have been somewhat hard on a liberty-loving Sagittarian Later, it was realised that the young Prince, true to his type, learnt far more quickly and thoroughly from travel and from personal intercourse with his fellow creatures than he would ever do from books There is a tremendous amount of strong practical common sense in this horoscope, a great kindliness and power of appreciation, a strong will and immense energy, nearly all of which was concentrated on the physical plane, making him efficient in what he undertook Jupiter, the ruler, sextile to Uranus and Semi-sextile to the Sun, would give insight and intuition. The only square is that of Neptune to the Sun, the only trine Neptune to Venus The first is bad for worldly wealth (♆ *being in the second house*) The King's income in his early days was insufficient for the claims upon it. The second suggests a wealth of happiness and of affection—Venus being especially powerful in her own sign of Libra—and very strong emotions generally

---

Pluto in Aries favours progressive movements, and adds vital energy, that "fiery" element being further strengthened by Pluto's trine to Jupiter in Sagittarius Note contradictory aspects. This warrior, by diplomacy and common sense, kept the peace.

ANALYSIS OF THE HOROSCOPE OF KING EDWARD VII.

A *Ascendant* :—SAGITTARIUS ♐. *Ruler* —JUPITER

DESCRIPTION

	According to Position of Signs.		*Modified by the Position of Planets.*	
Type	Original	*and*	Commanding	☉ in ♏
Watchwords	Liberty and Law	*and*	Utility	☽ in ♍
Method	Argumentative	*and*	Selective	☽ in ♍
Style	Vigorous	*and*	Concise	☽ in ♍
Intellect	Logical	*and*	Logical (*bis*)	☿ in ♐
Speech	Frank	*and*	Frank (*bis*)	☿ in ♐
Manner	Genial	*yet*	Authoritative	♄ in ♑
Bearing	Friendly	*and*	Adaptable	♂ in ♑
Temperament	Buoyant	*and*	Buoyant (*bis*)	Ruler in ♐

B *Zenith* :—SCORPIO ♏

Functions	Governor	*and*	Governor (*bis*)	☉ in ♏
Outlook	Fore-thoughtful	*and*	Romantic	♅ in ♓
Nature	Thorough	*and*	Thorough (*bis*)	☉ in ♏
Affections	Passionate	*and*	Tender	♀ in ♎
Attitude	Unflinching	*yet*	Diplomatic	♂ in ♑
Sex-attitude	Devoted	*and*	Protective	♂ in ♑
Disposition	Investive	*and*	Contented	♃ in ♐

C *Descendant* :—GEMINI ♊.

Mind	Fertile	*and*	Inquiring	♃ in ♐

D. *Nadir* :—TAURUS ♉.

Character	Trustworthy	*and*	Ambitious	♄ in ♑
Keynote	Peace	*and*	Power	☉ in ♏

SUMMARY OF THE HOROSCOPE OF KING EDWARD VII.

Influence of the Sun

☉ *in* ♏ Those born when the Sun is in Scorpio should find success in some sphere of activity which demands the exercise of concentration and of personal magnetism, or which is associated with the mastery of men or of natural forces; with work that is vitalising or regenerating or dominating in some degree, and in short with the use—or misuse—of *power*.

The driving force of this sign is excess of energy, which must find an outlet, and prefers to find it either in the generation or creation of new forms and fresh bodies, or in the destruction of those that are old and outworn At its best it is a vivifying, vitalising force, but when perverted, it takes a delight in hastening the work of destruction, degeneration and death

Influence of the Moon

♍ The Moon in Virgo gives practical and business-like methods of attacking work, habits of industry, and a critical rather than an appreciative turn of mind and style of expression, also, as a rule, a tendency to irritability (Probably cancelled in this case by Sagittarius, a genial sign, rising.)

Influence of the Ascendant

♐ Sagittarius as ascendant suggests attainment through some form of "sport"—mental or physical—that is to say through the eager pursuit of something which eludes capture; and, preferably, through the exercise of the reason and the searching out of such knowledge as will ultimately lead to true wisdom.

Influence of the Zenith

♏ Scorpio at the Zenith gives aspirations for perfect realisation of Divine strength, and practical ambitions for power over the lives of others through the exercise of the will. The point of view is that of the Governor, concentrated on the immediate future, and always on guard, vigilant, serious, and even inclined to be pessimistic; again Sagittarius would counteract this pessimism.

Influence of the Descendant.

♊. Gemini descending suggests the type of mind which is extremely fertile in ideas, but which does not always follow them up to a logical or practical conclusion; thus giving a certain impression of flightiness and irresponsibility

Influence of the Nadir.

♉. Taurus at the Nadir suggests, as the basis of character, stability and persistence—sometimes perverted into obstinacy This cancels the defect indicated in the previous paragraph

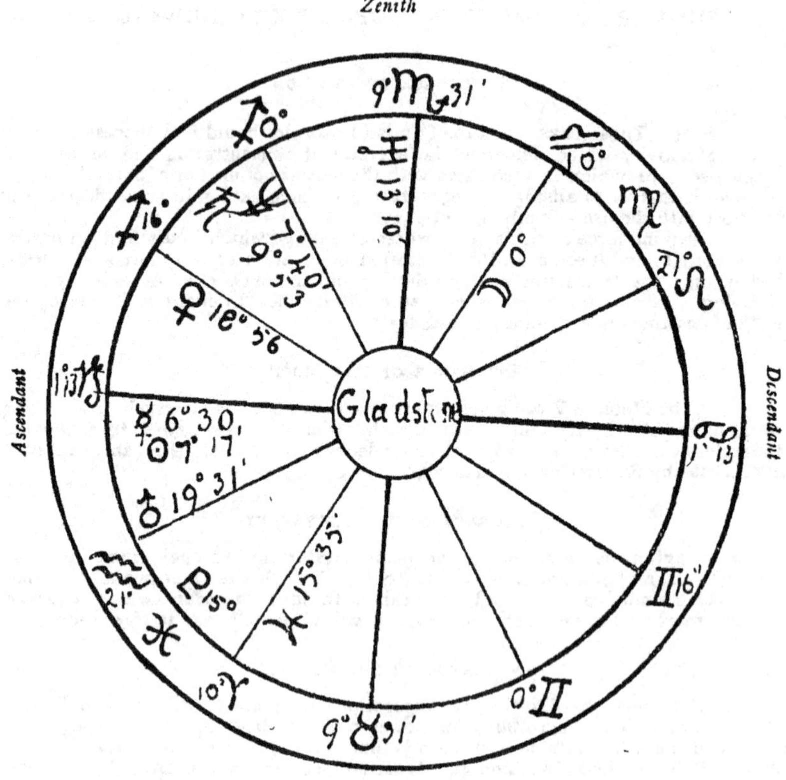

THE HOROSCOPE OF WILLIAM EWART GLADSTONE.

Born on December 29th, 1809, about breakfastime (i e., 8 a m.), Liverpool.

Data from "*The Astrologer's Magazine,*" Vol III , p 107

Horoscope copied, by kind permission from "*How to Judge a Nativity,*" p. 60, by Alan Leo

Pluto is in Pisces, adding good and bad aspects.

GLADSTONE

As is usual in the case of a very distinguished man, we get here a gathering of the forces indicated by conjunctions The Sun rising confers a radiating personality and in conjunction with Mercury suggests that the success will be an intellectual one Mars sextile both to Venus and Jupiter suggests that the mental energy and the happiness are closely associated Uranus at the Zenith makes the point of view an important factor in the career, and also a disturbing factor, for it is square to Mars and likely to provoke opposition. The clue to this will probably be found in the position of Jupiter in Aries—a progressive attitude of mind, leading to the alienation of old friends and former followers This note is accentuated by the powerful conjunction of Neptune and Saturn in eleventh house, which concerns the public and the native's relation to his fellow men The call to renunciation and the discipline of character both come from that quarter, and there must have been considerable suffering from adverse criticism, especially as one of the indications lacking in the horoscope is the influence that makes for a true sense of relative values—the saving grace of humour More and more is it borne in upon the writer, that Astrologers are right in attaching great importance to the personal factor in the success of those born with the Sun in the rising sign. It not only confers a certain kingliness but also, in many cases, such power and forcefulness and assurance of mastery as to suggest a Scorpio accentuation, even where it does not exist. Here the Scorpio Zenith, *plus* the rising Sun's forcefulness, fully accounts for the personal magnetism both of the orator and the man

ANALYSIS OF THE HOROSCOPE OF WILLIAM EWART GLADSTONE

A. *Ascendant:*—Capricorn ♑. *Ruler:*—Saturn ♄.

Description.

	According to Position of Signs		*Modified by Position of Planets*	
Type	Patriarchal	*yet*	Filial	☉ in ♑
Watchwords	Excelsior	*and*	Harmony	☽ in ♎
Method	Traditional	*and*	Weighing	☽ in ♎
Style	Ornate	*and*	Persuasive	☽ in ♎
Intellect	Profound	*and*	Profound (*bis*)	☿ in ♑
Speech	Fluent	*and*	Significant	☿ in ♑
Manner	Authoritative	*yet*	Genial	♄ in ♐
Bearing	Adaptable	*and*	Humane	♂ in ♒
Temperament	Devout	*and*	Buoyant	Ruler in ♐

B. *Zenith:*—Scorpio ♏

Functions	Governor	*and*	Priest	☉ in ♑
Outlook	Serious	*and*	Serious	♅ in ♏
Nature	Thorough	*and*	Zealous	☉ in ♑
Affections	Passionate	*and*	Honest	♀ in ♐
Attitude	Unflinching	*yet*	Forgiving	♂ in ♒
Sex-attitude	Devoted	*yet*	Dispassionate	♂ in ♒
Disposition	Investive	*and*	Generous	♃ in ♈

C. *Descendant.*—Cancer ♋.

Mind	Imaginative	*and*	Active	♃ in ♈

D. *Nadir:*—Taurus ♉.

Character	Trustworthy	*and*	Independent	♄ in ♐
Keynotes	Peace	*and*	Reverence	☉ in ♑

SUMMARY OF THE HOROSCOPE OF WILLIAM EWART GLADSTONE

Influence of the Sun.

☉ *in* ♑ Those born when the Sun is in Capricorn should find success in some sphere which gives scope for ambition—either personal or vicarious—and is associated with a recurrent possibility of promotion of some kind, preferably of a kind which is outwardly manifest to the eyes of men. Such ambition may be transmuted to aspiration and carry the energy wholly into the religious life, but even there, the outward and visible forms will absorb much of the attention, and the personal element—the office of mediator or ambassador to others, will be given tremendous weight

The driving force of this sign is reverence or devotion to the Highest, giving an earnest desire to attain This may be perverted into a dread of sinking to the lowest which either acts as a spur to exaggerated and unscrupulous efforts to climb rapidly and at the expense of others, or takes the form of a melancholy heaviness and discontent In Gladstone's case, the radiance of the rising Sun, would militate against melancholy

Influence of the Moon

☽ *in* ♎ The Moon in Libra gives a tendency to pass easily and naturally from one kind of work to another and to adapt oneself to changing conditions and environment and to make the best of them This position gives a well-balanced, lovable and loving nature and ensures a certain amount of popularity.

Influence of the Ascendant.

♑. Capricorn as ascendant suggests attainment through social and political ambition, personal or vicarious, leading either to strong concentration or to the development of diplomatic ability and the tendency to be all things to all men

Influence of the Zenith

♏ Scorpio at the Zenith gives aspirations for the perfect realisation of Divine Strength, and practical ambitions for power over the lives of others, through the exercise of the will The point of view is that of the governor, concentrated on the immediate future, and always on guard—vigilant, serious, and possibly inclined to be pessimistic

Influence of the Descendant

♋ Cancer descending suggests the type of mind which is imaginative and retentive, and inclined at times to fancifulness or brooding

Influence of the Nadir.

♉ Taurus at the Nadir suggests, as the basis of character, stability and persistence, sometimes perverted into obstinacy.

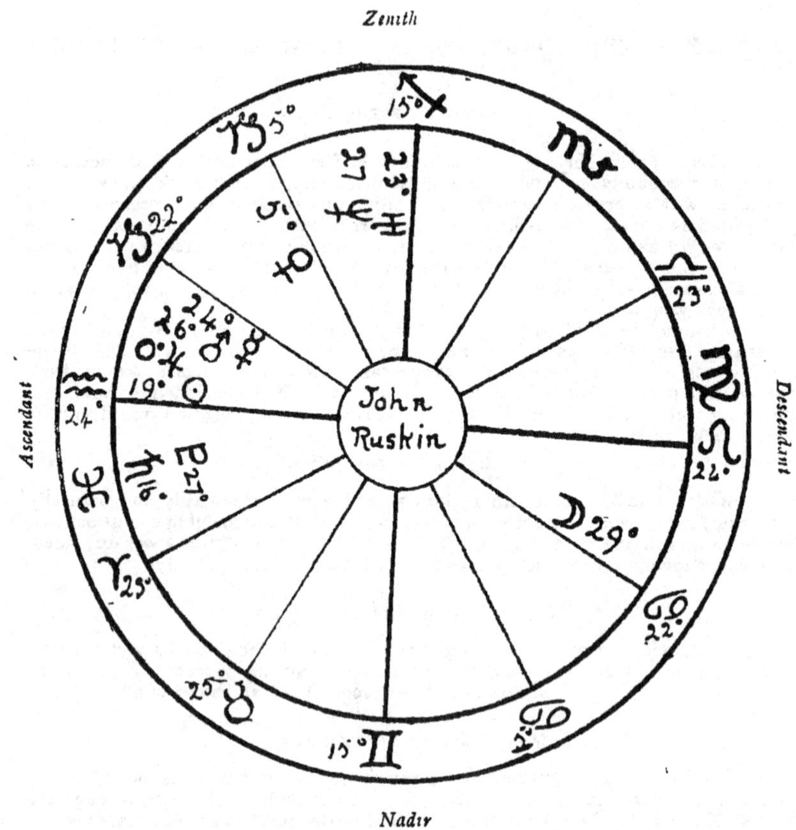

HOROSCOPE OF JOHN RUSKIN

Born February 8th, 1819, 7.30 a m , London

Data published in *The Life and Works of John Ruskin*, by W G Collingwood Published in one volume, by Methuen & Co in 1900 See Chapter II p 13 — "Into this family John Ruskin was born, on February 8th, 1819, at half-past seven in the morning" See also *How to Judge a Nativity*, by Alan Leo.

Pluto in Pisces, accentuating the Interpreter, with good aspects to Moon, Mercury, and Mars, but is square to Venus, Neptune, and Uranus.

RUSKIN

In looking at this horoscope the astrologer's eye would undoubtedly be first caught by the ruler—Uranus, right at the Zenith, in conjunction with Neptune, as the most interesting point about it These latest discovered planets are naturally the least understood, and anything that throws light upon them is correspondingly valuable. Neptune at the Zenith always suggests the possibility of direct inspiration from the higher planes, Uranus a tremendous widening of the horizon during the life In conjunction, well aspected, they should give extraordinary insight and intuition, the vision of the seer, and the power to interpret it They are both trine to the Moon, which is in Cancer, and is associated with the power to teach, so the message would certainly be delivered, but the Moon itself is afflicted by Mercury and Mars in opposition, so that worry, friction of some kind, or morbid imagination would be apt to hamper its delivery at times The Sun is rising, and those born at sunrise generally succeed in making their way in the world, while Venus, in the house of friends, promises happiness and help through them—and especially *mental* stimulus, for it is in excellent aspect to Jupiter, the planet of mind Many students still prefer, when reading Aquarian horoscopes, to take Saturn (its former negative ruler) as the true ruler, declaring that aspects to that planet are more important than those to Uranus for the majority of the children of this sign Naturally Saturn's position and aspects must be enormously important to Aquarians for that is the planet of character, and it is in virility or strength of character that they are apt to fail.

ANALYSIS OF THE HOROSCOPE OF JOHN RUSKIN

A *Ascendant*.—AQUARIUS ♒ *Ruler*.—URANUS ♅.

DESCRIPTION

	According to Position of Signs		*Modified by Position of Planets*	
Type	Scientific	*and*	Scientific (*bis*)	☉ in ♒
Watchwords	Tolerance	*and*	Sympathy	☽ in ♋
Method	Synthetic	*and*	Effective	☽ in ♋
Style	Descriptive	*and*	Picturesque	☽ in ♋
Intellect	Searching	*and*	Profound	☿ in ♑
Speech	Accurate	*and*	Significant	☿ in ♑
Manner	Earnest	*and*	Gentle	♄ in ♓
Bearing	Humane	*and*	Adaptable	♂ in ♑
Temperament	Serene	*and*	Buoyant	Ruler in ♐

B. *Zenith*.—SAGITTARIUS ♐.

Functions	The Sage	*and*	Truth-seeker	☉ in ♒
Outlook	Optimistic	*and*	Optimistic (*bis*)	♅ in ♐
Nature	Transparent	*and*	Sincere	☉ in ♒
Affections	Honest	*and*	Deep-rooted	♀ in ♑
Attitude	Uncompromising	*yet*	Diplomatic	♂ in ♑
Sex-attitude	Sincere	*and*	Protective	♂ in ♑
Disposition	Contented	*and*	Disinterested	♃ in ♒

C *Descendant*.—LEO ♌.

Mind	Large	*and*	Open	♃ in ♒

D. *Nadir*.—GEMINI ♊.

Character	Impulsive	*and*	Self-sacrificing	♄ in ♓
Keynotes	Joy	*and*	Truth	☉ in ♒

SUMMARY OF THE HOROSCOPE OF JOHN RUSKIN

Influence of the Sun

☉ *in* ♒ Those born with the Sun in Aquarius should find success in the sphere of the Truth-seeker—the Observer or Recorder of Phenomena They will probably engage in work which definitely alters their own outlook in life and possibly also enlarges the sympathies and the mental horizon of great numbers of their fellow creatures.

The driving-force of the sign is the craving for enlightenment, the passion for knowledge, and especially for knowledge of that occult or hidden Truth which underlies the mystery of manifestation This is often associated with a tendency to reject all incomplete or approximate statements which veil or distort the truth, a tendency which may be perverted into a depressed and depressing agnosticism

Influence of the Moon

☽ *in* ♋. The Moon in Cancer is associated with facility in teaching and tenderness in tending and sometimes with an inclination to employ effective and even startling methods, calculated to strike the imagination of the onlooker or listener.

Influence of the Ascendant

♒. Aquarius as ascendant suggests attainment through the constant observation and comparison of phenomena and of facts; through close investigation and research—possibly into occult matters, and through the unwearying study of the fundamental principles in nature or analysis of the mainsprings of action in mankind

Influence of the Zenith

♐ Sagittarius at the Zenith gives aspirations for perfect wisdom and understanding, and an ambition to make them of practical use to the world by carrying out the ideals grasped, and living according to conviction

Influence of the Descendant

♌ Leo descending suggests the type of mind which is large and comprehensive, but apt to lack clearness and precision.

Influence of the Nadir

♊. Gemini at the Nadir suggests, as the basis of character, a certain joyous impulsiveness which may possibly carry the native far in several successive directions.

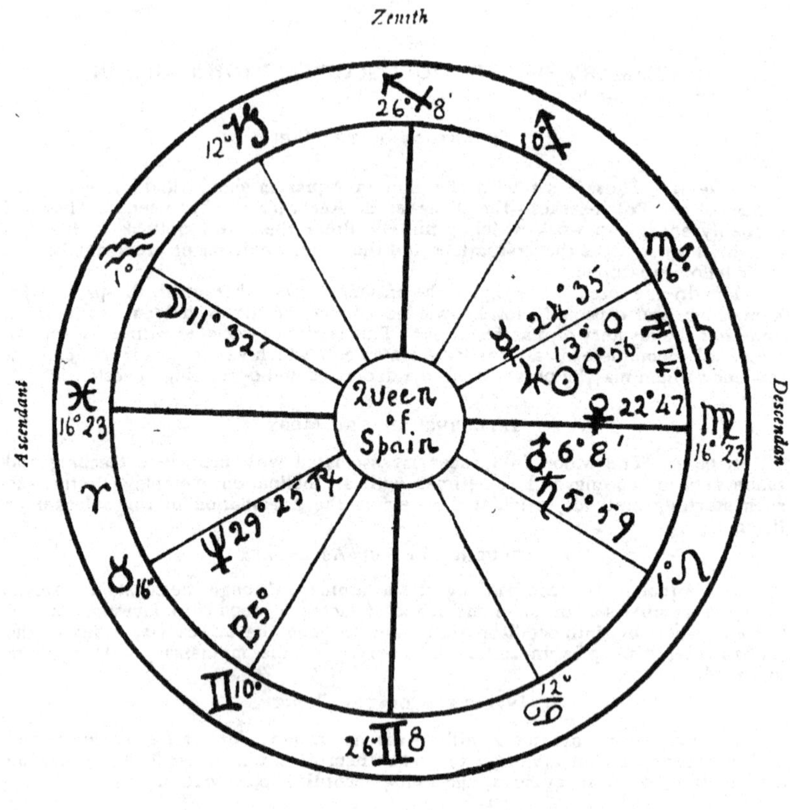

THE HOROSCOPE OF QUEEN VICTORIA EUGÉNIE OF SPAIN.

Born October 24th, 1887, at 3 45 p m , Balmoral, Scotland.

Copied, by kind permission, from *Modern Astrology*, July, 1910

Data from official announcements of the time

QUEEN VICTORIA EUGÉNIE OF SPAIN

In this horoscope the astrologer's eye is at once attracted to the house of partnership, and notes with satisfaction that Venus, the planet of love and happiness, sits smiling there, sextile to Mercury—the negative ruler of the King of Spain—and practically trine to Neptune, which is the positive ruler of the Native herself, and the presence of Uranus in the same house may be regarded with equanimity as well as with interest. In such a position it invariably indicates that the point of view will be changed and widened through marriage as must inevitably have been the case, for our English Princess has had to change the outer form of her faith, and adapt herself to the ways and customs of a Latin race, but the Moon—her habits and inherent tendencies—and Jupiter, the planet of Mind, would help the widening process to accomplish itself with the minimum of strain and stress There is a suggestion of intellectual worry in the opposition of the ruler to Mercury, and all the daughters of Neptune have something of the wistful element about them, born of the knowledge—conscious or unconscious—which belongs to the inner self—that *here we have no abiding city, but we seek one to come* The Moon's square to Jupiter may also give a tendency to take rather a grave view of life; and there is a great probability of psychic development.

Her throne was lost after this book was written, and a rather secluded life followed. The call of her ruler, Neptune, *to renounce* came from the house of possessions, ans is strengthened by its conjuction with Pluto, which is in Gemini.

ANALYSIS OF THE HOROSCOPE OF QUEEN VICTORIA EUGÉNIE OF SPAIN

A *Ascendant* :—PISCES ♓ *Ruler* :—NEPTUNE ♆

DESCRIPTION

	According to the Position of Signs		*Modified by the Position of Planets*	
Type	Inspired	*and*	Commanding	☉ in ♏
Watchwords	Unity	*and*	Investigation	☽ in ♒
Method	Meditative	*and*	Synthetic	☽ in ♒
Style	Illuminating	*and*	Descriptive	☽ in ♒
Intellect	Intuitive	*yet*	Penetrating	☿ in ♏
Speech	Suggestive	*yet*	Decided	☿ in ♏
Manner	Gentle	*and*	Stately	♄ in ♌
Bearing	Unassuming	*and*	Helpful	♂ in ♍
Temperament	Sunshiny	*yet*	Tranquil	Ruler in ♉

B. *Zenith* - SAGITTARIUS ♐

Functions	Counseller	*and*	Governor	☉ in ♏
Outlook	Optimistic	*and*	Impartial	♅ in ♎
Nature	Child-like	*yet*	Prudent	☉ in ♏
Affections	Honest	*and*	Well-regulated	♀ in ♍
Attitude	Uncompromising	*and*	Alert	♂ in ♍
Sex-attitude	Sincere	*and*	Faithful	♂ in ♍
Disposition	Contented	*yet*	Investive	♃ in ♏

C. *Descendant*.—VIRGO ♍

Mind	Clear	*and*	Clear	♃ in ♍

D *Nadir* :—GEMINI ♊.

Character	Impulsive	*and*	Merciful	♄ in ♌
Keynotes	Joy	*and*	Power	☉ in ♏

SUMMARY OF THE HOROSCOPE OF QUEEN VICTORIA EUGÉNIE

Influence of the Sun

☉ *in* ♏ Those born when the Sun is in Scorpio should find success in some sphere of activity which demands the exercise of concentration and personal magnetism; or which is associated with the mastery of men; with work that is vitalising or regenerating or dominating in some degree, and associated with the use—or misuse—of power.

The driving force of this sign is excess of energy, which must find an outlet, and prefers to find it either in the generation or creation of new forms and fresh bodies, or in the destruction of those that are old and out-worn At its best it is a vivifying and vitalising force, but when perverted takes delight in hastening the work of destruction, degeneration, and death

Influence of the Moon

☽ *in* ♒ The Moon in Aquarius is associated with habits of careful observation and an inclination to examine searchingly into the truth of any matter which comes up for discussion also sometimes a bent towards the study of natural or physical science.

Influence of the Ascendant.

♓. Pisces as ascendant suggests attainment through obedience or self-sacrifice, leading to the unification of body, soul and spirit, and possibly resulting in high achievement either in some kind of service to the State or to the race, or in excellence in some form of artistic interpretation, connected with music, colour, or word-painting

Influence of the Zenith

♐ Sagittarius at the Zenith gives aspirations for perfect wisdom and understanding, and an ambition to make them of practical use to the world by carrying out the ideals grasped and living in accordance with conviction, an ambition perverted by some into a tendency to make them square comfortably with the life The point of view is that of the practical philosopher or sage

Influence of the Descendant

♍. Virgo descending suggests the type of mind which is clear and practical, but somewhat lacking in imagination

Influence of the Nadir

♊ Gemini at the Nadir suggests, as the basis of character, a certain joyous impulsiveness, which may possibly carry the native far in several successive directions.

A SUGGESTION

In selecting the foregoing horoscopes for publication the writer has fallen far short of her original scheme, which was to have twelve great examples taken from men and women whose horoscopes had not hitherto been published, whose hour of birth was accurately known, who had greatly distinguished themselves in literature, and who had all been the subjects of faithful biographers. The task proved impossible, and the list has been made up largely through the kindness and courtesy of other students of astrology, whose best efforts to gather satisfactory statistics have revealed the fact that it is extremely difficult to obtain them The rooted convictions of the astrologer as to the soundness of the particular theories he or she may hold depend very little upon such examples and almost entirely on personal observation of ordinary men and women whose horoscopes are of no particular interest to the world at large If he works along these lines of private investigation, the favourite question, "Do you do this for amusement or do you really believe in it?" may still embarrass him, after years of study; for the "it" stands for so very much and needs such careful definition, that the careless questioner is not to be answered all in one breath. Whether much of ancient theory will have to be actually discarded when scientific inquiry on the subject is further advanced, it is difficult to say; but the writer is inclined to think that the majority of students who attempt to formulate their astrological beliefs, fail to give sufficient importance to the particular planetary influence which must surely be the most powerful of all, as far as our own evolution is concerned, namely, the influence of our own kindly Mother Earth, and véry tentatively, and with all due humility, she ventures a suggestion The work she has done so far, and the classification she has attempted to make, may be fairly accurate without its affording any proof that the planets exert any direct influence upon the sons of men That they influence the earth—even physically—is indubitable, for she swings out of her true path to greet them as they pass Granted the astrological belief that she is intensely alive, body and soul and spirit, just as we are, it is conceivable that she has many moods, that these moods are influenced by telepathic intercourse with her kind, and also that these moods, in their turn, influence her progeny Thus she has her mood in which she greets her brother Mars, or that Greater Being yet, who is represented by the symbol of Aries, and in that mood she sends forth her warrior children. Then follows a restful and tranquil mood, and the peaceful Taureans draw their first breath, and so on through the twelve signs, each one of which is something of a contrast to its predecessor These moods succeed each other in a definite order, sweeping over and around her, like waves, and it is actually possible to time them, at least approximately, though as the Earth is a living organism, pulsating in every atom with divine energy, it is not very probable that such timing can ever be exact The clock which the ancients used in attempting this task of timing was the great belt of the Zodiac, and although she has altered her relation to it since astrologers first began their observations, the moods succeed each other still, and the Prophets, and Kings, and Poets, are born in the same order as they were thousands of years ago. Yet this succession of moods is only an illusion after all, for all of them persist always *when viewed from the centre* While the warlike mood prevails in England and the children of Aries are being born there, the sons and daughters of Libra are opening their eyes in New Zealand; and during the same space of time the children of all the other signs are drawing their first breath in the various other regions of the globe Only patient investigation and the gradual accumulation of trustworthy statistics can possibly show us the real scientific basis of this old classification of mankind into types, and after that foundation stone has been well and truly laid, astrology will gradually be raised to its true position in the West again, as at once a Science and a Religion, for when we go back to its foundation principles we find a platform upon which the man of Science and the Mystic can meet, and on which the two can join hands with the poet and the prophet.

And for this reason the fixed stars were created as they are, being divine and eternal living creatures, ever abiding and revolving after the same manner . . . and the other stars which change their motions and wander, were created in the manner already described. . . . The Earth which is our nurse, He made . . . first and eldest of gods that are in the interior of Heaven. Vain would be the labour of telling about all the figures of them, moving as in a dance, and their meetings with one another, and the return of them in their revolutions towards each other, and their approximations; and to say which of them in their conjunctions meet, and which of them are in opposition, and in what order, and when they get behind and before one another, and are severally eclipsed to our sight and again re-appear, sending terrors and intimations of things about to happen to those who can calculate them—to attempt to tell of all this without looking on the models of them would be labour in vain. Let what we have said about the nature of the created and visible gods be deemed sufficient, and have an end.

THE TIMAEUS OF PLATO.

THE POWERS

			Physical Manifestation.	Mental Manifestation
♈	ARIES	*The Ram*	Impetus	Enterprise
♉	TAURUS	*The Bull*	Inertia	Steadfastness
♊	GEMINI	*The Twins*	Expansion / Contraction	Eagerness / Despair
♋	CANCER	*The Crab*	Flexibility ?	Adaptability
♌	LEO	*The Lion*	Radiation	Faith
♍	VIRGO	*The Virgin*	Crystallisation	Discrimination
♎	LIBRA	*The Scales*	Equilibrium	Balance
♏	SCORPIO	*The Scorpion (formerly the Eagle)*	Chemical Action	Determination
♐	SAGITTARIUS	*The Archer*	*Spiral Rotation ?	Reason
♑	CAPRICORN	*The He-goat (also called the Crocodile)*	*Vibration	Concentration / Relaxation
♒	AQUARIUS	*The Water-bearer*	Absorption	Curiosity
♓	PISCES	*The Fish*	Solution	Insight

* Possibly Vibration and Spiral Rotation should be reversed ?

CHARACTERISTICS OF ARYAN PERSONIFICATIONS OF DIVINE ASPECTS

♈ THE WAR GOD, or God of Victory bright, hopeful, handsome, strong and young Patron of Athletics.

♉ MOTHER EARTH, naturally revered as *Queen of Heaven* by those who believed that she was the centre of the Universe—Sun, Moon and Planets revolving around her A maternal deity, patroness of education, upholder of law and order, and of fidelity to contract, sometimes severe, or jealous Consort of the creative mind, and also his daughter

♊ THE GOD OF INVENTIVE INTELLECT, youthful, precocious, quick, eloquent, resourceful, always able to overcome difficulties and find a way Sometimes shifty, evasive, thievish

♋ DAME NATURE, kindly, tender to all young things, protectress of motherhood, associated with seed-time and birth, and with the free life of the forest

♌ THE SUN GOD, golden haired, handsome and young, patron of arts and sciences, a healer and a musician Generally manifesting on Earth as well as in Heaven, and so doubly represented—Apollo and Bacchus, Froh and Baldur, etc

♍ THE SMITH AMONG THE GODS, or the God of the Hammer, who forges the thunderbolt, and builds the palaces of the gods, assisted by the Giants or Titans Very powerfully built, mirthful, or the cause of mirth in others, sometimes lame

♎ THE GODDESS OF LOVE, beautiful, youthful, lovable, unexacting, musical and a patroness of art, happy and laughter-loving, tender and sympathetic to fallen womanhood

♏ FATE OR DESTINY, the Ruler of the Underworld or Physical Plane, a realm which becomes a veritable hell for the evil-doer This is the Lord of Karma, the incorruptible judge who metes out to men just exactly what they have deserved of good or evil fortune in lives past or present His is a vivifying and regenerating force, fertilising seeds of every kind, stimulating and regenerating the life, while destroying out-worn forms A stern and somewhat stately deity, very powerful The third Person, approached through action

♐ THE ALL-FATHER, or Creative Mind, the Father of gods and men, the Ruler of the Mental Plane, benevolent and kind, the hearer of prayer, comprehending all forms of activity but dwelling on the mountain-tops among the clouds Represented as elderly and dignified, with a noble forehead and thoughtful countenance This deity is associated with lightning and enlightenment The first Person, approached through the understanding

♑ OLD FATHER TIME, the Grandfather of the gods, who sets limits and marks off boundaries A rhythmic deity, sometimes a harper, always associated with the orderly succession of times and seasons Represented as very aged, venerable, hoary Fittingly approached through ritual and sacrifice

♒ THE GOD OF SPACE, or Lord of the Firmament, the Great-grandfather of the gods, all-seeing, all-knowing, always in the back-ground and at the root of all manifestation The silent watcher, or All-seeing Eye. Realised in meditation.

♓ FATHER OCEAN The Saviour. Ruler of the Astral plane, the mediator between the All-Father and the God of Destiny, having power to transmute Karma—through whom comes Salvation The second Person, fittingly approached through adoration Husband or Father of the goddess of Love

SUGGESTED SYNTHESIS OF THE POWERS

	Latin	*Greek*	*Scandinavian*	*Irish or Welsh*	*Hindoo*
♈	Mars	Ares	Tyr	Nuada ?	Kartikeya
♉	Juno	Hera	Frigga	Danu	Sarasvati
♊	Mercury	Hermes	Loge	Lugh	Ganesa
♋	Diana	Artemis	Iduna	Brigit	Párvati
♌	Apollo (*Bacchus*)	Phoebus (*Dionysos*)	Froh (*Baldur*)	Beli (*Con ?*)	Surya (***Krishna***)
♍	Vulcan	Hephaestos	Thor	Goibniu / Govannon	Bhîma sena
♎	Venus	Aphrodite	Freya	Dwynwen	Lakṣmi
♏	Pluto	Hades	Vilje	Morrigu ?	Siva, Kali
♐	Jupiter	Zeus	Odin	Gwydion	Brahma
♑	Saturn	Chronos	Bor	Dagda	Sami
♒	Coelus	Ouranos	Bur ?	Nwyvre	Iṣvara or Varuna ?
♓	Neptune	Poseidon	Ve ? or Aegir	Llyr or Ler	Vishnu

It is natural to look for such correspondences as these suggested above, among the deities of all Aryan races; but identification is difficult, for each deity has its male and female aspect and manifests as benevolent or baleful, and different bards tend to exalt and emphasise those aspects which are locally or racially appropriate. They also modify the myths, blending with them actual historical events. It should be noted that although the incarnate deity always approximates to the Sun God, having power to heal and to harmonise, and is usually associated with the idea of death and resurrection, he is generally considered as an *incarnation* of the second Person of the Trinity—the Saviour or Preserver—and yet at the same time as a ***child*** of the First Person. The All-father is always regarded with peculiar reverence, and rarely appears to man, except in Scandinavia. The Warrior Maiden, his firstborn daughter, who often represents him, is recurrent in Minerva, Pallas and Brynhilda, and could probably be traced elsewhere. These lists are very diffidently submitted in the hope that they may arouse further interest in this line of study among readers competent to deal with these questions. Comparative folk lore and mythology make fascinating pursuits. The carrying off of Sita in India and of Helen in Greece have many equivalents, and the limitations imposed upon deity in each successive generation are very suggestive. Ouranos is mutilated and Saturn imprisoned. Odin loses an eye. Manifestation means limitation, and is consequently invariably associated with suffering, even in the Highest.

SUGGESTED SYNTHESIS OF THE POWERS

Christian Descriptions and Saints		*Angels and Archangels, Zodiacal and Planetary*		
The Lord of Hosts	St George	Malchidiel	Zachariel	*The Man of God*
The Eternal (*Queen of Heaven*)	St Catherine (*of Alexandria*)	Asmodel	Tzaphkiel	*Encompassed of God*
Divine Wisdom ?	St Paul ?	Ambriel	Raphael	*Healing of God*
Divine Grace (*Virgin Mother*)	St. Margaret	Muriel	Gabriel	*Strength of God*
The Logos or Word (*Jesus Christ*)	St Sebastian	Verchiel	Michael (*The Messiah*)	*Like unto God*
The Almighty	St. Clement	Hamaliel	Uriel ?	*Fire of God*
The All-merciful (*Our Lady*)	Mary Magdalen	Zuriel	Anael	*Sweet Song of God*
The Holy Spirit	St Augustine ?	Barbiel	*Azrael ?	*Help of God*
The Father	St Peter	Adnachiel	Zadkiel ?	*Righteousness of God*
The Ancient of Days	St. Nicholas	Hanael	Arifiel	*Hour of God*
The Infinite	St Jerome ?	Cambiel	Chamuel	*One who sees God*
The World Saviour	St. Francis	Barchiel	Jophiel	*Beauty of God*

In studying Christianity it is absolutely necessary to remember that we have a blending of Aryan and Semitic influences, difficult to reconcile and equally difficult to disentangle. The Hebrew Sages kept much of the teaching concerning the Powers secret, probably in order to discourage the exaltation of any one aspect; and although winged Seraphim were allowed as Temple decoration, and placed as supporters of the vacant throne in the Holy of Holies, there was no sex distinction permitted nor were human attributes bestowed The very names of the angels were a precious mystery, to betray which was, in some cases—in the sect known as the Essenes at any rate—punishable by death The Jewish High Priest wore twelve sacred stones associated with the Zodiac on his breast plate, each one standing for a tribe of Israel. Astrological traditions and interpretations were studied by the priesthood, but strictly forbidden to the people, probably with good reason Oriental nations—and indeed Westerners also—are too prone to be discouraged and disheartened by evil aspects to make prognostication desirable

The first list of Hebrew Angels is Kabalistic and I have not found the meanings of the names given anywhere The other list is compiled from two which varied, one making Michael the Angel of Jupiter Jewish students assure me that he is always associated with the Sun, Gabriel with the Moon, Anael with Venus and Raphael with Mercury The position of the others is never openly declared Some people give *Satan* as the angel of Saturn, but this seems unlikely, for though Time tries all things, the real tester is Scorpio Compare with the ancient conception of Saturn the description of deity as "The first and the last" in Rev. I

---

* Azrael is the Angel of Death Other Angel names to choose from are Cassiel, Samael, Salamiel, Sachiel, and there are Angels of the Seasons as well as of the months *Cf*, Demeter, Proserpine, etc.

The student will most easily learn the order of the signs by memorising the following doggerel list, which is ascribed to Allan Cunningham.

The Ram, the Bull, the Heavenly Twins
And, next the Crab, the Lion shines,
The Virgin, and the Scales.
The Scorpion, Archer and He-goat,
The Man that holds the Watering-pot,
And Fish with glittering tails.

In drawing the horoscope, the correct position of six signs only is given in the published tables. It is therefore necessary to fill in the others as follows:—

♈ *exactly opposite* ♎	♋ *exactly opposite* ♑
♉ *exactly opposite* ♏	♌ *exactly opposite* ♒
♊ *exactly opposite* ♐	♍ *exactly opposite* ♓

Lift up your heads, O ye gates;
And be ye lift up, ye everlasting doors;
And the King of Glory *shall come in.*

INDEX

* Error. Marconi born September 23rd.

CPSIA information can be obtained
at www.ICGtesting.com
Printed in the USA
FSOW03n0942170318
45848FS